Families, relationships and intimate life

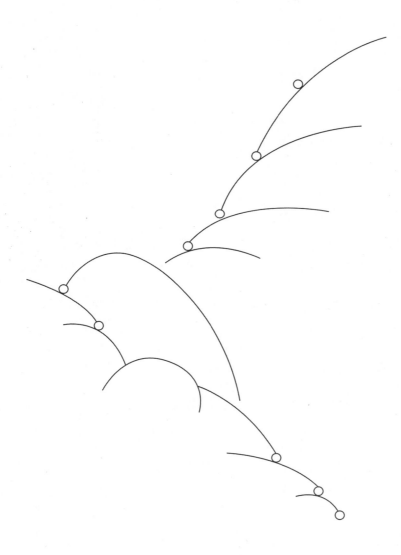

Families, relationships and intimate life

Jo Lindsay and Deborah Dempsey

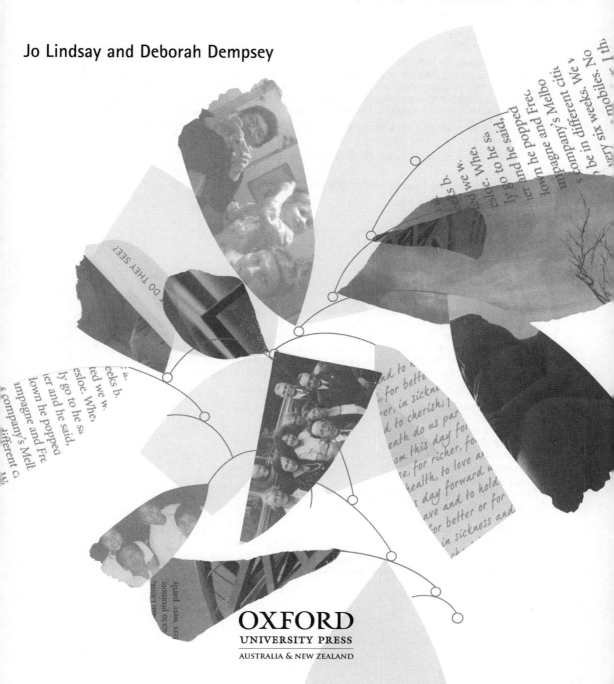

OXFORD
UNIVERSITY PRESS
AUSTRALIA & NEW ZEALAND

OXFORD
UNIVERSITY PRESS

Oxford University Press is a department of the University of Oxford.
It furthers the University's objective of excellence in research,
scholarship, and education by publishing worldwide. Oxford is a registered
trademark of Oxford University Press in the UK and in certain other
countries.

Published in Australia by
Oxford University Press
253 Normanby Road, South Melbourne, Victoria 3205, Australia

First published 2009
Reprinted 2010, 2011

National Library of Australia Cataloguing-in-Publication data

Lindsay, Jo.
Families, relationships and intimate life/Jo Lindsay; Deborah Dempsey.

ISBN 978 0 19 556202 6 (pbk.)

Includes index.
Bibliography

Family.
Interpersonal relationships.

Dempsey, Deborah.

306.85

Reproduction and communication for educational purposes

For details of the CAL licence for educational institutions contact:

Copyright Agency Limited
Level 15, 233 Castlereagh Street
Sydney NSW 2000
Telephone: (02) 9394 7600
Facsimile: (02) 9394 7601
Email: info@copyright.com.au

Edited by Liz Filleul
Cover design by Streamer Design and Communication
Text design by Streamer Design and Communication
Typeset by diacriTech, Chennai, India
Indexed by Russell Brooks
Printed in Hong Kong through Sheck Wah Tong Printing Press Ltd.

Contents

Chapter 7: Relating Beyond the Cohabiting Couple Household · 106

Chapter 8: Fertility, Technology and Family Change · 123

Chapter 12: Violence and Intimate Relationships   197

Chapter 13: Ageing, Care and Intergenerational Relationships   213

Chapter 14: Conclusion: New Families, New Relationships?

Preface

Families, relationships and intimacy are ideal subjects for sociological study. Using a sociological imagination allows us to see the play of social forces, biography, culture and history in the trajectories of our interpersonal relationships and family ties. The aim of this book is to explore the changing social terrain of families and relationships in Australia and other industrialised countries, redressing the token treatment sometimes given to non-Western families and non-heterosexual relationships. The concept 'intimate life' embraces the theoretical and social emphasis we give in this book to meaningful relationships within and beyond notions of family, heterosexuality, coupledom and cohabitation.

The themes we explore draw on our long research and work histories. For Jo, this includes research on unmarried cohabitation, young people and relationships, lesbian families, and heterosexual families managing work and care. For Deb, this includes formative years spent as a counsellor and project worker in a women's domestic violence crisis service, and research into same-sex-attracted young people, gay and lesbian family formation and primary carer fathers.

This project is very much a shared intellectual endeavour that emerges from our mutual enthusiasm for teaching the sociology of families and relationships, to culturally and sexually diverse undergraduate and postgraduate students. We wanted to create a book that would do justice to the complexity of contemporary international scholarship and speak meaningfully to the breadth of students' experiences. The book itself is the product of many collegial hours spent debating, occasionally arguing, and mostly agreeing about what are the central themes and trends in late modern relational life.

We owe our thanks to many people who helped us along the way. Lucy McLoughlin at Oxford University Press was instrumental in getting the project off the ground and provided helpful feedback on early drafts. Katie Ridsdale and Rachel Saffer were always encouraging and astute in their subsequent editorial guidance. We also thank Tim Campbell, Liz Filleul and other production staff at OUP, who so capably took the book through to publication. Deb would like to thank sociology colleagues at Swinburne University of Technology, Karen Farquharson, Paula Geldens, Michael Gilding and Joshua Mullar for their encouragement throughout the project. Jo would like to thank colleagues in sociology and the School of Political and Social Inquiry at Monash University, who generously supported both the writing and production of this book. We are both grateful to Briony Horsfall, who provided outstanding research assistance and was unflagging in her dedication to the project, and to our students, who have engaged with and challenged our ideas over the years.

On a more personal note, heartfelt thanks go to our friends and family. Fab Superina very generously provided us with a writing retreat by the sea. Deb would like to thank Letizia, Joy and Noel for their ongoing love, care and support, and Charlie for fun and diversion. Jo would like to thank Paul, Isobel and Hugo, Russell and June and the rest of the clan, for the intimate life they share.

Acknowledgments

The authors and the publisher wish to thank the following copyright holders for reproduction of their material.

Photos

123RF/Solovei Olga, p. 180; AAP Image/Hambury Daniel, p. 84 right; AAP Image/Porrit Alan, p. 136; AAP Image/Proepper Heribert, p. 84 left; Aquarius Collection/BBC, p. 30 top right; Aquarius Collection/Gold Circle Films, p. 13 bottom; Aquarius Collection/United Artists (Mike Nichols), p. 13 top left; CASA Forum, p. 197; 'dids.inc', Dads in Distress, p. 188, courtesy of Tony Miller; Duluth Domestic Abuse Intervention Project, p. 200; Fairfaxphotos/De La Rue Andrew ADL, p. 69 left; Fairfaxphotos/Taylor Andrew, p. 123 right; Fiveash Tina & Kelly Deborah, © 2001, p. 123 left; iStockphoto/Jansen Silvia, p. 149; iStockphoto/O'Claire Sandra, p. 1; iStockphoto/Prescott John, p. 13; Lindsay Jo, p. 213; Newspix/Town Jay, p. 142; State Library of Victoria/Pictures Collection, p. 160, picture by Porter Carol, 'Man's Final Frontier'; Shutterstock/Pawlowska Edyta, p. 69 right; Human Rights and Opportunity Commission, p. 34, cover of the *Bringing Them Home* report, photo by Heide Smith, 1996, <www.humanrights. gov.au/social_justice/bth_report/index. html>; Southern Start Entertainment P/L, p. 106.

Text

Carter Meg, for extracts reproduced on pp. 170–1, from 'It's Easier just to do it all Myself: Emotion Work and Domestic Labour', paper presented at the 2003 TASA conference, University of New England, 4–6 December.

De Vaus David, for extracts reproduced on pp. 219–20, from *Letting Go*, Oxford University Press, 1994, Melbourne.

Goodfellow Joy, for extracts reproduced on pp. 225–6, from 'Grandparents as Regular Child Care Providers: Unrecognized, Under-valued and Under-resourced', *Australian Journal of Early Childhood*, 2003, vol. 28, no. 3, pp. 7–17.

Taylor & Francis, for extract reproduced on p. 223, from Baldassar Loretta, 'Transnational Families and Aged Care', *Journal of Ethnic and Migration Studies*, vol. 33, no. 2, <www.informaworld.com>, reproduced by permission of Copyright Clearance Centre.

Tables

ABS data, reproduced on pp. 37–8, 91, 126, 182, used with permission from the Australian Bureau of Statistics, <www.abs.gov.au>.

Federation Press, for figure on p. 169, from Pocock B, *The Work/Life Collision*, © Federation Press, 2003, Sydney, p. 24.

Commonwealth of Australia, for tables on pp. 168, 172, from deVaus David, *Diversity and Change in Australian Families: Statistical Profiles*, Australian Institute of Family Studies, Melbourne, 2004, pp. 286–7, reproduced with permission of Commonwealth of Australia.

Commonwealth of Australia, for figure on p. 163, from *Women in Australia*, Office of the Status of Women, 2004, p. 58, reproduced with permission of Commonwealth of Australia.

SAGE Publications, for table reproduced on p. 185, from Amato & Previti, 'People's Reasons for Divorcing', in *Journal of Family Issues*, 2003, vol. 24, no. 5, reprinted by permission of Copyright Clearance Centre.

United Nations, for table reproduced on p. 125–126, from *World Population Prospects: The 2006 Revision*, World Population Database, <http://esa.un.org/unpp>.

Every effort has been made to trace the original source of copyright material contained in this book. The publisher will be pleased to hear from copyright holders to rectify any errors or omissions.

01 Introduction

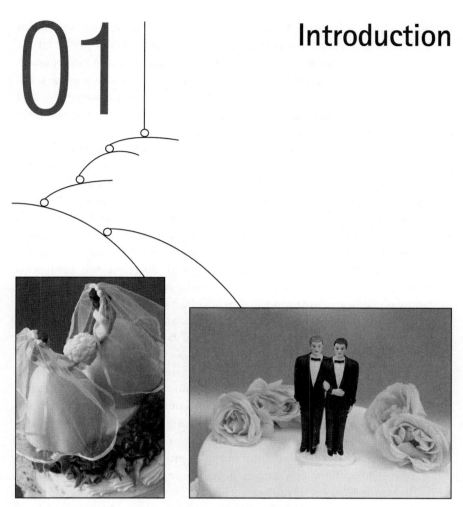

Figure 1.1: Will Same-sex Marriage be Legalised in Australia?

IN 2004, THE AUSTRALIAN FEDERAL government changed the *Marriage Act 1961* by adding the words 'man' and 'woman' to a previously gender-neutral clause. These changes were the initiative of the then Australian Prime Minister, John Howard, and aimed to make it more difficult for lesbian and gay activists in Australia to claim that same-sex couples, not just heterosexual couples, should have the right to marry. Following the legislative changes, policy directives were issued to marriage celebrants about the required content for wedding vows. It is now a formal requirement in Australia that the words 'husband' and 'wife' are used in all wedding vows rather than alternatives, such as the word 'partner'.

The example of marriage rights and vows is just one of many we could have drawn on to emphasise how **relationships** are controversial and contested.

In Australia and most parts of the Western world, the relationships we tend to think of as our most private and personal are subject to considerable public debate. Controversies about families and relationships tend to arise as a consequence of a number of demographic changes. The average age of first marriage has risen over the past three decades, with many people having a number of sexual relationships and/or living with their partners before they get married. Fewer people are getting married in the first place and many marriages are no longer for life. Over a third of all marriages will end in divorce, meaning many children now experience their parents' separation. Some children will have sole parents or only one active parent, or will grow up in a step or blended family. Further to this, there is increased social visibility of same-sex relationships and practices.

For socially and morally conservative members of society, these trends represent social and moral decline. Many take for granted the view that marriage should be confined to a couple comprised of a man and a woman. Similarly, it is often stated that the 'intact' (that is, not divorced) nuclear family comprised of mother, father and children who all live together, is the only legitimate site for raising children and sustaining adult sexual relationships. However, for more liberal members of society, contemporary relationships are perceived as more complex than our conventional definitions and laws can accommodate. The **family** is regarded as a more flexible entity and can be more broadly defined to keep up with the changes occurring in how people live their personal lives. In this view, definitions, laws and policies should move along with the times, and new conventions and moralities will necessarily come to the fore to support the adults and children living within new configurations of family life.

Families and relationships are often contradictory for those who live within them. On the one hand they are about our most profound, joyful and important social connections. They are the privileged setting for expressions of social connectedness and love. On the other, they are also about power, exploitation and violence. As Bittman and Pixley (1997) argue, for the people who participate in them, families have a 'double life'. Changing relationships potentially offer women, children and men more freedom than they have in the past, but at the same time they offer new challenges and constraints.

The controversies and contradictions inherent to contemporary families and relationships make them an enthralling topic to study. This book seeks to do justice to the complexity of this topic from a sociological perspective.

Defining families and relationships

THE CHAPTERS OF THIS BOOK look at a range of contemporary themes relevant to families and relationships. Here we begin to map the parameters of these two concepts in current sociological thought, as a preliminary to discussing them in greater depth throughout the book.

Relationships

AT THEIR MOST BASIC, THE relationships we discuss in this book are connections between people, but not just any connections. In the first instance, a relationship can be an objective connection based on biological relatedness ('blood') or marriage. In Western and some non-Western cultures, biological and legal ties between people are objectively acknowledged as relationships, whether or not the people concerned ever see each other or have any feelings towards each other. Although husbands and wives and biological brothers and sisters usually do have an emotional connection, they also have a relationship in the eyes of the law or cultural convention regardless of whether they have a social or emotional connection.

Relationships can also be thought of as intimate connections to other people; that is, they can be defined by their qualities rather than any kind of objective status. Jacqui Gabb (2009) observes that **intimacy** has often been discussed in the context of sexual relationships, but it is equally relevant to 'affective interactions' between friends or parents and children. For Lynn Jamieson (1998), intimacy may include caring, sharing, physical closeness, love, 'deep' understanding, and privileged knowledge. For instance, friendship is a type of relationship determined largely on the basis of its qualities. People become our friends because we choose them or they choose us, rather than for objectively determined reasons such as blood or marriage. Sometimes intimate relationships also involve a sexual component—for example girlfriends, boyfriends, lovers.

In this book we are concerned with both kinds of relationships, those that have objective status as blood or marriage ties and those that are more subjective in the sense that they exist by virtue of emotional connections. It is important to give due attention to both kinds of relationships because for many people today their most significant relationships of love and care are not those determined by ties of blood or marriage.

Family

GILDING (1997) CONTENDS THERE ARE three main ways in which family can be defined: as a specific set of people, in keeping with the objective definitions used by demographers and government organisations; as a set of fixed social functions, or the roles it fulfils as a social institution; or in more subjective terms, as a set of personal meanings or ideas about what constitutes family. It is worth exploring these in some detail. While there is a good deal of fit between the first and second ways of thinking about family, with regard to the relationships that are included and excluded, the third definition may considerably contradict the first two ways of thinking about family.

Family as an objectively defined set of people

IN THE LEGAL AND POLICY arena, relational terms such as 'father', 'mother', 'parent', 'child', 'aunt', 'grandmother', 'husband', 'wife' and so on designate people who are connected by blood, marriage (more recently de facto marriage or **cohabitation**), or adoption, who by virtue of these objectively defined relationships are assumed to have certain obligations and entitlements. Objective definitions of family inform collections of official statistics such as the Australian Census. They also inform a range of government laws and policies. For instance, if you are legally defined as a mother or a father, you have certain financial and social obligations to support the people legally defined as your children, if they are less than 18 years of age. If you are legally defined as a deceased person's aunt, and you are their only surviving relative by blood or marriage, you may be entitled to make a claim to inherit their wealth. If you are married to or cohabiting with your partner, who becomes unemployed while you are working, your relationship status legally determines the government benefits to which your partner is entitled.

Although these official definitions of family greatly influence how social obligations and entitlements are determined by law in any given society, and are based on dominant cultural norms about family relationships, they tell us nothing about the meaning or function of the relationships. In other words, assumptions are made about the social support content of relationships, based on biological relatedness, marriage, co-residence or a combination of these elements. This means the definitions and associated obligations or entitlements are very powerful. Yet they often lag behind observable social change. For example, until the late 1980s, de facto heterosexual couples were counted in the Australian Census as unrelated adults living in a house together. Until the late 1990s, same-sex couples were counted as unrelated adults. The relationships that law- and policy-makers take to be family relationships may not be keeping up with what is actually happening in people's lives. A more recent example relates to cohabiting lesbian couples who have conceived children in the context of their relationship. Although their children may call both members of the couple 'mum', only the birth mother can claim the legal rights or responsibilities of motherhood in some Australian states, such as the right to have the child live with her if the women separate, or to sign permission slips for school excursions. The lag between official, objective definitions of family and social reality can create distress and difficulties for those living in less conventional family relationships. As sociologists, we need to be mindful of these objective definitions because they are relevant to the distribution of social and economic resources, and thus greatly influence people's lives.

Family as a set of functions

A FAIRLY RIGID VIEW OF family was taken by sociologists working in the post-World War II era such as Talcott Parsons and George Murdock, who were keen to determine what role families served in industrialised Western societies. Murdock's definition of family was as follows:

> a social group characterized by common residence, economic co-operation and reproduction. It includes adults of both sexes, at least two of whom maintain a socially approved sexual relationship and one or more children, own or adopted of the sexually co-habiting adults (Morgan 1985, p. 20).

In this view of family, which largely conforms to the two-parent nuclear family **household**, the family is a basic building block of society, in the sense that it has four fixed main purposes or functions that ensure the social survival and well-being of its members, namely, common residence or setting up a household; financial support or cooperation; reproduction of children; and sexuality. We discuss the functionalist perspective on families more in Chapter 4. At this point it is sufficient to say that although this definition conforms to what many people think a family is and does, there have been many criticisms of Murdock's and other functionalist definitions of family.

One of the major flaws in the definition is that it is so fixed and thus unable to accommodate how assumptions and practices among people who consider themselves family members have changed in a relatively short period of time. Consider these contemporary examples that problematise Murdock's definition:

- Throughout the Western world, there are growing numbers of married or cohabiting couples who remain child-free through choice or infertility. Does this mean these couples are not each other's family members?
- Family members may not co-reside (one partner may need to live interstate for work purposes or be posted overseas in the armed services).
- Sexuality is not always reproductive or socially approved (heterosexual couples practise contraception, same-sex relationships are still stigmatised) and monogamy (having sex exclusively with one person) is not always practised among couples who live together (gay male couples often negotiate 'non-monogamy' in their relationships).
- People who live together in a sexual relationship may maintain economic independence from each other. For instance, many cohabiting heterosexual couples and gay couples do not pool money and may own property independently of each other.

Family as an idea

THROUGHOUT THE 1990S, CHANGING SOCIAL trends such as those listed above indicated considerable challenges were occurring to the nuclear family and household. Retaining family as a concept, while moving away from the notion that it performs fixed social functions or is a specific set of objectively determined blood or marriage relationships, characterises a significant proportion of contemporary family sociology, particularly work that seeks to understand people's relationships from their own point of view. In this way of thinking, family relationships are conceptualised and ordered in different ways according to different criteria at different times. In other words, family signifies 'the subjective meaning of intimate connections rather than formal, objective blood or marriage ties' (Silva & Smart 1999, p. 7).

One illustration of this point is the fact that 'family' as a concept has enormous appeal among gay men and lesbians as a descriptive term for their most valued social relationships, despite the fact that many lesbian and gay relationships are not legally recognised and remain socially stigmatised. For instance, the partners of lesbian and gay biological mothers and fathers may have no legal status as family members even if they are actively involved in parenting, but they may still call themselves mothers and fathers to reflect their social status in the children's lives. Weeks, Heaphy and Donovan (2001) also argue that lesbians' and gay men's most significant relationships may be with friends who come to perform many of the social functions conventionally associated with family members, and are referred to as brothers and sisters, rather than as friends. Using the language associated with family relationships stakes a claim to social and legal recognition of important and meaningful relationships that fall outside convention.

In accepting a shift away from objective definitions of family, it is important not to lose sight of a manageable focus. As Gubrium and Holstein (1990) point out: 'The familial is not … an undisciplined, unfettered interpretive brainstorm' (p. 155). By this they mean that there are limits to the kinds of relationships and phenomena the concept 'family' can describe. In conventional and unconventional usage, family continues to bring to mind associated terms such as 'belonging', 'household', 'home', 'privacy', 'intimacy', 'connectedness' and 'kinship', terms we will consider further in the chapters to come. The term 'family' continues to evoke meaningful, enduring and emotionally significant relationships.

In concluding this discussion of 'family' it is also important to point out that sociologists are beginning to ask whether the concept 'family' is flexible enough to describe the kinds of relationships and personal connections contemporary people value. Some recent scholarship draws instead on the concept '**personal life**' in order to better capture the fluidity and variety of contemporary relational lives, without the historical baggage that may accompany the concept of family (Roseneil & Budgeon 2004; Smart 2007). There will be many opportunities to reflect on the relative merits of 'family' as opposed to 'personal life' as you read your way through this book.

Thinking sociologically

FUNDAMENTALLY, SOCIOLOGISTS THINK OF CHANGE in families and relationships as inevitable. This is because change in personal lives cannot be separated out from social change more broadly. Three basic assumptions that guide this book are as follows: that social forces shape the decisions in our lives that seem most natural, personal or private; that the social forces of late modernity made possible by global capitalism are a particularly important influence on contemporary relationships; and that more localised ethnic, religious and historical traditions and practices continue to influence the way we think, feel and act out our relationships. Below we discuss each of these assumptions in turn.

1. Social forces shape our personal decisions

What's in a name?

'As most parents do, we took the naming of our child, our daughter, very seriously. My name is "Joanne", which I had never really liked. It felt like a common and plain suburban name to me. In the 1970s the Joannes were there with all of the Karens and Sharons. I wanted to avoid that for my first child. But at the same time I didn't want to give my baby a name that was too unusual, something that would stand her apart from the crowd too much and inhibit her chances of conventional middle-class success. The name "Isobel" emerged as a front runner—it was a traditional name that could be taken seriously if she had a leadership position, but it could also be shortened in a number of ways. Depending on her preferences and her emerging personality, she could be "Belle" or "Issy" or "Isobel". I found out later that the most popular name for girls in 1999 was "Isabella"—I had called my daughter the "Sharon" of the 1990s! She is now at school surrounded by many other Isobels and Isabellas, with a variety of spellings, just to make it annoying (Jo Lindsay).'

Above, Jo reflects on the choice of a name for her daughter Isobel. Jo's anecdote illustrates the degree to which her cultural background, her sense of positioning within a social class, and prevailing fashions in names had a profound influence on one of the most personal decisions she and her partner have ever made. It is challenging to think of personal life being shaped by social forces. Our relationships often feel so natural and individual that it is difficult to examine them with an analytical or critical lens—but without this we are unable to fully understand the present, the past and the future of family configurations. As we will explore in this book, families and family practices such as naming children illustrate continuities with the past. Although we may seek to make different decisions from our parents' generation, we find ourselves reproducing some of their social values and ideas. Yet relationships and families are also historically specific. Their shape, structure and function and the experience they offer have changed and will continue to change over time. Social categories such as **gender** and **social class** have become less deterministic and more fluid in the last half century but, as we will explore in the chapters that follow, both gender and class continue to shape our relationships and choices in profound ways. A further key insight is that the changing nature of global capitalism has an enormous influence on the way we live our intimate and family lives. This brings us to our second assumption.

2. Globalisation and associated processes of individualisation influence personal lives

MOST SOCIOLOGISTS BROADLY AGREE we are living through a period of immense economic and societal transformation, largely accelerated by the now global dominance of free-market capitalism. Since the late 1970s and 1980s we have witnessed far-reaching changes such as the demise of many national communist and socialist governments and the greater reach of neo-liberal economics. The influence of these changes can be felt most keenly in the world of work, where secure employment conditions and the notion of a 'job for life' have given way to the 'downsizing' or demise of many traditional industries and the casualisation of the workforce. Along with the de-regulation of national economies, consumerism has further encroached into private life, as credit has become more freely available in Western countries. As Pamela Kinnear (2002) explains, these kinds of economic changes force people to become increasingly self-reliant and take individual responsibility for their own circumstances. The precariousness of work and the tendency of neo-liberal economics to emphasise a minimal welfare state fosters a way of thinking about and acting in the world in which 'the politics of the individual prevail over the politics of the collective' (p. 22). What this means is that people are increasingly fending for themselves and being required to draw on their own resources in their personal lives.

Many contemporary sociologists contend that this contemporary focus on the individual is the continuation of processes that began to become evident in industrialised societies much earlier in the twentieth century. Broadly, we can refer to these processes as **individualisation**. For instance, English sociologist Anthony Giddens (1992) argues that an emphasis on personal growth and self-identity is what distinguishes the contemporary historical era from previous times. The spread of democracy and the rapid pace of social change in industrialised societies have, to some degree, undermined the authority and predictability of social categories such as gender, class, religion and status group. Decisions ranging from who to love, how to express that love, and whether to marry, stay single or have children are more and more taken at the level of the individual rather than following taken-for-granted expectations of family or community.

Although personal lives have become more individualised under global capitalism, **globalisation** has also fostered new and hitherto inconceivable forms of social connection. Increasingly, affordable technologies that make the world feel much smaller, such as cut-price air travel, the internet, mobile phones and satellite TV also influence the way we practise and experience family and intimate relationships. For instance, with the aid of these globalised technologies, parents and children retain day-to-day relationships of care across national borders in a new social phenomenon, 'transnational caregiving' (Baldassar, Baldock & Wilding 2007). Emotionally committed couples are able to sustain their love and sexual relationships while 'living apart together' (Levin 2004).

3. Local cultures and traditions maintain influence over personal relationships

OUR THIRD SOCIOLOGICAL ASSUMPTION is that despite individualisation and globalisation, relationships and families need to be viewed in their local social and historical context. We must attend to factors such as **ethnicity**, religion, the migration experience and local history. It is important to maintain a comparative perspective that illuminates the local contexts and settings in which families and relationships are conceived and practised. Despite broader social changes such as individualisation, high levels of family obligation and support continue to thrive in some communities. We compare practices customary to some South, South-East and East Asian families—such as arranged marriage, obedience to and respect of one's parents and ancestors, and the formation of multi-generational households—with increasingly smaller Anglo-Australian families and their fragmented family ties.

Why study families and relationships?

A THOROUGH EXPLORATION OF THE controversies, contradictions and broad patterns that characterise contemporary relationships and families is crucial for a variety of reasons. This knowledge is important for designing sound economic and social policy. It enables us to predict, monitor and comprehend population change; particularly fertility patterns, the age structure of our society, and family instability and the consequences for family care of the dependent—babies and children, the sick and disabled and the aged.

We hope the thinking you will do as you read this book will be useful to you in two major ways. You may develop a career in policy-making or service delivery in the health and community services, and we aim to foster your ability to think broadly about the issues you will encounter in these environments. For instance, how do various social divisions such as gender, socio-economic status and the migration/refugee experience shape a person's behaviour and opportunities? Sound knowledge of the social forces underpinning beliefs and practices about families and relationships is important in designing effective social policy with social justice outcomes.

Secondly, this book will provide you with a deeper understanding of the social forces influencing your own personal life, with regard to the choices you are making and the constraints on choice. It may help you to make sense of those personal questions like:

- Why can't I find a partner?
- Can I commit to a long-term relationship?
- Why can't I get my partner to do their share of domestic labour?
- How should the government support me in balancing and maintaining work, family, and relationships of love and care to significant others?

It may be a consolation to learn through reading this book that despite our personal views we are all in it together in navigating the complexity of contemporary families and relationships. We live in interesting times and face distinctive opportunities and challenges conducting our relational lives under current social conditions.

Structure of the book

THE FIRST FOUR CHAPTERS PROVIDE the conceptual scaffolding necessary to analyse contemporary relationships and families. In Chapter 2, we examine families in their historical context. We concentrate primarily on the development of Western families in countries such as the UK, the USA and Australia. We trace the ways in which relationships and families have changed alongside economic development, from pre-modern traditional families to modern nuclear families and then to our current environment of late-modern families (sometimes termed post-modern families). As a comparative contrast we will examine the history of Chinese families, which provides a background for comparisons with South-East Asia running through the book.

In Chapter 3 we examine cultural differences in relationships and families. We begin by discussing the key elements of the organisation of relationships in Western, industrialised countries, with a focus on the organisation of gender and sexuality. Next there is a section discussing the distinct elements of Indigenous Australian families, followed by the section on variations between immigrant families in Australia. We then trace the ways in which social inequality continues to shape family experiences and end with a section on lesbian and gay families and relationships.

In Chapter 4 we lay out the major sociological perspectives used to analyse families. We explain how these theories developed in concert with historical change and identify which theories are currently 'live' in contemporary scholarship.

Following this groundwork we then move to more substantive chapters organised loosely around traditional dominant heterosexual life stage transitions—dating, marriage, parenting and labour. Due to the processes of individualisation discussed earlier, a fixed and linear notion of life stages is hard to sustain and we offer a taste of the contemporary complexities characteristic of youth, middle-age and old age as we move through the text.

In Chapter 5 we examine young people, relationships and sexuality in the context of what is sometimes known as 'new adulthood'. In Chapter 6 we explore love, commitment and the implications and significance of cohabitation and contemporary marriage for heterosexuals and same-sex partners. In Chapter 7 we consider how personal lives can be lived beyond notions of family or the couple-based household. Chapter 8 provides an opportunity to think through the implications of changing fertility patterns and of assisted reproductive technologies (ART).

The changing nature of parenthood and childhood is outlined in Chapter 9 along with childcare debates, which are particularly fraught in Australia. Chapter 10 critically examines how far feminism has come in changing domestic labour arrangements and the potential for anyone to achieve work/family balance in rapidly de-regulating paid labour markets. The implications of the normalisation of divorce are traced in Chapter 11. In Chapter 12 we discuss the exploitation and violence that still (all too often) characterises family life. Chapter 13 discusses ageing and family ties across generations and geographic locations. We conclude the book with an assessment of the present relational landscape and consider the potential for free, fair and satisfying intimate relationships in the future. We ponder how we are faring with developing the new moral frameworks that some sociologists claim are needed for these changing times.

Key concepts

Family

Relationships

Intimacy

Personal life

Cohabitation

Ethnicity

Household

Globalisation

Individualisation

Discussion questions

1   Which social forces do you think have the greatest influence on families—the global economy, gender or localised cultural practices?

2   What does family mean to you? Do you find objective or subjective definitions more useful?

3   Which relationships in your own life are particularly important at this time in providing you with social and emotional support? Are these all 'family' relationships?

4   Can you think of an example of what seemed like an intensely personal decision on intimate relationships being made by you and many of your friends at the same time? Can you see evidence of a social trend or pattern in the way this decision was being made?

Recommended further reading

Gilding, M. 1997, 'Sociology of the Family', in *Australian Families: A Comparative Perspective*, Longman, South Melbourne.

Silva, E. & Smart, C. 1999, 'Introduction: The "New" Practices and Politics of Family Life', in E. Silva & C. Smart (eds), *The New Family?*, Sage, London.

Smart, C. 2007, *Personal Life: New Directions in Sociological Thinking*, Polity, Cambridge.

02 Relationships and Families Over Time

Figure 2.1: The Nuclear Family: 'A Dying Species'?

Introduction

In the above picture of a nuclear family, a mother, a father and their children are represented as a discrete and self-sufficient unit. There is considerable anxiety about the impending demise of this family type. For example, a similar picture in a Melbourne newspaper, *The Age*, was accompanied by the headline 'The Australian nuclear family could be extinct by the end of the century' (Crawford 2000). The quote suggested something is threatening this kind of family, just as an animal species may be endangered due to an introduced predator or disease. The word 'extinct' encouraged us to view this family as a kind of species that occurs in nature, which, we were told, was in danger of dying out.

This is a good example of how **sociobiology** often dominates popular media representations of family. Sociobiology is a school of thought that has become very popular in recent times in order to explain everything from why women can't read maps to why men cannot help but be unfaithful to their wives. The basic idea is that women and men have very different roles to play in life and things are the way they are because this is hard-wired into our brain chemistry or our genes. Sociobiologists are usually very keen to regard human beings as just another type of animal that has natural, programmed instincts and drives designed to maximise survival of the human species.

So why begin a chapter on the history of families with this anecdote about media representations of natural families? We do so to emphasise the contrast between a sociological and a popular view of family. Sociologists take a keen interest in the history of the family precisely because history teaches us that the family is not natural. Foremost, history tells us about the process and the dynamics of social change (Gilding 1997). Through studying the history of the family we learn the extent to which our beliefs and practices with regard to families change over time. Differences are revealed between what we took for granted there and then and what we take for granted here and now. Taking a historical view also enables us to see the close connection between economic change and the dominant forms families take even though the interaction between the economy and families is often complex, contradictory and uneven.

Below, we provide a historical overview of the development of Western and some non-Western families. In taking this comparative perspective, we also emphasise the extent to which culture influences family history. For instance, Chinese and Singaporean families have developed in the context of Confucian values and beliefs that are quite distinctive from the economic and moral traditions influencing the European family. Family historians differ in the approaches they take—some emphasise demographic change and the shape and size of households in particular (see Anderson 1980), others focus on emotions, sentiments and changing ideologies about how family life should be (see Shorter 1975) while others focus on links with the economy or the state (Reiger 1991, 2005; Gilding 1997). Despite the heated academic debates and complex historical data on families over the centuries it is useful to trace dominant patterns and broad shifts so we can understand the heritage of contemporary families and relationships.

First we look at the history of the European family, taking the view that it is appropriate to view non-indigenous families in the UK, USA and Australia as having their roots in European history. We use the following terms to describe the three major patterns in the history of European families. These are **'pre-modern families'**, **'modern families'** and **'late-modern families'**. Pre-modern refers to the period in history prior to the Industrial Revolution. Modern refers to the period from the time of **industrialisation** up to about the mid twentieth century and late-modern refers to the current era—from the 1970s to now.

Pre-modern families (circa pre-eighteenth century)

SOCIOLOGISTS PRIOR TO THE 1970S TENDED to divide the Western family into two main types: the **nuclear family**, consisting of parents and their children living under the one roof, and the **extended family**, consisting of parents, children, grandchildren and possibly other family members. The extended family was believed to be the most common family form in pre-modern societies, and the nuclear family form was believed to have become more common with industrialisation because it was better suited to the needs of societies concentrated in cities with large populations. However, research by historians of the European family such as Laslett, Stone, Shorter and Flandrin argued that these assumptions about pre-modern families were wrong.

Laslett (1972) did most of his work using both parish and census records for various English villages from a time frame between the late sixteenth century and the early nineteenth century. This is called the **demographic approach**. His focus was on broad patterns within the population, with regard to marriage, having children and household size. Contrary to the prevailing view, he found that before industrialisation, most people lived in relatively small households, averaging about 4 to 5 persons, a size that corresponds much more closely to what we expect of a nuclear family. He also found that considerably large numbers of people never married or lived with other single people, or lived alone. This led him to argue that the idea of large extended family households in pre-modern times was a figment of social scientists' imaginations.

Other historians of the family were critical of Laslett's focus on household size and structure and were more interested in how people in households interacted. They took the view that knowing who lived in various households tells us nothing about how those people related to each other, or understood their relationships. Stone, Shorter and Flandrin whose work is consistent with this **'sentiments' approach** looked to more personal, intimate sources such as diaries, letters between family members and doctors' case notes. They also looked at household architecture. For instance, through studying architecture it was possible to understand the priorities given to privacy among household members.

Stone (1977) was interested in the values that were associated with families, rather than family size or structure and argued that there have been at least three main types of family in Western Europe between 1500 and 1800. The **open lineage family** was characterised by lack of privacy, extensive kin ties, lack of close relationships between spouses and between parents and children. This was superseded by the **restricted patriarchal nuclear family**, characterised by loyalties to the Church and State rather than to one's immediate kin or community, with the father being the unquestioned head of the household. The third family type identified by Stone was the **closed domesticated nuclear family**, which he believed became popular around the mid seventeenth century. This family type he associated with stronger bonds of emotion between parents and children, and increased privacy within the home. Stone was also of the view that particular historical periods were characterised by the predominance of these different types of family, but this view has been largely discredited by more recent research that found substantial diversity in family size and shape in these periods (Gittins 1985).

Flandrin (1979) took quite a different view, finding greater diversity within historical periods in his study of regional French families. Flandrin's argument was that it was very misleading to claim that a particular family type predominates at any given point in history. He was also quite dismissive of work like Laslett's that attempted to find broad patterns in the population at the expense of focusing in on detailed variation between families. Knowing who lived in a house, for instance, does not tell us much about the role of servants in households or how they were regarded by other household members. To Flandrin we also owe the observation that the word 'famille' (family, in French) did not always mean mother, father and children living together under one roof. This definition of family included servants living in the household.

Role of the family in society

DESPITE THEIR DIFFERING APPROACHES TO the study of pre-modern families, historians generally agree that pre-modern European families constituted units of production and consumption. That is to say families were involved in agricultural work and produced goods for their own use including food and clothing. Others were involved in small-scale cottage industry, making and selling goods for local consumption beyond the household. Family members tended to labour together on interdependent tasks. Women's and men's labour was mutually dependent and they could not survive without each other. Men, women and children worked in a wide range of economic activities, often interchanging these according to household situation and the availability of work (Gittins 1985).

Stacey (1990) argues that pre-modern families were held together by economics rather than emotions and marriage was an affair of the purse rather than the heart. Arranged marriages, for instance, were customary in sixteenth and seventeenth century England, particularly among wealthier families. These placed the interests of the wider network of kin relationships above and beyond the compatibility or affection of the man and woman getting married. Upper-class families used marriage to make alliances and control large areas of land while poor people married for economic survival (Reiger 2005).

There was a stark difference in the way life was lived between rich and poor families: for instance, the landed gentry compared to peasant farmer families. The poorer the person the harder and more precarious life was. At the same time, there were some similarities among lifestyles of the rich and poor.

Obligation and duty was an important part of family life and behaviour was tightly controlled by the community. A person couldn't survive without being connected to a family household. Privacy was a limited resource in both rich and poor households. In upper-class households there were often guests and servants present in large rooms. In poor European households family members or servants and apprentices were known to share sleeping quarters and even beds in order to fend off the cold (Flandrin 1979).

Role of children

CHILDREN WERE USEFUL AS ECONOMIC assets; they participated in household labour working alongside their parents. Babies were welcomed as future labourers and a source of future security for their parents. Children between the ages of five and seven assumed a variety of work responsibilities such as caring for younger children, undertaking household tasks and tending animals. In many non-Western cultures today children in agricultural families remain productive workers and continue to undertake these tasks (Zelizer 1994).

Before disease prevention measures improved, infant mortality was highly likely and even adults did not tend to live much past what we now refer to as middle age. Therefore death was an omnipresent part of life that shaped and re-shaped families continuously. Because children so frequently died, in some families two living children were given the same name on the assumption that one would die before adulthood. In poor families in particular it was likely for children to have lost siblings and one or both of their parents by the time they grew up (Gittins 1985, p. 9). Because life expectancy was low and the age of marriage was relatively high (around 25) there were few extended families as grandparents rarely lived long enough to see their grandchildren (Gittins 1985).

It is argued that under these circumstances, people were much more restrained about the emotional investment they made in relationships. Relationships between husbands and wives, and parents with their children, were, historically, not always defined as close and intimate. Relationships were more subsumed with survival needs maintained by a network of other important and inter-dependent kin relationships. Shorter (1975) argued that children were routinely maltreated and abandoned, although some now believe he overestimated the extent of this. Writers such as Philip Aries and Laurence Stone argued that in a time of high mortality rates parents remained relatively aloof from their children but as mortality rates improved emotional bonds between parents and children deepened (Zelizer 1994, p. 10). However the evidence for the argument about children being less valued in times of high mortality remains highly speculative. Some writers such as John Demos pose the opposite argument that a high death rate may have encouraged 'a special concern for and tenderness toward infants' (Zelizer 1994, p. 11).

Because of high mortality rates and poverty there were many diverse and blended families. Women frequently died in childbirth so step-parenting was not unusual.

Birth was also a regular feature of life and following marriage, women tended to bear children every few years from their mid 20s to their late 30s—until they died or reached menopause (Gittins 1985). Women were frequently pregnant or breastfeeding, which they combined with caring for young children and other time-consuming productive tasks (Reiger 2005).

Balancing the size of your household in pre-modern times was fairly difficult and servants were required to fill labour shortages in both large households and smaller farms. According to Gittins (1985) over half of the young people in pre-modern England would have experienced a time of living in another household as a servant. Poorer families with large numbers of children would have been forced to send their children to work elsewhere. In richer families boys were more likely to be sent to live as apprentices while girls remained at home until they married. Joining the household or becoming a servant for family members (uncles, aunts, brothers or sisters) was relatively common (Gittins 1985).

Service was an important means by which people whose families had little property or wealth could accrue enough savings to be able to set themselves up in marriage. It also regulated household size, as well as being a vital source of both geographical and social mobility for young people. Pre-modern society was both mobile and varied, and so were the families and households within it (Gittins 1985, p. 16).

Modern families (eighteenth–mid twentieth century)

IN BROAD TERMS, THE INDUSTRIAL era became established in the USA and UK in the late 1700s, in Canada in the mid 1800s and in Australia in the late 1800s. Industrialisation shifted the locus of production away from the family household towards workplaces such as factories and offices that were geographically distant from the home. There were four major changes to family and household organisation largely attributed to the influence of industrial capitalism. There was a growing split between paid and family work, marriage was given a new emotional significance, and family life became increasingly privatised as distinct from the public world of paid work. Finally, gender relations were re-defined with this division of labour so that men came to specialise in paid work while women came to specialise in domestic and emotional work (Stacey 1990). We discuss each of these in turn below.

Once the capitalist economic system became dominant, households began to sell their labour rather than produce everything required for their own needs in their immediate home or village setting. This had consequences for how family members perceived their dependence and independence on the family unit. For instance, the possibility of leaving home to work for strangers freed up children from needing to depend on inheritance of the household farm or cottage industry for their livelihood. They could sell their labour to outsiders and form new family units quite separate from the parental home.

There is little doubt that the nineteenth century European family became far more characterised by notions of privacy and domesticity. At this point in history, the family became more inward looking and centred around conjugality, or the relationship between the married couple, as separated from other kin and the broader community. We can perhaps see this most strongly in changes in domestic architecture. According to Flandrin (1979), domestic architecture in the sixteenth and seventeenth centuries was characterised by rooms that were multipurpose and not specifically designed to preserve privacy between members of the household. The room where you had dinner could be the same room where you would later lay down to sleep. As Gilding (1997) comments, the bedroom as a discrete and segregated room from the public rooms in the house, was a nineteenth century invention. Corridors separating the private rooms of the house from those that guests could have access to, also became a popular architectural form in this period.

Marriage was given a new emotional significance. Marriage was increasingly perceived to be about love, companionship and voluntary commitment. The economic aspects of family life became less obvious and shifted to the background. Mortality rates improved so that by 1800 there were more people surviving to adulthood each year. As wage labour grew and the ability to set up households became easier people began marrying younger (Gittins 1985, p. 22).

The fourth major change was a re-making of gender relationships and a new sexual contract between men as '**breadwinners**' and women as '**homemakers**'. Tilly and Scott (1978), two influential feminist historians, emphasise how the growth of workshops and factories as the focus for paid work, rather than the home, influenced the role of women in society at large, and the increasing differentiation between men's and women's roles in the family. There were new difficulties that arose for women having children if they had to go out to work. Women's paid work had to become irregular and still largely focused around domestic duties that could keep them close to where the children were. It became customary for women to alternate between reproductive and productive work rather than do both at once, as they had in earlier times when the household was the site of production. The fact that paid work became largely separate from the home meant that women from more wealthy households tended to stop paid work altogether. This led to the sharp distinction between a domestic sphere of activity and a separate sphere of paid work. Along with this separation, the home came to be idealised as something of a haven or refuge from the fast pace of city life, and a complete contrast to the values of the world of work.

Modern families are sometimes called 'bourgeois' families because of the rise and increased dominance of the middle classes under industrialisation. The bourgeois family overtook both the peasant and upper-class modes of family organisation. Middle-class families were the first to adopt the gendered public and private distinction. Women's labour remained crucial to working-class families and many women participated in factory work, sometimes on a casual or seasonal basis. 'Outwork' or labour undertaken at home such as making matchboxes or gloves, or needlework was undertaken by working-class women alongside their caring responsibilities (Gittins 1985, p. 29).

The emergence of 'childhood'

DURING THE NINETEENTH CENTURY, CHILDHOOD became increasingly split off from other parts of the life cycle as a special time of development and learning. In the USA for example, by the mid nineteenth century the urban middle class had come to see the period of childhood as separate from adulthood and a sacred and emotionally important part of the life cycle. Children became less of an economic asset to the family as they stopped undertaking labour and were encouraged to focus on education. At the same time, class differences were apparent with regard to the meaning and experience of childhood. Working-class urban families remained dependent on the wages of older children and the household assistance of younger ones. But this was set to change. The introduction of child-labour laws and compulsory education for all children meant that by the 1930s working-class children had become as economically useless and emotionally priceless as their middle-class counterparts (Zelizer 1994, p. 6).

The changes to the family given impetus by industrialisation can be summed up as follows. As capitalist economies developed, they needed a healthy, well-disciplined and educated labour force. Men became breadwinners and were expected to economically support their wives and children. Women became homemakers—domestic specialists and mothers. Mothering came to be seen as a natural vocation for women. Children were to concentrate on their education while women cared for and socialised children and took care of male workers' household needs (Zelizer 1994, p. 9). Over the course of the late nineteenth to early twentieth century, these changes gradually became 'naturalised' in Western countries with capitalist economies—they came to be seen as natural and inevitable.

The modern Australian family

FOR MANY YEARS THERE WAS an implication that the Australian family did not have a distinctive history of its own, and merely followed European patterns. White settlers could not comprehend—and were barely influenced by—traditional Aboriginal families or their ways of life. (We discuss Aboriginal families further in the next chapter.) Feminist historian Patricia Grimshaw (1983) contends that the Australian family was 'born modern' or very much modelled on the European, nuclear form. With the extended family left behind in Europe, husband and wife couples had to draw on their own resources in establishing households and families. Grimshaw also looked to the specific circumstances of life in the Australian colonies as meaningful for the development of the Australian family. For Grimshaw, the generally harsh, pioneering conditions in the Australian colonies supported more interdependent working relationships between women and men that in turn fostered more egalitarian intimate relationships. For instance, Australian women obtained the vote before women in European countries, and Grimshaw believes this was the result of their relatively high status in the Australian family of the time.

Michael Gilding (1991) analyses the changing character of the Australian family in the period between 1870 and 1930. He contends that the Australian family changed a great deal in that 60-year period, and traces the social forces that brought the changes about. While largely supportive of Grimshaw's work on the Australian family, Gilding departed from her argument in two main ways. He believed Grimshaw overemphasised the imported modernity of the Australian family in the early colonies, and also the uniformity of Australian families. Gilding saw much more evidence of complexity and diversity in the family and household arrangements of the late nineteenth century Sydney families he studied.

For instance, Gilding saw evidence that the form households adopted largely depended on people's means. Business men and other kinds of professionals were able to form large households that included extended kin, long-staying guests and servants. Households grew bigger or smaller depending on whether or not extended kin required economic support. Among the less wealthy, things were quite different. According to Gilding, the Sydney economy of the late nineteenth century necessitated a lot of casual labour that could relocate at short notice. Boarding houses became popular to cater to this. Many families took in lodgers from this casual and mobile labour force to supplement the family income. Sometimes parents, children and grandparents or other family members lived together for periods of time to help each other out. Servants were still commonly members of wealthier households. However, Gilding found that as the twentieth century progressed, this diversity in household form narrowed. Servants disappeared, domestic service for girls in wealthy households became less common, and the practice of lodging became less widespread. Extended family households became less evident. Economic restructuring and the development of welfare policy promoted smaller and more nuclear households. The nuclear family household came to predominate due to a particular constellation of circumstances based on 'regulation from above and improvisation from below' (1991, p. 10). In other words, Gilding encourages us to look at the history of Australian families as the product of changing economic circumstances, government policy-making in response to these, and how ordinary people creatively respond to government intervention and economic realities.

For Gilding, a crucial aspect to this changing experience of family was the continuous reconstruction of the language through which family relationships were understood. For instance, between the late nineteenth century and the present day, many new words and concepts entered the language of family, and shaped taken-for-granted beliefs about family. Other older words changed their meanings. Words such as 'breadwinner' and 'housewife' to explain men's and women's distinctive roles in the family emerged. Concepts such as 'delinquency' and 'motherhood' were defined differently. Gilding claims that the previously very clear class distinction in Australia between 'ladies' and 'women' collapsed as the concept 'housewife' emerged in the lexicon. Women of all classes began to do work that was more and more privatised and less acknowledged as work, meaning gender increasingly came to shape women's experience rather than notions of class. The idea that children were 'dependants' had become mainstream by the 1930s, whereas before the 1880s, children were expected to work and contribute to the household economy.

In *The Disenchantment of the Home* (1985), Kerreen Reiger's interest was in a similar period to Gilding's: between 1880 and 1940. However, her focus was on how the Australian family became an object of intervention 'from above' or of great interest to experts over that period of time. Childrearing, in particular, came to be seen as a much more specialised task. Professionals such as doctors and teachers became increasingly concerned with regulating family life, taking the care of children out of the hands of parents and into the hands of professionals with specific expertise. In the late nineteenth century, for instance, schooling became compulsory for Australian children, whereas prior to this the responsibility for educating children was largely the job of parents. Reiger documents how in the early part of the twentieth century, the monitoring of babies' health by infant welfare nurses became the norm. All of this reflects changing beliefs about the value of children and childhood. Childcare had become too important and specialised to be left in the hands of mothers. People, notably women, had to be told how to do it.

The aberrant 1950s family

THE HEIGHT OF THE NUCLEAR family occurred in the mid 1950s in Australia, the USA and the UK. The economic boom following the end of the War, led to good conditions for marriage and household formation. More people got married, and they got married earlier than ever before. In the mid 1950s the average age of a first marriage was 21.5. Romantic love and sexual attraction were viewed as the main basis for marriage rather than economic security. There was also a **'baby boom'** along with the favourable economic conditions in which fertility rates increased and most families had 3 to 4 children (Reiger 2005).

In this post–World War II era, the breadwinner/homemaker model reached its pinnacle as the template for organising family life. At this time, Talcott

Parsons, a famous family sociologist, developed the functionalist understanding of the role of the family in industrialised societies (Parsons & Bales 1955). Parsons argued that family members had different functions according to their gender. Men had mainly 'instrumental roles' and specialised in paid work and public life. By contrast women specialised in 'expressive roles', managing emotions and socialising children. We will discuss Parsons's perspective in more depth in Chapter 4.

The high rate of marriage in early adulthood and high fertility that characterised the 1950s nuclear family was aberrant if we consider the broader sweep of European history. It was soon to lose its demographic dominance but its ideological dominance has largely continued. There is continued rebellion against and/or nostalgia for this model of family life (Stacey 1990).

Families and relationships in late modernity

WE NOW TURN TO CONSIDER the contemporary social landscape for our relationships and families. The development of the post-industrial economy coincided with new changes in family life. This occurred from the 1960s onwards in the USA and from the 1970s onwards in Australia. The last four decades have been characterised by a 'marriage bust', a 'baby bust' (Bittman & Pixley 1997), an increased period of dependency on parents by young adults and greater diversity in relational and household forms.

The **marriage bust** consists of a series of interrelated developments. Increasingly, young people began choosing to delay marriage or not to marry at all. The proportion of young people cohabiting outside marriage rose substantially in the 1980s in Australia so that by the early 1990s, the proportion of people choosing to cohabit before marriage was greater than the proportion marrying without prior cohabitation. In 2006 the vast majority of couples marrying (76 per cent) cohabited prior to marriage (ABS 2007c). Alongside the delay and retreat from marriage is the substantial rise in the divorce rate. In Australia in 1975, legislation was passed to allow divorce without the need to assign fault to a guilty party. The divorce rate has grown steadily since then, reaching a high point in 2001 but declining slightly in recent years. Over the last two decades the number of divorces has increased by more than 30 per cent (ABS 2007a). It is reasonable to argue that in Western countries such as Australia divorce has become 'normalised' (Beck-Gernsheim 2002). For example, the stigma surrounding divorce has largely dissipated and divorce is a viable proposition for all married couples. It is estimated that a third of Australian marriages entered into in 2000–02 will end in divorce (ABS 2007d). The economic and emotional changes in the basis of marriage have undermined it as an institution. In late modernity it became possible for men and women to live outside marriage as cohabiting couples or single people. Marriage is no longer essential economically as both women and men can make a living in the paid labour market. Instead marriage became the focus of emotional fulfilment. However as Stephanie Coontz argues in her history of marriage, 'personal satisfaction' is an inherently unstable foundation for marriage (Coontz 2005).

The **baby bust** coincided with the marriage bust (Bittman & Pixley 1997, p. 14; Paice 2003). Couples have delayed having children and had fewer of them. In comparison to pre-modern families, children were no longer a financial necessity or insurance against old age but a definite burden. The financial burden of having children is now calculated by government agencies and discussed in the media. According to recent estimates, raising two children from birth to age 20 costs about half a million dollars ($448,000) or $310 a week, or 23 per cent of a couple's gross income (Percival & Harding 2003). To ameliorate some of the initial costs of having children the Australian government has introduced a baby bonus to be paid at the birth of each child.

The experiences and responsibilities characteristic of young adulthood have also changed, as young people spend a longer time in education and tend to delay the responsibilities that accompany marriage and childrearing. Increasing proportions of young people stay in the family home until their mid 20s and beyond. Age 30, rather than 21, is the age for 'settling down' in the twenty-first century. For Australians the median age of first marriage is 30 for men and 28 for women (ABS 2007c) and the median age of mothers giving birth in 2006 was 31 and the median age for men having a child was 33 (ABS 2007b).

Second wave feminism developed in the 1970s and it was to have major impact on the way family life was explored academically and experienced personally. Much of the focus and success of feminism was in the domain of paid work for women. Women, including married women with children, entered the paid workforce in unprecedented numbers. In the post-industrial economy women continue to be regarded as a cheap and flexible workforce that can meet labour market demands.

Feminist analysis turned to the domestic sphere and housework was recognised as a form of labour supporting the paid labour market. Women continued to undertake the bulk of domestic labour even as they entered the paid labour market and men were slow or resisted taking a greater share of domestic labour. Housework was no longer highly regarded. Paid work has increasingly become valorised as central to adult identity and according to some writers we now enjoy and privilege work over sex (Trinca & Fox 2004). Domestic labour has become largely denigrated as a meaningful activity (Lloyd & Johnson 2004).

The feminist movement and other liberation movements of the 1960s and 1970s and the availability of effective contraception have meant that sexuality has become largely freed from reproduction. For the majority of young people with Anglo-Celtic backgrounds in Australia marriage is no longer a prerequisite for having sex. The opportunity for casual sexual relationships has re-shaped dating and courtship patterns, an issue we will explore in more depth in Chapter 5.

As we move to increased labour market flexibility and post-industrial work time schedules, households are becoming even smaller. It can be argued that consumer capitalism requires flexible, mobile workers available around the clock, so in response families become smaller and the divorce rate continues to grow (Beck-Gernsheim 2002). The proportion of smaller households is projected to grow. There is now a greater prevalence of single people, sole parent families and the elderly than in other times in history.

Where does this leave the family? It is reasonable to argue that the family has been so de-institutionalised it can no longer be taken for granted as a social institution with fixed functions. The divorce rate is high and unmarried cohabitation is an increasing phenomenon. New family forms are emerging in that lesbian and gay couples and single women are increasingly engaged in child-rearing. LAT couples have emerged, these are partners who are 'living apart together' in a relationship but maintaining separate residences. As Judith Stacey, an American sociologist argues, in Western countries we are moving towards a social context where there is no single dominant pattern of relationships or families. Instead relationships are contested, ambivalent, undecided, diverse, fluid, unresolved and fragile (Stacey 1990).

History of East Asian and South-East Asian families

The history of East and South-East Asian families is substantially different to Western families and a brief comparison is useful to contextualise family change. These cultures and countries are extremely diverse but they share some common elements in terms of family history. The ideal family over a number of centuries is the extended family, a tightly knit social group involving three generations. Parents, their married children and spouses (or at least one of their children) and their children's children live in the same household or compound or at least in the same neighbourhood (Quah 2003, p. 2). The three generation family ideal is favoured in China, Japan, Korea, Malaysia, the Philippines, Singapore, Taiwan, Thailand and Vietnam (Quah 2003).

The histories of East and South-East Asian countries vary dramatically in terms of colonisation, war and mass migration. In terms of colonisation there is the history of the Dutch in Indonesia, the British in Singapore and Malaysia and the French in Vietnam and Cambodia. Wars radically changed everyday life in Vietnam, Cambodia and Korea as did the introduction of communism in China, Vietnam and Korea. Mass migration from the Philippines and Vietnam dramatically increased the proportion of transnational families. The lived realities of families in these countries vary in marked ways in response to these wider social forces. In this book we are unable to provide a comprehensive account of family history or family change in East and South-East Asian families but we use examples throughout the chapters to illustrate culturally diverse family practices and experiences. We end this chapter with a brief discussion of the history of Chinese families to illustrate how economic development and family change have played out in a distinct cultural and historical context.

Chinese families

EAST ASIAN COUNTRIES SUCH as mainland China, Korea, Japan, Taiwan and South-East Asian countries such as Singapore and Vietnam, are all heavily influenced by the philosophical school of thought known as **Confucianism.** The Confucian tradition places emphasis on family hierarchy, **filial piety** and parental authority. This means the wider kin group and parents, in particular, played a major role in spouse selection, the timing of marriage and where the married couple would live (Quah 2003, p. 27). The theme of women's subordination is also a very strong element of the Confucian tradition. Loyalty and obedience are central virtues so sons are subordinate to fathers, wives are subordinate to husbands and subjects are subordinate to rulers (Quah 2003, p. 121). In the traditional Chinese family there was strong patriarchal authority and **patrilineal** descent and the expectation that the oldest son would marry and continue to the live with the parents and other sons and daughters would marry and leave the family unit (Logan, Bian & Bian 1998).

Local historical and political factors are also important. For instance, in China, the adoption of communism in 1949 had a radical impact on family life. The egalitarian ideology of the Cultural Revolution provided women with education and paid employment, which increased the age of marriage (Quah 2003). Women joined men in working outside the home but they were also expected to continue doing domestic labour tasks within the home (Entwisle & Henderson 2000). The recruitment of young people as paid workers or volunteers for a range of public activities took young people away from their families and undermined the traditional system of the superiority of age. Customary large wedding celebrations were banned by the state (Quah 2003).

The one-child policy was introduced in 1979 to radically reduce population growth. This has been 'the most aggressive, comprehensive population policy in the world' (Short et al. 2001, p. 913). The fertility rate declined dramatically from 6 in 1969 to 2.7 in 1979. The policy is not always strictly one child and many rural families are allowed to have two children if the first child is a girl. The one-child policy has had a profound effect on Chinese family life and will continue to do so in the future. A shift towards more child-centred parenting has emerged as children have become scarce (Short et al. 2001). However, the strong preference for male children has been intensified by the one-child policy and there is a gender imbalance in the Chinese population from selective abortion (Short et al. 2001). The implication of this gender bias is that there are a large proportion of Chinese men who will not find partners to marry in the future.

Although urbanisation and industrialisation proceeded and women now enter the labour force outside the home, the pattern of intergenerational living arrangements has remained a central feature of Chinese family life. Logan et al. (1998) argue that the living preferences of Chinese families have been constrained by the State. First, there was limited investment in urban housing during the 1950s and throughout the Cultural Revolution and housing shortages have forced families to live together. There is evidence that the state has tacitly supported **patrilocal** preferences and couples are more likely to find housing through the husband's work unit instead of the wife's. Second, public services for children and the elderly have been limited. The state has emphasised women's employment but has not provided adequate childcare. At the same time responsibility for the elderly has been assigned to adult children. Both of these encourage co-residence and people look for solutions to work and care issues within their family (Logan et al. 1998). In summary, the example of families in China illustrates how broad historical developments—the shift to communism, the upheavals of the Great Leap Forward and the Cultural Revolution and the realities of contemporary policy—profoundly shape the day-to-day lives of families.

Conclusion

FAR FROM BEING NATURAL OR biologically given, families change over time. In this chapter we have discussed the complex links between historical developments and notions of gender, relationships and families. Our main focus has been on the development of Western families. Pre-modern families were diverse but being attached to a household was crucial for economic survival. Life was difficult and precarious—the mortality rate was high and life expectancy was low. Modern families emerged alongside industrialisation and involved a new gendered contract between male breadwinners and female homemakers. It is argued that there was a new emphasis on emotional life and love and companionship in marriage. Late-modern families signify a return to the household diversity of pre-modern times. However, families are frequently re-shaped by divorce now rather than death. The strict division between the public and private is waning as women's paid labour is increasingly viewed as a necessary contribution to contemporary households.

In this chapter we have emphasised historical change as changing economic circumstances but social changes such as liberation movements and technological developments also shaped the possibilities for personal life in important ways.

There are many versions of the history of families and relationships to be told but the key argument we have presented in this chapter is that social forces, such as the organisation of the economy, play a large role in the ways in which people establish relationships and families. In the following chapter we examine cultural diversity as an influence on families and relationships.

Key concepts

Sociobiology

Pre-modern families

Modern families

Late-modern families

Nuclear family

Extended family

Industrialisation

Demographic approach

Sentiments approach

Open lineage family

Restricted patriarchal nuclear family

Closed domesticated nuclear family

Patrilineal

Confucianism

Second wave feminism

Discussion questions

1   Why is it important to study the history of families?

2   What are the main differences between pre-modern, modern and late-modern families?

3   Which social factors have most influenced change in Australian families over the past 50 years? Provide examples.

4   What are the main social forces shaping the history of Asian as opposed to Western families? Are there similarities and differences in trends over the past 50 years?

Recommended further reading

Gilding, M. 2001, 'Changing Families in Australia 1901–2001', *Family Matters*, no. 60, pp. 6–11.

Quah, S. 2003, *Home and Kin: Families in Asia*, Eastern Universities Press, Singapore.

Reiger, K. 1985, *The Disenchantment of the Home: Modernising the Australian Family 1880–1940*, Oxford University Press, Melbourne.

03 | Relationships, Families and Cultural Diversity

Figure 3.1: Images from the films *The Birdcage*, *Billy Elliot* and *My Big Fat Greek Wedding*

Introduction

EACH OF THE POPULAR FILMS illustrated above presents the viewer with what could be called a culture clash. In *My Big Fat Greek Wedding* the importance of the extended family group shapes Toula's everyday life—both in its controlling and generous aspects—in comparison to the quiet reserve of her fiancé Ian's Anglo-American family. In *The Birdcage* we see Val's gay fathers and mother being forced into role-playing a traditional nuclear family configuration to impress Barbara's ultra-conservative middle-class parents. Finally, in *Billy Elliot* we see working-class notions of appropriate masculinity pushed to the limits as Billy's working-class father and brother struggle to allow Billy to enter the 'feminine' world of ballet.

Families and relationships vary enormously according to cultural context. There are substantial cultural differences between and within different countries. Embracing a multi-faceted discussion of cultural diversity as encompassing ethnic, racial, sexuality and class dimensions, this chapter elaborates the substance and consequences of cultural diversity in families. First, the distinction between traditional and contemporary Indigenous Australian families is discussed. Second, we look at immigrant families from non-English speaking backgrounds and we discuss the ways in which these families are similar to each other and different from Anglo-Australian nuclear families. Third, we consider same-sex families and relationships. Finally, we outline the manner in which **social class** shapes family experience.

Diversity beyond the nuclear family

IN WESTERN SOCIETIES SUCH AS Australia, the **nuclear family** remains a dominant cultural ideal. Most people live in a nuclear family household comprised of mother, father and children for at least some of their childhood or adult lives, and this family form enjoys the support of major social institutions such as the government and organised religion. Despite this cultural dominance of the nuclear family, a range of different values, assumptions and expectations influence the expression of family and intimate relationships. Many Australians do not spend their entire lives in nuclear family households, and embrace diverse notions of interdependence, intimacy and support beyond this idea and form of family life.

Cultural diversity exists when people have different values and beliefs about family and intimate relationships that are, in turn, expressed in their practices. The notion of cultural diversity often brings to mind 'multiculturalism', or the idea that Australian society is made up of a number of distinctive, immigrant ethnic groups, each with their own family structures, customs and traditions. This is one aspect of cultural diversity. Vasta (1993) comments that there has been a tendency to view the concept 'culture' in a very static way in Australian discussions of multiculturalism, as if culturally and linguistically diverse immigrants come to Australia with uniform, unchanging and decidedly different views about family from their Anglo-Australian counterparts. An alternative understanding of cultural diversity, which can be extended to other contexts, assumes culture is a more dynamic process. The complicated intersections between history, tradition, the changing nature of the migration experience and local practice need to be taken into account when considering cultural diversity in immigrant families and relationships. With regard to indigenous families and relationships, the history of European colonisation, remote or urban geographic location, and local patterns of migration, all influence how cultural diversity is expressed. Bottomley (1997) argues that culture is informed by: 'ideas, beliefs and practices through which people negotiate their conditions of existence' (p. 3). In other words, culture shapes and is shaped by the people who live it, and is constantly transformed through social interactions in local contexts.

Sexual and class diversity can be thought of as cultural diversity, because different ideals from the nuclear family standard often exist when it comes to interdependence, intimacy and social support. Historically, lesbians and gay men have lived in fear of social rejection by members of their families of origin, leading to some loss of faith in the permanence of these relationships (Weston 1991; Weeks, Heaphy & Donovan 2001). Lesbian and gay relationships and households raise the prospect that family is more a question of who sustains us in our day-to-day existence, rather than relationships defined by heterosexuality, biological relatedness, co-residence or legal status. Class differences, like other cultural differences, are often overlooked, but class has a profound influence on assumptions about families and personal relationships, and we consider class in the final section of this chapter.

- -

Indigenous Australian families

VERY DIFFERENT NOTIONS OF **KINSHIP** (that is, relatedness to others) were evident among Indigenous Australians from the beginning of contact with European colonists. As in other hunter-gatherer societies worldwide, the extended family was the locus for political, social and economic organisation (Healy, Hassan & McKenna 1985). The traditional Aboriginal concept of kinship is complex, diverse and very different from the nuclear family model. It encompasses siblings, aunts, uncles, grandparents and other connections reckoned in ways often completely unfamiliar to Western notions of relatedness. For instance, marriage with certain kinds of biological cousins is considered highly desirable among some groups. Mothers' sisters may also be referred to and treated as mothers in some groups. Traditional Indigenous kinship rules also specify kinds of relationships that should be socially avoided. Among some groups, brothers and sisters were not allowed to freely mix socially after they became adults, and a prohibition regarding social contact between a man and his wife's mother exists (Berndt & Berndt 1977). Kinship could also be attained through certain kinds of social contact. Many anthropologists coming into contact with remote Indigenous groups have achieved kinship status by virtue of acceptance into the local community.

As Gilding (1997) notes, it is very hard to understand the details of a kinship system pertaining to a different cultural setting because we take our own assumptions about relatedness so much for granted. Consider the complexity of this description of relatedness among the Mardu people of the Western Desert district of Australia:

> My father's brothers are classed together with my father and are all called by the same term, which in Mardu is *mama*; similarly, my mother's sisters are called yagurdi (mother). Therefore, my parallel cousins on both sides of my father (mother's sisters' children and father's brothers' children) I classify as 'brother' and 'sister' because they are children of the people I call 'mother' and 'father'. In turn, I call the children of my male parallel cousins 'son' and 'daughter' since any woman my brother calls 'wife' I will also call 'wife' (Tonkinson, cited in Gilding 1997, p. 9, original italics).

In traditional Indigenous cultures, place was central to notions of kinship and identity. Attachment to land or country, and ancestral stories or Dreamings about the spirits inhabiting particular places strongly influenced understandings of belonging and relatedness. European settlers did not recognise the significance of land to Indigenous Australians, because Indigenous Australians did not have similar concepts of buying, selling and ownership of discrete plots or allotments. The early white settler notion of Australia as 'Terra Nullius' or 'empty land' ripe for colonisation and ownership demonstrated this lack of understanding or respect for Indigenous notions of belonging to country. For traditional Indigenous Australians, there is no such thing as empty space, all people are produced by and in turn produce place. In traditional families, children explore place or country alongside relationships with people from birth. Children learn to understand themselves as produced by the land, its resources, wildlife, the food it produces, and understand these features of the land as part of themselves. Hartley (1995) notes that remote Indigenous Australians still living their lives according to traditional cultural values tend to place one another by asking 'Where do you come from?' rather than 'What is your name?'.

It is important not to over-generalise and systemise Indigenous kinship from one part of Australia to another. Anthropologist John Avery (2002) argues that individual behaviour, competition between groups occupying adjacent geographic areas and highly specific coalition building in particular places, are key to understanding the character of Indigenous kinship and social life in the Northern regions of Australia. For instance, some traditional groups may emphasise birth order and seniority in ways that others do not. The way kinship ties are reckoned with regard to status or the strength of spiritual connections to land or place may also differ from group to group, and change over time.

Early anthropological accounts of Indigenous Australian kinship emphasised that responsibilities for raising children tended to be shared among extended kin rather than the biological mother and father, as was the European norm. The anthropologist Bronislav Malinowski, who did extensive fieldwork in the

1930s in Central Australian Indigenous communities, came to the conclusion that children were treated affectionately, yet very leniently in Indigenous communities. Many writers have noted that children in Indigenous families were historically taught to respect an extended notion of kinship, and the value of keeping close contact with and providing support and sustenance to kin. Traditionally, although children were reared by the extended family group, mothers, mothers' sisters and grandmothers played a pivotal role in rearing children. Through this process of socialisation by grandmothers and mothers, children learned to identify their kin connections and know who they could and couldn't associate with.

There are no Indigenous Australian communities that remain entirely untouched by Western culture and influence (Healy, Hassan & McKenna 1985). However, in remote areas of Western and Northern Australia, many Indigenous Australians continue to live and organise kinship according to traditional culture, where 'traditional' is defined by practices such as initiation ceremonies, following other forms of tribal law, and speaking an Indigenous language rather than or in addition to English. Polygyny, or marrying multiple wives, according to tribal law continues to be practised in some remote Western Australian and Northern Territory communities. In the southern regions of Australia, traditional ways of living have been far more disrupted by a succession of Australian Government policies invested in removing Indigenous people from their land, institutionalising children in government missions, and removing whiter skinned children from their families of origin.

The Stolen Generation

Australian director Phil Noyce's 2002 film *Rabbit-Proof Fence* examines the eugenicist thinking that informed the removal of Indigenous children from their families for most of the twentieth century. According to political scientist and social commentator Robert Manne, Noyce's film offers a clear historical interpretation of the early phase of Aboriginal child removal in Western Australia, which was strongly motivated by the ideas about racial purity that informed the White Australia policy. The film tells the story of three 'half-caste' girls from the

Figure 3.2: Cover of *Bringing Them Home* Report

Aboriginal settlement at Jigalong in the West Australian north, who were seized by the police in the early 1930s and transported to the Moore River Native Settlement, but who escaped and, managed to walk over 2400 kilometres home. The so-called Chief Protector of Aborigines at the time, A.O. Neville, was strongly motivated to 'cleanse' society of half-castes, albeit for what he believed was their own good. There was a very deliberate attempt on behalf of Australian government authorities to erase black people from the population through removing mixed race children from their families and encouraging them to marry each other or whites. Through these means, it was believed, aboriginality would eventually be bred out of the population. In 1997 an Australian government enquiry entitled 'Bringing Them Home' (illustrated on previous page) documented the devastating and long-term impact of the removal of children from Aboriginal families. In February 2008, in a historic, nationally televised event, Australian Prime Minister Kevin Rudd apologised to the **Stolen Generation** in Parliament for the irreparable pain and suffering caused by the interventions of successive Australian governments and their officers into the lives of Indigenous families.

Historian Anna Haebich (2000) explains how in the 1950s and 1960s, in most Australian states, there was an increase in the removal of children from Aboriginal families. In addition to the racist motive of attempting to breed aboriginality out of the population, removal policies were partially due to the imposition of mainstream white cultural values with regard to standards of housing and parenting. Interventions directed at and surveillance of Aboriginal families were designed to make these families conform to the nuclear model. To take the example of one Australian state—New South Wales—in excess of 5000 Aboriginal children were removed from their birth families between 1909 and 1969 (Read 1983). The Australian Bureau of Statistics found that in 1994, 10 per cent of Indigenous Australians aged over 25 said they had been removed from their families of origin and reared apart from family networks.

Contemporary aboriginal families

IN SPITE OF THE SHAMEFUL history of white Australia's maltreatment of Indigenous families, Indigenous family life endures in cases where people have grown up quite separated from extended family and country. Contemporary Indigenous urban families continue to experience higher levels of poverty, unemployment and ill-health in comparison with other groups in the Australian population. Their families and households tend to be much larger than other Australian families, and they have lower incomes. There are also larger numbers of sole parents on social security payments among Indigenous Australians. Daly and Smith (2003) note that in 2001, the proportion of Indigenous families in Australia receiving a Parenting Payment Single (PPS) allowance from the Australian Government was twice that of other families. In many urban communities such as Fitzroy in inner

Melbourne and Redfern in Sydney, Indigenous families have to contend with poverty, racism, alcoholism and much poorer health and life expectancy than their white Australian counterparts.

Poverty and hardship are also not the only stories to be told about growing up in an indigenous family. Some urban, middle-class Indigenous families have similar patterns of employment, education and notions of home and place to their non-indigenous counterparts. Many Indigenous Australians, particularly in the southern states of Australia, live in nuclear families, marry people from other cultural backgrounds and speak English as their first or only language, in which case their familial expectations and ways of life bear more resemblance to dominant European patterns than traditional cultural values. Yin Paradies (2006) contends that contemporary indigenous families and notions of identity are characterised by hybridity, fluidity and complexity. By 'hybrid', Paradies is referring to the fact that many contemporary urban people of indigenous background see their aboriginality as one component of a multi-faceted identity that includes whiteness, as well as gender, sexuality, socio-economic status and educational background. Many contemporary Indigenous Australians inhabit an in-between space where they are both black and white, Indigenous and non-Indigenous by virtue of their racial and cultural heritage, and how they are treated by others as a result of this. In arguing that Indigenous and non-Indigenous Australians need to embrace the multiplicity of family and cultural identities, Paradies describes his family and cultural background in the following way:

> I identify racially as an Aboriginal-Anglo-Asian Australian … My personal history compels me to identify as more than just indigenous and as other than exclusively white, while moving beyond this dichotomy in also recognizing my Asian heritage … Descended from both Indigenous and Euro-Australian ancestors I am both colonizer and colonized, both Black and consummately White … Due in large part to my grandmother being a part of the Stolen Generation, I do not speak an Aboriginal language, I do not have a connection with my spiritual lands or a unique spirituality inherited through my indigeneity. I have little contact with my extended family and the majority of my friends are non-indigenous. Also due to this same history, I am a middle-class, highly educated professional working in the field of indigenous research (Paradies 2006, pp. 357–8).

Culturally and linguistically diverse immigrant families

BEFORE THE AUSTRALIAN CONSTITUTION WAS drafted in 1900, there was a history of encouraging migration to Australia from a number of non-English-speaking

European, and Asian countries. However, the *Immigration Restriction Act* came into effect in 1901—the so-called White Australia policy—which severely curtailed the possibility for immigrants of non-English-speaking origin to settle in Australia. By 1947, Australia had one of the most culturally and ethnically homogenous societies in the world, with only three per cent of the population born overseas (other than in the UK or Ireland) (Storer 1985).

In 1947, the exceedingly difficult English language dictation test underpinning the White Australia policy was discontinued, and immigration from a number of non-English-speaking European countries was encouraged for economic reasons (Storer 1985). Since this time, immigration has been one major influence on the cultural diversity of Australian families and in excess of 5.5 million people have migrated to Australia from 170 countries (Batrouney & Stone 1998). Although the main source of migration to Australia between 1947 and the present day continues to be from English-speaking countries such as England, Scotland, Ireland and New Zealand, considerable numbers of continental European immigrants arrived throughout the 1950s and 1960s from the Netherlands, Italy, Greece and the former Yugoslavian countries (Serbia, Croatia, Slovenia). With the complete dismantling of the White Australia policy in the early 1970s, Asian immigrants increased in number, and large groups from Vietnam, China, Hong Kong, Sri Lanka, the Philippines and Indonesia now reside in Australia (Batrouney & Stone 1998). The most recently arrived groups in Australia include refugees from the Eritrea, Ethiopia, Somalia and Sudan, and a number of Middle-Eastern countries such as Iraq and Afghanistan.

Table 3.1: Regions of birth, Proportion of Australia's population— Selected years at 30 June

	1997 %	2002 %	2003 %	2004 %	2005 %	2006 %	2007 %
Australia	76.7	76.7	76.4	76.2	75.8	75.4	75.0
Oceania and Antarctica (excl. Aust.)	2.3	2.6	2.7	2.7	2.7	2.7	2.8
North-West Europe	8.2	7.5	7.4	7.4	7.3	7.3	7.3
Southern and Eastern Europe	4.8	4.4	4.3	4.3	4.2	4.1	4.0

(continued)

Table 3.1: (*Continued*)

	1997 %	2002 %	2003 %	2004 %	2005 %	2006 %	2007 %
North Africa and the Middle East	1.2	1.2	1.3	1.3	1.4	1.4	1.5
South-East Asia	2.8	2.9	2.9	3.0	3.0	3.1	3.2
North-East Asia	1.6	1.8	1.9	2.0	2.1	2.3	2.5
Southern and Central Asia	0.9	1.1	1.2	1.3	1.4	1.6	1.6
Americas	0.9	0.9	0.9	1.0	1.0	1.0	1.0
Sub-Saharan Africa	0.7	0.9	0.9	1.0	1.0	1.1	1.1

Source: ABS 2008, *Migration Australia*, cat. no. 3412.0 p. 48

Despite the cultural differences between the different immigrant communities in Australia, some similarities with regard to the organisation of family life and intergenerational relationships have been observed. In the following section, three dimensions of similarity between different non-English-speaking background immigrant families are elaborated; the tendency for the interests of individuals to be subordinate to the interests of extended kin and community, the tendency towards family and household structures that privilege extended or dispersed family networks; and the notion of 'generation gap' between overseas-born parents and their second or third generation children.

Interests of individuals subordinate to interests of the broader group

ANGLO-AUSTRALIAN, BRITISH AND AMERICAN nuclear family values tend to emphasise individuality, self-reliance and assertiveness among family members once they reach certain age-based milestones. For instance, there is strong expectation that children will grow up, move out of the family home, choose their partners and their line of work, and establish a new family home when they are ready to have children of their own. Although young adult children who go into tertiary education may be financially dependent on parents for much longer, children in Western countries are basically encouraged to establish quite separate lives from their parents. Most elderly Australians do not live with their adult children, and are responsible for managing their own finances (de Vaus 2004). It is also reasonably common for elderly parents to move into retirement villages or supported accommodation once they are no longer able to meet their own daily self-care and grooming needs. This is not to say 'Anglo' extended family members are not involved in each other's lives. Rather, it is to point out that a considerable measure of independence from each other and negotiated commitments based on individual capacity are often seen as ideal (see Finch & Mason 1993).

However, as Robin Hartley (1995) notes in her study of ethnic family values in Australia, in both Asian and continental European families, the interests of the extended family tend to be emphasised over and above the interests of the individual. McDonald (1991) argues that this is consistent with the values of the traditional **patriarchal family**. Stronger paternal authority over women and children in many non-English speaking immigrant families tends to go along with other attributes such as, a tendency towards higher fertility and earlier marriage, and an influential and engaged network of relatives who exert pressure on key relationship decisions such as marriage.

Eastern cultural practice is predicated on notions of generational inter-dependence, mutual exchange and obligation (Sheng & Settles 2007). East and South-East Asian societies remain strongly influenced by the belief system known as Confucianism, which places emphasis on children's obligations to care for their elderly parents. This is because caregiving is consistent with **filial piety**, or showing respect, obedience and gratitude to elder parents and grandparents (Kwok 2006; Ikels 2004). Children are taught from an early age that elderly relatives are their responsibility, not only their parents' responsibility. Chinese elderly people are likely to rely on their adult children for economic support and daily care in later life. Daughters may be expected to look after parents or elderly relatives in their homes and sons may be expected to support parents and elderly relatives financially (Sheng & Settles 2007; Kwok 2006). Ikels (2004) points out that filial piety is expressed in different ways in different Asian countries, and is very much shaped by local histories, economics, population change and individual family circumstances. Also, processes of globalisation and modernisation are changing the manner in which filial piety is expressed, meaning there is sometimes a gap between elders' expectations and the kind of support their children are willing to provide (see Ikels 2004).

The continuing popularity of arranged marriages among some non-English-speaking immigrant groups is another aspect of how the interests of extended kin may take precedence over the interests of individuals (more discussion of this in Chapter 6). Lebanese Muslims and Indian Hindus are two immigrant groups in the Australian population who actively participate in arranged marriage. For instance, Hindu religious views on marriage mean immigrant Indian groups may see marriage as a means of fulfilling social obligations to a broader community, rather than as 'love matches' between two individuals. Western practices such as dating and pre-marital sex may be frowned upon, with love, commitment and devotion between couples expected to develop after marriage has taken place (Goodwin & Cramer 2000).

Family and household structure

CONSISTENT WITH THE FACT THAT family values privilege obligations to an extended kinship network, it is more common for some immigrant family groups from non-English-speaking backgrounds to form **multi-family households**. The 2001 Australian Census indicates that only three per cent of all family households in Australia are multi-family households, and immigrant and Indigenous Australian families make up the majority of these. Immigrant couples with children from South-East Asia and China, the Middle East and North Africa are more than twice as likely as Australian-born non-Indigenous couples to live in a multi-family household (de Vaus 2004). Most multi-family households among non-English-speaking immigrant groups are comprised of families related by blood or marriage. The majority also consist of families of two consecutive generations, that is, where married children live with their parents (ABS 2001). To look at extended family as a broader network of support beyond the multi-family household, many immigrants from various parts of the world, including the Pacific Islands, southern Europe, the Middle East, some Asian countries and Indonesia retain strongly interdependent relationships with parents and siblings. Even when they do not live together, relatives often live next door or round the corner, help out extensively with the children, share money and help each other with employment and housing.

However, in the globalisation era, elderly parents, adult children and other family members are increasingly separated because of migration, and extended family households may be separated by national borders and spread over vast distances. Particularly in Asian countries, a huge increase in international migration in recent years has precipitated considerable social change in the practice and process of family life. **Transnational families** may be formed at the point of marriage to an overseas person, or when temporary and permanent work takes family members abroad, and in each case intergenerational relationships —between fathers and other family members, domestic worker mothers and their young children, or older adults and elderly parents—are transformed. They must be lived on a daily basis through complex networks of communication maintained through global travel and technologies, gendered strategies of organising work and care, as well as processes of imagination and memory (see Yeoh, Huang & Lam 2005; Baldassar, Baldock & Wilding 2007). Transnational family practices are beginning to be documented in many different national and social contexts such as when Chinese mothers accompany their children to Singapore for the duration of the children's study (Huang & Yeoh 2005), Australian immigrant families organise care of and return visits to elderly parents back home (Baldassar, Baldock & Wilding 2007) or when Taiwanese businessmen practise 'transnational business masculinities' through maintaining work and mistresses in China and dependent wives and children in Taiwan (Shen 2005).

Is there a generation gap between immigrant parents and their children?

SOCIOLOGISTS HAVE ARGUED IN THE past that among Australian immigrants from non-English-speaking backgrounds, the values associated with the home country may persist long after people in the home country have moved on to newer ways of thinking (see Bottomley 1979). In this view, a strong notion of **core culture** or the ideals and beliefs characteristic of the country of origin at the time of departure may persist, in resistance to **host culture** ideals and practices. For instance, one study conducted in the early 1980s in the Australian Greek community showed that Australian Greek mothers were more likely than mothers in Greece to support arranged marriages (Smyrnios & Tonge 1981). Arguably, it is becoming less and less possible for parents to maintain a notion of core culture, when societies are increasingly interconnected through media, telecommunications and other technological advances. The constant flow of information around the world and the fact that air travel and telecommunications have become less expensive set the scene for a greater blurring of the boundaries between so-called core and host cultural values and practices. For instance, it is less possible to romanticise as unchanging the values and practices common to one's country of origin when daily news coverage and frequent telephone or email contact is a possibility.

However, some persistence of core cultural values may reinforce perceptions and experiences of a pronounced 'generation gap' between children being raised in Australia and their overseas-born parents. Children's language fluency in their parent's language tends to decrease over first and second generations after migration, and in tandem with this process, children become more inclined to want to take on the values and beliefs they consider to be Australian. Research by Mak and Chan (1995) found that Chinese immigrant parents find it difficult to influence their children to accept the importance of maintaining their language and family of origin culture, and the values of respect for the elderly, obedience to parents and deference to familial sources of authority. This is not a problem voiced only by Chinese parents: for instance, Pacific Islander parents have expressed similar frustrations. Mak and Chan also found that teenage children of Chinese parents believe their parents are too controlling and put too much pressure on them to achieve in an educational sense.

It is also important not to overgeneralise about the nature and extent of the generation gap between immigrants and their Australian-born children. Pallotta-Chiarolli and Skrbis (1993), in their study of second generation young Australians, emphasised the complexity with which young Australians from

Italian, Croatian and Slovenian non-English-speaking backgrounds engage with parental expectations. These researchers found at least three distinct ways of dealing with parental pressure to conform to core cultural values among the young people they interviewed: they could act passively in the face of parental coercion; they could actively embrace the values of their parents; or they could resist the values of their parents.

Those who acted passively towards parental pressure believed it was important to keep peace and harmony in the family by pretending to go along with dominant cultural values (for example, a father's authority, a woman's place). These young people feared ostracism from their family and community members and did not want to face rejection. Those who demonstrated active acceptance of their parents' values tended to emphasise the benefits of having large social networks of extended family, such as cousins and aunts, due to the care, recreation and support these family ties could provide. This was particularly characteristic of the young women and men from Croatian and Slovenian backgrounds. Patterns of acceptance of and resistance to parental values were also mixed among the young people. For example, 16-year-old girls from Italian backgrounds resisted the idea of a traditional Italian wedding and marrying someone from an Italian background, yet they participated with pride and enjoyment in their Italian socio-cultural environments and agreed with their parents about the importance of 'family togetherness', 'spending time with the family' and 'respecting and visiting relatives' (Pallotta-Chiarolli 1990).

Somali families in Australia

In addition to the cultural and social upheaval of immigration, the refugee experience creates specific life challenges for families from non-English-speaking backgrounds settling in Australia. Separation from family members under distressing, if not traumatic, circumstances often characterises the refugee experience.

Somali people began to come to Australia in the early 1990s, many to the state of Victoria, as a result of the United Nations (UN) Refugee and Humanitarian program. Violence between clan-based rivalries erupted in Somalia in the early 1990s, leading to thousands of civilian deaths. Around one million Somalis fled to neighbouring African countries seeking escape from starvation and persecution, and hundreds of thousands lost their lives. UN intervention proved unsuccessful in resolving the civil conflict and Somalia has been without a central government since 1991.

Somali people speak Somali, and also use written Arabic for religious instruction and rituals. Somali did not have its own written language until the 1970s. Islam is the religion of 98 per cent of the population. Somalis are born into clans, and the clan name is passed down from one generation to the next. Marriage is permitted between most clans but forbidden between some.

Somali women tend to have five or six children, and family networks are extended. A great degree of financial and social interdependence between different generations of family members is customary (McMichael & Ahmed 2003). The refugee experience is likely to have severed or fractured these family networks either through death or geographic distance. There are many young single mothers in Somali communities in Australia, due to the fact that many of their husbands were killed or reported missing in the war. Many of these young women are from rural areas, illiterate and lack family support for themselves or their children. Finding suitable public or private rental accommodation can also be difficult, given average family size is far larger than the Australian norm. Australian resident sons face pressures to financially support elderly parents still in Somalia, or try to relocate them to Australia where they can be looked after. It is becoming more difficult to bring out family members on refugee visas, as Somalia has not been considered a priority country by the Australian Government since the war ended.

Members of Australian Somali communities may also experience a degree of intergenerational conflict, particularly between young people and the elderly, as the younger generation try to adapt to Australian youth cultures. Above and beyond these generation gap issues common to many groups of immigrants, Somali young people are very likely to have lost many family members and witnessed violence first hand, which may result in behavioural problems due to grief or loss (Immigrant Resource Centre in the North East 2002).

Sexual diversity, families and intimate relationships

As STATED AT THE BEGINNING of the chapter, when we consider cultural diversity in families and relationships, this can also include concepts of family and relationships among people living their lives beyond heterosexual family relationships. This is not to suggest lesbian, gay, bisexual or otherwise 'queer' couples or singles inhabit a separate cultural space, in which relationships with parents, brothers and sisters are irrelevant, or the idea of family relationships based on blood and marriage is meaningless. Rather, as Weeks, Heaphy and Donovan (2001) explain, there is something about the collective experience of identifying as lesbian, gay, bisexual or otherwise 'queer', that may open up different ways of experiencing relationships and attributing meaning to relationships:

> The collective coming out experience of many self-identified lesbians and gays, and the creation of a sense of collective identity associated with developing communities of interest … has opened up new opportunities for personal experimentation (p. 57).

The Australian Bureau of Statistics began to acknowledge same-sex couples in the 1996 Census collection, indicating the increasing social acceptance of same-sex relationships. The 2001 Census identified 11,000 male same-sex couples and 9000 female same-sex couples in Australia, although given the stigma still attached to same-sex relationships and practices, it is likely that this number under-represents the actual numbers of gay and lesbian couples. Same-sex couples are more likely not to have children than heterosexual couples: 95 per cent of male same-sex couples and 81 per cent of female same-sex couples, compared with 43 per cent for heterosexual couples, were not living with children (ABS 2005). The Australian Census only counts same-sex couples and couples with children which in many cases may not capture the complexity of lesbians' and gay men's intimate relationships and family lives.

The importance of friendship in lesbian and gay notions of kinship was first written about by anthropologist Kath Weston in *Families We Choose* (1991). Weston conducted a large interview-based study of lesbians and gay men living in the Bay area of San Francisco in the USA, observing that the participants in her study tended to talk about their relationships with family of origin members as subject to choice and individual intention. It was the experience of many of her participants that friendships were the relationships that provided love, care and other forms of social support, whereas the blood ties with mothers, fathers, brothers and sisters may be tenuous social relationships. Weston advanced the idea that lesbians and gay men reverse dominant cultural ideas that friendships do not last because they are chosen, while biological ties with family are enduring and supportive. As her study documents, this was particularly true to the experience of the thousands of gay men who became infected with HIV/AIDS during the 1980s, a time when infection with the HIV virus generally led to death from an AIDS-related illness. Many dying men were cared for on a daily basis by close networks of friends in their communities rather than the families of origin who had rejected them because of their sexuality.

Weeks, Heaphy and Donovan (2001) in a more contemporary British study document what they call **life experiments** characteristic among lesbians and gay men. For instance, although many do live in cohabiting couple relationships, many choose not to, well into adulthood, and may live alone or with friends rather than setting up house with a partner. Further to this, supportive communities of friends tend to be more prominent in fulfilling needs for social interaction, care and household favours in situations where heterosexuals would often turn to their family members. Another observation these authors make about lesbian and gay relationships is the greater sense of fluidity between the categories 'sexual partner' and 'friend'. It is common for lesbians' sexual relationships to develop out of pre-existing friendships, and for sexual partners to remain friends once the sexual relationship has ended. Finally, they discuss gay men's sexual cultures, noting that **monogamy** or sexual exclusivity with the one partner may be less important to the maintenance of long-term emotional commitments. Many gay men's emotional commitment to long-term partners co-exist with a negotiated agreement about non-monogamy, or having other sexual partners outside the relationship.

This negotiated relationship ethic to which Weeks, Heaphy and Donovan refer is also evident in the kinds of unconventional parenting relationships being arranged between lesbian couples and the gay men who agree to become their children's biological fathers. Dempsey (2006b), in her study of concepts of family and kinship among Australian lesbian and gay parents, documents the parenting agreements that some prospective lesbian and gay parents write together as part of the process of negotiating how family relationships and responsibilities for children will socially unfold. These agreements describe how relationships between the unborn child's biological parents and extended kin are re-imagined and re-configured beyond the conventional nuclear family model, in a manner that is attentive to enabling stability and flexibility in children's upbringings.

One of the agreements in Dempsey's study was between lesbian couple Felicity and Fiona and their long-term friends, gay male couple, David and Karl. Their child had been conceived by self-insemination at home using David's sperm, which meant that under Australian law, Felicity was the only one of the four adults involved to be legally defined as a parent. Felicity is the biological mother and David is the biological father, but the intention is for Felicity and Fiona to jointly raise the child at their home, with regular visits from the men. The written agreement the adults made prior to the birth of their baby sets out some principles to guide everyone's understanding of how family relationships will be socially understood, given that their arrangement does not follow normative social or legal assumptions about family.

> We Felicity, Fiona, David and Karl are embarking on a new and exciting journey. We understand we are all committing to a long-term relationship between the four of us and any child born. This document serves to clarify the rights, responsibilities and best wishes we have for the child born of our arrangement … The child will live with Felicity and Fiona who will be socially and legally acknowledged as primary carers. We intend that David and Karl will be acknowledged as fathers and have the opportunity to develop a non-resident, yet caring relationship with the child. We imagine there will be lots of visits between all four of us and the child, and although our extended families will not have any rights in respect of the child, we value their love in their roles as aunties, uncles, grandparents and cousins (Dempsey 2006b, pp. 260–1).

Also apparent, in agreements such as those above, is Weeks, Heaphy and Donovan's observation that choosing the form and content of family relationships can be very attentive to principles of living ethically and well with others. They reject the idea that chosen relationships represent 'the triumph of individual need over collective responsibility' (2001, p. 46) in favour of arguing freedom to choose is based on standards and principles deemed ethical precisely because they are negotiated. Sexual relationships, couple relationships, parental and childcare commitments, all become subject to this negotiated ethic based more on the sentiments associated with friendship rather than with notions of duty or obligation, or taking what relationships mean for granted.

Social class

RESEARCHERS IN THE UK, USA and Australia have documented the different family practices and assumptions of working-class families in comparison to their middle-class counterparts. It is important not to overgeneralise but some tendencies are evident in the available research on class and family life.

Social class is a hotly debated term in sociology, it is somewhat fluid and not always easily observable. Education, occupation and income are often used as class indicators in social research. In recent theoretical debates about class, there has been a shift in emphasis from relations of 'production' or the economic, to relations of 'consumption' that focuses more on cultural locations and processes (see Crompton 1998; Pakulski & Waters 1996).

In this book we prefer to use a dynamic understanding of class. Class involves two major interconnected sets of relations: material and cultural. Material relations include production, labour and economic resources while cultural relations include consumption, cultural capital and discursive practices (see Barrett 1992; Bradley 1996). Class is a dynamic that is constantly being made and remade. Social classes are much more difficult to identify than in the past and class relations are more complex, but systematic forms of social inequality continue to operate around occupations and levels of education and income and this in turn shapes people's relationships and intimate lives.

In comparison to middle-class families, women and men in working-class families tend to lead more separate lives (Komarovsky 1987). Deb Warr in her study of disadvantaged young people and their relationships found that men were unable or unwilling to do the 'disclosing intimacy' expected in contemporary relationships, or share their innermost thoughts and feelings with partners (Warr 2006). Social disadvantage puts pressure on established relationships and may also have a negative impact on forming relationships. There is evidence emerging that young people living in poverty feel unable to marry or begin families because they do not have the resources to do so (Birrell et al. 2004; Heard 2008). Over the last decade there has been a reversal in the relationship between education and marriage among women. More highly educated women are more likely to be partnered and more likely to be married than women without post-school qualifications. The relationship between education and partnering is even starker for men. For example, for men aged 40–44, those with a higher level of education were more likely to be partnered than men with no post-school qualifications (84 per cent compared to 68 per cent) and higher educated men were more likely to be married than those without post-school qualifications (76 per cent compared to 57 per cent) (Heard 2008).

A major difference between working-class and middle-class families is that working-class families have greater attachment to and dependence on families and local networks in order to survive (Stack 1974). Working-class families are often stigmatised while middle-class families and their values are promoted as the best way to construct family life. Working-class families are viewed as pathological—and this is particularly the case for working-class single mothers— and a threat to social order. Terms such as 'welfare mothers' or 'council estate slags' in the UK or 'crack babies' in the USA represent working-class parents as deviant (Skeggs 1998). Beverly Skeggs in her study of young working-class women in the UK found that 'respectability' emerged as an important ideal. When the women were young respectability was linked primarily to sexuality but as they got older it was linked to family and caring practices. Respectability is a marker of class and an aspiration for the women—to not be respectable is to have little social value or legitimacy (Skeggs 1998, p. 3). Susan describes her experience of visits to her home by a health visitor:

> You know they're weighing you up and they ask you all these indirect questions as if you're too thick to know what they're getting at and you know all the time they're thinking 'she's poor, she's not good, she can't bring her kids up properly' and no matter what you do they've got your number. To them you're never fit, never up to their standards (Skeggs 1998, p. 3).

Val Gillies (2007) argues that material and economic resources play a major role in shaping decisions, experiences and actions and often middle-class privilege makes it difficult for policy-makers, educators and politicians to see the strengths of working-class family life. The vilification of lone mothers as 'lazy, irresponsible and indifferent to the needs of their children' shows little understanding of the constraints lone mothers face (Gillies 2007, p. 46). These women do not walk away from their responsibilities for child rearing but struggle to manage with the resources available to them. 'This meant sheltering, feeding, clothing and schooling children on an income barely sufficient to sustain one individual, while actively compensating for the day-to-day experience of disadvantage through love, protection and humour and affirmation' (Gillies 2007, p. 47).

Gillies talks about the differences between working-class and middle-class childraising in the UK. Working-class families cultivated close social relationships that were necessary for emotional, practical and financial support. This context was at odds with valuing individualism that fitted within the context for middle-class families. Middle-class families in the UK and USA engage with a process of 'concerted cultivation' where parents develop skills in their children by engaging in a variety of structured after-school activities. Middle-class children are encouraged to see themselves as unique and distinct and able to exploit opportunities available to them (Lareau 2003; Gillies 2007). By contrast, working-class parents emphasise 'fitting in' rather than 'standing out' in their childraising practices. In working-class families 'children are told what to do, in contrast with middle-class households where reasoning strategies and negotiation are employed' (Gillies 2007, p. 79). Encouraging individuality is not feasible for working-class parents because they do not have the resources to support it and children's defiance is more likely to be constructed as threatening to society instead of struggling towards independence as it may be for middle-class children. In working-class contexts being seen as an exceptional individual is more likely to result in social exclusion rather than admiration as it threatens relational ties and support systems (Gillies 2007).

At the other end of the spectrum rich families tend to protect their privileged position and take the project of transmitting wealth and positioning their children for success very seriously (Gilding 1997). Upper-middle-class children are under substantial pressure to perform at a very high level in educational settings, which sometimes has a negative impact on their self-esteem and psychological health (Gillies 2007; Walkerdine, Lucey & Melody 2001). Social class and economic advantage or disadvantage continue to shape the way families relate to their local communities and go about their daily business of work, intimacy and care. These different contexts are often ignored by policy-makers and politicians ready to scapegoat dysfunctional working-class families for a variety of social problems.

Conclusion

IN THIS CHAPTER WE HAVE demonstrated how cultural difference shapes families and relationships in profound ways. Sometimes the effects of cultural difference are relatively benign. At the other extreme, families outside the white, middle-class, nuclear, heterosexual ideal are harshly discriminated against or actively oppressed and opportunities for children and adults to flourish become very difficult. It is also important to bear in mind that even though we have presented cultural difference under discreet headings, in practice most of us inhabit multiple, fragmented identities; we are insiders in some respects and outsiders in others. The structures and practices of relationships and families are diverse and we must be cautious not to use our own assumptions and experiences as the only measure. We will revisit specific instances of cultural diversity many times in the chapters that follow.

Key concepts

Kinship

Ethnicity

Patriarchal family

Core culture

Host culture

Monogamy

Filial piety

Multi-family households

Transnational family

The Stolen Generation

Life experiments

Social class

Discussion questions

1   What is it about the migration experience that may create a generational divide between non-English-speaking immigrant parents and their children?

2   What do you see as the main social challenges for people who have 'non-heterosexual' families and relationships?

3   What are the main consequences for Indigenous Australian families of Stolen Generation policies and practices?

4   Are you aware of class differences in expectations or understandings of family relationships? Describe some of these differences.

Recommended further reading

Baldassar, L., Baldock, C. & Wilding, R. 2007, *Families Caring Across Borders: Migration, Ageing and Transnational Caregiving*, Palgrave Macmillan, Houndmills, Introduction.

Haebich, A. 2000, *Broken Circles: Fragmenting Indigenous Families 1800–2000*, Fremantle Arts Centre Press, Fremantle.

Paradies, Y. 2006, 'Beyond Black and White: Essentialism, Hybridity and Indigeneity', *Journal of Sociology*, vol. 42, no. 4, pp. 355–67.

Warr, D. 2006, 'Gender, Class and the Art and Craft of Social Capital', *The Sociological Quarterly*, no. 47, pp. 497–520.

Weeks, J., Heaphy, B. & Donovan, C. 2001, *Same-Sex Intimacies: Families of Choice and Other Life Experiments*, Routledge, London, Chapter 2 'Life experiments'.

04 | Sociological Perspectives on Relationships and Families

Introduction

IN THIS CHAPTER WE OUTLINE the major theoretical perspectives used for understanding families and relationships. Each theoretical perspective allows us to focus on some aspects of family and intimate life rather than others. A key insight for grasping each of the perspectives is that they were developed according to their historical and social context. It makes sense that new theories are more suited to today's context than those developed half a century ago. Some theoretical perspectives such as **individualisation** are more in favour now than others. We can think of these as living theories. Others have had their time in the limelight, such as structural functionalism, and are less popular with contemporary family researchers.

In theorising about the family there are two key continuums. First, there is the continuum between theories that emphasise social structure and theories that emphasise individual agency. Theories at the structural end emphasise the way that society (and social structures such as gender and class) shapes families and relationships, while those at the agency end emphasise individual freedom and choice in the shaping of personal life. The second continuum is between the material and the cultural. Theories at the material end emphasise economic relations and the organisation of labour as having the most influence on families and relationships, while theories at the cultural end emphasise cultural influences such as moral values, the role of religion, ideology or belief systems in the way we shape our personal lives.

Structural functionalism

WE BEGIN WITH FUNCTIONALISM, WHICH is a structural theory of families in that it emphasises the ways in which societal structure shapes behaviour. Functionalism offers a consensus model of society in the sense that society is comparable to a biological organism: each part has its role to play to ensure a healthy system. The classic functionalist perspective on society was developed by French theorists Auguste Comte (1798–1857) and Emile Durkheim (1858–1917), both of whom are often called the fathers of sociology. Talcott Parsons (1902–79), the prominent American sociologist, considerably refined the functionalist perspective and emphasised its relevance to the study of families (Parsons 1951; Parsons & Bales 1955). Functionalism dominated sociological scholarship on families until at least the mid 1970s (Gilding 1997).

The basic idea of functionalism is that societies are structured with many interlocking parts that together contribute to how the whole of society works. Family, religion, government, education and the economy are all different parts that make up the system and each plays a different role in ensuring the whole system functions as it should. Parsons argued that the family had lost some of its earlier functions after industrialisation and had become a progressively more specialised institution. He believed that the conjugal or nuclear family had become more isolated as a logical consequence of industrialisation, in the sense that a greater sense of obligation and duty had developed towards the nuclear family unit than to the extended family network beyond the conjugal household. For Parsons, the development of paid work outside the home and a main male breadwinner explained declining dependence on extended family for economic support. The extended family was also no longer needed so much for reasons of status, because status came from the job held by the breadwinner father. For Parsons, there were obvious benefits in terms of efficiency and effectiveness in the nuclear family form. Having just the one breadwinner meant families could move around if they needed to with minimum fuss.

In the functionalist view of family, men and women performed distinctive masculine and feminine sex roles. Parsons' contention was that the family has two main functions: first, the socialisation of children into appropriate gender roles and second, the stabilisation of adult personalities. **Socialisation** is a key concept and Parsons argued that 'families are the factories that produce human personalities' (Parsons & Bales 1955, p. 16). With isolation from extended family, mother and father could depend on each other's mutually beneficial and complementary roles in parenthood (Parsons 1951). Within families, roles between women and men had also been differentiated into expressive and instrumental roles. The **instrumental role** was characterised as masculine and was orientated to the public world and paid work to economically support the family. By contrast the **expressive role** was characterised as feminine and oriented to the private world of unpaid work and emotional nurturing of children in particular.

Critique of structural functionalist view of families

IN ACADEMIC CIRCLES THERE HAVE been numerous critiques of Parsons and many of his ideas have fallen from favour. Functionalism has been criticised for three major reasons: first, because the focus is on one single family type as a logical response to the demands of industrialised societies; second, because the theory assumes cooperation and consensus among family members; and third, because it neglects inequality, power dynamics and change within families.

In the first instance, functionalism could not explain why there is such variety in family values and formations in different industrialised settings. If we take two different industrial societies, such as Japan and Australia, it is apparent that they display very different dominant family patterns and values with regard to assumptions about intergenerational relationships. For instance, it is customary in Japan for elderly parents to move in with their adult children in later life, but this is not the case in Australia. Under these conditions it is difficult to maintain the argument that one family form is a logical response to or the best fit with industrialisation. The extent to which the nuclear family is actually isolated from extended kin is also questionable. Litwak (1960), a contemporary of Parsons, made this observation in coining the term '**modified extended family**'. There is substantial evidence that family members may not live in the same household but many continue to rely on each other for emotional support and the exchange of resources. In particular, sociological research conducted in working-class neighbourhoods in London and black neighbourhoods in urban America throughout the 1950s and 1960s have often contradicted the idea that nuclear families were isolated, self-sufficient units (Young & Willmott 1957; Stack 1974).

Feminist scholars have perhaps been the most uncompromising in their critiques of functionalism. This is not surprising, given the extent to which Parsons viewed families as vehicles for the expression and reproduction of relatively fixed gender roles. Although Parsons acknowledged some tensions in the nuclear family form, in that women had less access to 'activities that were taken seriously and importantly rewarded' (1951, p. 193), there was little acknowledgment that women and children were often deeply disadvantaged within the nuclear family form. However, with the development of second wave feminism in the 1970s, women and men were shown to have different and competing interests. Speaking broadly, feminists argued that confining women to the role of housewife had primarily benefited men rather than the whole of society. Feminists understand rigid gender roles as restrictive and perpetuating of inequalities between men and women rather than necessary to harmonious social functioning. Furthermore, Parsons' theory, in its emphasis on harmonious systems, was particularly ill-equipped to explain cases of extreme conflict and violence in nuclear families.

The third major problem with functionalism is that it cannot account for change. Functionalism does not examine class or ethnic differences in family life and cannot account for the fundamental changes that occurred in families in the developed world from the 1960s onwards.

Political economy perspective

THE **POLITICAL ECONOMY PERSPECTIVE**, SOMETIMES known as historical materialism, Marxism or socialist theory, is also a structural theory that emphasises how family and relationships are shaped by wider social structures, particularly economic relations and social class. In stark contrast to the consensus seen by functionalists, the political economy perspective focuses on conflict between different groups and the operation of power. Socialist critical theories of the family emerged in the late 1960s and 1970s in the USA and UK at a time of immense social unrest. **Feminism**, black civil rights, gay liberation and anti-Vietnam war protests were all occurring around this time.

Socialist theories about families were largely derived from the nineteenth century work of Friedrich Engels, who was a close friend and colleague of Karl Marx. In *The Origins of the Family, Private Property and the State* (1972), first published in 1884, Engels adapted Marx's economic theory of class conflict to account for the emergence of the nuclear family under capitalism.

Engels believed that with the development of capitalism, **matriarchal** families changed to a nuclear family form characterised by patriarchal subjugation. In this view, family groupings had originally been controlled by women and were egalitarian and communal, but changed after people learned how to domesticate and exchange animals: a key moment in the origin of private property. Engels contended that the origin of private property—the underpinning of a capitalist ethos and economy—first put economic power into men's hands and resulted in 'the overthrow of mother right' or the 'world historic defeat of the female sex' (1972, p. 120).

Engels argued that the origin of private property was crucial to the development of the nuclear family because this property had to be passed on when its owner died. For Engels, a capitalist system of owning property meant it was in men's interests to know who their children were and to control women's sexuality in order to do so. Monogamous marriage guaranteed the man's paternity and the legitimacy of children so property could be passed on from one generation to another. For this to occur, women had to become men's sexual and economic property, which they were in nineteenth century European and Australian marriage law.

Inspired by Engels' insight that the 'private' sphere of family life is not separate from the economic realm of 'public' life, socialist family theorists in the 1960s and 1970s were keen to explore the relationship between economic production, the state, private property and the family. For instance Zaretsky (1976) focused on the family as the site where women's unpaid labour was appropriated and exploited. He argued that the relegation of women to the so-called private sphere of the home served to isolate them from a public sphere of industrial development, and enabled male supremacy to flourish. In later work, Zaretsky (1982) turned his attention to the interactive relationship between families and state welfare systems, arguing that state policies often effectively strengthen the idea that the family is a self-sufficient economic unit. Other socialist theorists were keen to explore how classist ideology was perpetuated through state intervention into the nuclear family. Christopher Lasch (1977) argued that through 'scientific management' the capitalist state was keeping working–class family life under surveillance through the intervention of experts such as doctors, teachers and psychiatrists.

Critique of political economy perspective

THE CLASSIC POLITICAL ECONOMY PERSPECTIVE has also been critiqued over time. The three major criticisms are that its focus was too limited to the economic, that it was unable to account for diversity and that it had difficulty conceptualising the positive rather than the oppressive and controlling aspects of families and relationships.

The political economy perspective lost momentum due to broader socio-political developments. This included the collapse of communist/socialist regimes worldwide during the late 1980s—as symbolised by the fall of the Berlin Wall in 1989—and mounting lists of human rights atrocities accruing to various regimes. At the same time, the emergence of other social movements throughout the 1980s, based on notions of identity beyond class such as sexuality or ethnicity, could not readily adapt the political economy perspective. Finally, the theory was seen as an overly economic view of class and gender relations. The more ideological strands of Marxist critique tended to portray men and women as capitalist dupes with little power of free thought or agency, and issues such as intimacy or love could not really be analysed except as forms of labour or ideological traps. Nevertheless, the insight that families involve labour relations and power continues to have a profound influence on contemporary family research, as will be evident in the discussion later in this book on families and labour (see Chapter 10).

Feminism

FEMINIST PERSPECTIVES ARE DIVERSE, ALTHOUGH in common they emphasise conflict between women's and men's interests and take women's subordination as their starting point. The emergence of second wave feminism in the 1960s and 1970s radically changed family studies. It put women's experiences in families at the centre of new intellectual work demonstrating how patriarchal values had shaped family life.

Ann Oakley's *The Sociology of Housework* (1974), published in the UK, paved the way for the themes that were to dominate sociological feminist family scholarship throughout the 1970s and 1980s. The first chapter of Oakley's book was entitled 'The Invisible Woman' and argued that sociology was characterised by sexism, given its lack of attention to women and gender in prevailing theories about social stratification and power. Based on interviews with forty young city-dwelling housewives, Oakley's book documented women's feelings about the unpaid work they did at home, their difficulties with combining housework and motherhood, and their sense of satisfaction and dissatisfaction with various aspects of housework. Oakley made a strong case for the importance of undertaking scholarly work from the perspective of women themselves, for viewing housework as real work, and for placing domestic themes at the centre of sociological scholarship. These principles remain central to the discipline today.

Feminist scholarship from the 1960s to the early 1980s was often aligned with liberal, socialist or radical feminist politics, which have different intellectual heritages and concerns.

Liberal feminism

LIBERAL FEMINISTS EMPHASISED EQUAL ACCESS for women to education, paid work beyond the home and other rights. They drew on the Enlightenment intellectual heritage that began with Mary Wollstonecraft's *A Vindication of the Rights of Women,* published in 1792. The idea was that individual women should have access to paid work and education in order to realise their full potential as individual human beings. Betty Friedan's *The Feminine Mystique,* for instance, was published in 1965 and implicitly challenged the functionalist view of women's place in the home as logical and fitting with the demands of industrial capitalist societies. Friedan wrote of what she called 'the problem with no name', or the immense feelings of loneliness, boredom and dissatisfaction experienced by many mothers and housewives who had no access to paid employment, stimulating company or sufficient support with raising children once they were married. It was Friedan's view that women's subordination in the home would continue unless they were given equal rights to paid work and education, and these claims were central to the activism of the 1970s Women's Liberation Movement.

Radical feminism

FOR RADICAL FEMINISTS, PATRIARCHY WAS the central concept in understanding women's oppression. Kate Millett, whose book *Sexual Politics* (1970) popularised the concept, defined patriarchy as the universal oppression of women, children and younger men by older men, although other radical feminists used the term to include all men.

Radical feminists were highly critical of gendered power relations within the heterosexual nuclear family. A common theme in radical feminist critiques of the nuclear family was that women should support each other to organise their personal lives beyond this family form. For instance, Janice Raymond (1986) argued for the complete rejection of the nuclear family. She advocated that women should refuse to become wives and mothers in favour of devoting themselves to strong female friendships and political work within communities of women. In *Of Woman Born* (1976), Adrienne Rich proposed that motherhood within the patriarchal nuclear family was an institution within which women were oppressed and controlled by men:

> Through control of the mother, the man assures himself of possession of his children; through control of his children he insures the disposition of his patrimony and the safe passage of his soul after death. It would seem therefore that from very ancient times the identity, the very personality of the man depends on power, and on power in a certain specific sense: that of *power over others*, beginning with a woman and her children (Rich 1976, p. 64, original italics).

Rich distinguished between motherhood as a potential relationship any woman has to her natural ability to reproduce, and motherhood under patriarchy, which she saw as the main source of women's enslavement. For Rich, patriarchal culture produces full-time motherhood as akin to solitary confinement while fatherhood gives a man rights and privileges over children towards whom he assumes minimal responsibility. According to Rich, the key to social change was the repossession by women of their bodies (through acquiring greater knowledge about pregnancy and childbirth) *and* women-centred social organising beyond the nuclear family.

Radical feminism was very important and influential in putting issues such as male violence and sexual assault on the public agenda for analysis and response from social welfare organisations. This intellectual work often coincided with political work to obtain government funding for women's refuges and sexual assault services.

Socialist feminism

SOCIOLOGISTS ARE PARTICULARLY WELL-REPRESENTED among socialist feminists. Socialist feminists grafted the notion of patriarchy onto Marxist analysis. They emphasised the gendered division of labour, particularly the exploitation of women's domestic labour under patriarchy and capitalist systems. Women's work within the home was a subject that had been largely ignored by sociologists prior to **socialist feminism**.

For instance, in *The Main Enemy* (1977), French socialist feminist Christine Delphy proposed that men and women belong to separate classes under capitalism. She believed there were two modes of production: one industrial and the site of capitalist exploitation; the other domestic, which was the site of patriarchal production. Marriage served to locate women within a gender class in which their labour was appropriated by men and the oppression of all women by men was perpetuated. Delphy also proposed that women should be paid wages for the work they did in the home.

The Anti-Social Family (1982), by UK sociologists Michele Barrett and Mary McIntosh, marked an important transition in socialist feminist critiques of the nuclear family because it emphasised the extent to which nuclear families were repositories of ideology and values. In other words, the family operates at the level of beliefs and ideas about how we should live, work and raise children together, as much as it exists as a tangible set of social and economic relations. In calling the family 'anti-social', Barrett and McIntosh highlighted the extent to which values of privacy and 'looking after one's own' were perpetuated within dominant familial ideology, rather than a broader sense of social responsibility to all members of society. Writing at the time of the conservative Thatcher Government in England, Barrett and McIntosh argued that the version of family relations supported by the capitalist state appealed to 'the family' (that is, to women) as the appropriate site of care-giving responsibility for children, the sick, the disabled and the elderly.

Critiques of early second wave feminist theories

As GILDING (1997) NOTES, SECOND wave feminist theories dating from the 1960s and 1970s were often challenging and controversial in presenting the darker side of family life which functionalist theories largely ignored. The theory of patriarchy permeated the politics of the Women's Liberation Movement and changed many women's expectations and lives. However, liberal, radical and socialist feminist theoretical approaches were extensively critiqued during the 1980s for a number of reasons.

Liberal and radical feminist approaches were charged with universalising cross-cultural experience, in generalising the experiences of white, Western women to non-Western women and black women. Black feminists in the USA were particularly critical of this universalising tendency, because patriarchy as a concept had never been able to explain why black men have not reaped the benefits of white patriarchal relations (Gittins 1985, p. 37). Socialist and radical feminist theories relied heavily on the concept 'patriarchy', which was increasingly criticised as an ahistorical concept that could not adequately account for differences in gender relationships in different social groups or classes, different cultures and different eras of human history. The question begged was: 'Are women always so similar and powerless all the time, in every culture?'.

The main problem with the concept of patriarchy as formulated in classic radical and socialist feminist theories lay in its rather monolithic understanding of power. Radical and socialist feminist analyses assumed institutionalised gender inequality and understood power as a structural controlling force wielded by men and social institutions such as the state. As such, these analyses could not effectively explain why some women took such pleasure in their families and relationships, without resorting to the idea that women were victims of 'false consciousness' or ideological dupes.

Contemporary feminist and gender theories

DESPITE THE DECLINING INFLUENCE IN overarching theories of patriarchy, feminism continues to shape contemporary theorising about families and intimate life. During the 1980s and 1990s, newer conceptualisations of how gendered power is exercised arose that were more capable of taking into account historical, social and situational diversity in gender relations. Gender, in the sense of how various femininities and masculinities are performed, now tends to be understood as a more dynamic process, rather than as a relatively rigid or universal component of social stratification.

Candace West and Don Zimmerman (1987) argued that gender is an activity, process or accomplishment that is sustained and contested within interpersonal relationships. Importantly, these do not have to be relationships between men and women. Gender can be enacted in relationships among men or among women. Pre-figuring the work of postmodern feminist theorist Judith Butler (1990), West and Zimmerman advanced the idea that gender is not a fixed 'role' or an attribute of self, but is performed through various emotional displays and behaviours. Gender relations are changeable, and always constituted through everyday experiences. West and Zimmerman's work has been particularly influential in exploring the gender dynamics of participation in domestic and paid labour, among heterosexual, lesbian and gay couples (see Chapter 10 for examples of this work).

The post-structuralist theorist Michel Foucault offered feminist thought a more nuanced account of how power operates. Foucault (1977) argued that power was not held by central agencies or groups in society, but was more widely dispersed. Foucault's concepts of discourse and subjectivity offered new ways of thinking through how gender and sexuality were constituted. These were taken up by feminist and family scholars from the 1990s onwards (for example, Lawler 1999; Walkerdine, Lucey and Melody 2001; Allen 2003—see Chapter 5).

In recent years, R.W. Connell's gender theory has sought to synthesise the insights of structuralist and post-structuralist concepts of power. Connell's (1987) gender theory developed in part out of dissatisfaction with the feminist concept of 'patriarchy'. For Connell, the theory of a universal patriarchy in which all men have power over all women could not really explain how it was that some men were able to oppress not just women, but also other men (for instance, gay men). Connell (2005, 2002) describes gender as a social and historical process in the sense that gender relations and gendered identities are perpetuated and changed by social structures such as the state, but also by the possibilities for gender interaction that arise through everyday practice. One way in which Connell's gender theory has been useful in the arena of families and intimate life is to explore how various masculinities are enacted in relationships. Hegemonic masculinity refers to the fact that in most social settings there are dominant ways of enacting masculinity. Connell argues that masculinities and femininities are (at least in part) relational and changeable rather than fixed and structural (see Totten 2003 on young marginalised men and girlfriend abuse in Chapter 12).

- -
Micro sociological perspectives

IN CONTRAST TO THE FUNCTIONALIST and political economy perspectives, micro sociological perspectives emphasise individual agency and choice (although this may be constrained by wider social structures) and the creation of meaning. For instance, **symbolic interactionists** focus on people's own understandings and how these are created in interaction with the social world around them. The founding theorists of this perspective include Mead (1934) and Goffman (1959), who emphasised how meanings were made and identities performed in everyday life. This theoretical perspective complements qualitative research that focuses on social processes and the everyday construction of meaning in families and relationships.

An example of applying the interactionist perspective is in the paper by Lindsay and colleagues (2006) on the ways in which lesbian-parented families presented themselves in the mainstream contexts of schools. The perspective was useful for conceptualising the ongoing performance work and anxiety involved for lesbian parents and children in negotiating potentially hostile mainstream organisations. The article describes the ways in which individuals in lesbian families actively manage information about the lesbian identity of the parents or 'coming out'.

British family sociology is heavily influenced by micro sociological perspectives. As Carol Smart (2004, p. 1046) contends, 'families are conceptualised as spheres of intimacy and interaction, and where the meanings attributed to and generated by relationships are constructed by family members (in a cultural and historical context) rather than in relation to naturalistic reproductive and/or socialisation functions' as American family sociology tends to be. Contemporary micro-sociological theorising includes the concepts of 'performance', '**family practices**' and 'display'. Commitment to family and care of family members remains central to everyday life for most people even though families have become more diverse. It is clear that commitment to family life, intimacy and care remain but the format of family obligation can no longer be taken for granted. Instead, family relationships must be made and re-made on an ongoing basis. To help understand our increasingly flexible family arrangements, in terms of both meaning and labour, more dynamic and interactive concepts have been developed. David Morgan's concept of 'family practices' is useful. For Morgan, families are understood as 'activities' rather than structures—family is in the doing rather than the being (Morgan 1996). Building on this further is Janet Finch's proposition that 'displaying' families is as important as 'doing families'

(Finch 2007). In the contemporary social context it is not only non–conventional families that need to display their commitment:

> In a world where families are defined by the qualitative character of the relationships rather than by membership, and where individual identities are deeply bound up with those relationships, *all* relationships require an element of display to sustain them as family relationships (Finch 2007, p. 71, original italics).

Critique of micro sociological perspectives

CRITICS HAVE ARGUED THAT MICRO sociological perspectives fail to see the powerful influence of broader social forces (such as capitalism or patriarchy) behind commonsense beliefs. Others have argued that micro sociologists inconsistently present some elements of social reality as 'objective' and other elements as 'constructed' (Giddens 2001).

However, micro sociology remains a useful framework for understanding family meanings and dynamics, and has informed a substantial amount of qualitative research on families and relationships. This research has worked to critique or extend the broader scale perspectives such as the political economy and individualisation approaches (Smart 2007).

- -

Postmodernism

MARILYN POOLE (2005A) ARGUES THAT 'confident theorising' about the family is at present a thing of the past, given the ever increasing pace of social change. There is debate about what to call the historical period we are living through— some argue that we are in postmodernity while others argue that we are in late modernity. Postmodern (or poststructural) thought is characterised by a critique of grand theory and universal thought. Instead, the emphasis is on difference, diversity and contradiction. Postmodern theoretical work has focused on language, text or meaning and power. Postmodern theory has influenced many of the critiques of feminism and political economy theory outlined above. In recognition of these critiques, we can no longer talk of 'the family' as a single entity but must speak of 'families'.

In terms of family theory, **postmodernism** is fairly underdeveloped, and 'postmodern' has often been used as a convenient label to describe the diversity of contemporary families. Edward Shorter (1975) is given credit for coining the phrase 'postmodern family', referring to the idea that the family is always changing, varied and that the nuclear family form is becoming increasingly fragile. According to American sociologist Judith Stacey, contemporary families have 'contested, ambivalent, undecided' characters (Stacey 1990, p. 16).

Postmodernist thought has been critiqued on the grounds that it cannot be readily applied to political action or social change or the study of real lives. However, queer theory is consistent with a postmodernist perspective and, since the early to mid 1990s, has proved useful to sociologists who are interested in the complex interrelationship between sex, sexuality and gender. More recently, queer theory has become influential in the sociology of intimacy and relationships.

Queer theory

IN MODERNIST SOCIOLOGY, SEX, GENDER and sexuality are often thought about as discrete attributes of the self that can be constructed in binary or dualistic ways. For instance, bodies are either female or male, sexuality can be heterosexual or gay/lesbian, and gender can be masculine or feminine. Each category of the binary pair is established as the opposite of the other and assumed to bring with it an essentially different way of being in the world. In this model, it is often assumed that everyone has one sex, one gender and one sexuality, which are stable and fixed for life. Counter to this, queer theory provides ways of thinking about sex, gender and sexuality that presume sexual and gender identities are not fixed or stable categories that conclusively determine who we are. It seeks to deconstruct or undo the conventional way of combining and opposing these categories, in order to better understand the complexity of sexualities, genders and relationships.

Heteronormativity (see Warner 1993) is a concept derived from queer theory that has proved very useful for sociological work on families and relationships. Berlant and Warner (2000) define heteronormativity as the 'institutions, structures of understanding, and practical orientations that make heterosexuality seem not only coherent—that is, organized as a sexuality—but also privileged' (p. 312). In this view, a range of social processes and structures serve to constitute heterosexuality as normal or natural, and therefore construct homosexuality as its marginalised and denigrated 'other' or binary opposite. 'Heteronorms' are often internalised through exposure to the understandings about gender and sexuality perpetuated in school curricula, the opinions and behaviours of authority figures such as parents and elders, and the mass media. They are apparent, for instance, in the unexamined assumption that a person is heterosexual unless proven otherwise, or that sex education lessons to children by their parents or teachers should only provide information about heterosexuality. Heteronormativity also refers to the way in which gender and sexuality are interrelated in fairly prescriptive ways. For instance, in Western cultures, a man or boy who presents as too feminine is often believed to be gay, irrespective of his sexual desires and behaviours. A masculine-looking woman may be thought to be a lesbian. Following on from this, heteronormativity does not so much describe the prevalence of open abuse or prejudice about homosexuality (homophobia), as the silences, absences and assumptions that mark out homosexuality as deviant or different.

Importantly, a queer analytic perspective on relationships is different to treating gay men and lesbians as a minority group in society. It refuses to minoritise or 'ghettoise' homosexuality, in favour of investigating how relationships are enacted across the heterosexual/homosexual binary. It assumes that sexual desire or object choice is only one axis of difference between people, and may not be the central one, with regard to how people perceive and live their relational lives. Roseneil (2000a), for instance, includes in her research people of all sexualities who live beyond what she calls **heterorelationality**, or cohabiting, monogamous, couple relationships. If we think of heterorelationality as being a particular package of assumptions about sex, intimacy and household, it is not necessarily something only heterosexuals do, although it is a way of relating that is historically central to the Western social institution of marriage. In other words, gay men and lesbians may adopt heterorelational values, and heterosexuals may refuse them. The insight of queer theory here is to draw attention to the tendency to trivialise relationships between adults that do not conform to the heterorelational type (for example, friendships, or non-monogamous relationships). If we only consider the kinds of relationships that underpin the dominant nuclear family model as 'mature' and worthy of research attention, we are substantially limiting our point of view (see Chapter 7).

Individualisation

AN INFLUENTIAL BODY OF THEORETICAL work on families and relationships in recent years has been the reflexive modernisation or 'individualisation' perspective. Several key thinkers are important here, such as Anthony Giddens (see *The Transformation of Intimacy* 1992); Ulrich Beck (see *Risk Society* 1992); Zygmunt Bauman (see *Liquid Love* 2003); Ulrich Beck and Elisabeth Beck-Gernsheim (see *The Normal Chaos of Love* 1995) and Elisabeth Beck-Gernsheim (see *Reinventing the Family* 2002).

Sociologists who adhere to individualisation theories broadly agree that the immense economic and societal transformations of the late twentieth century, including globalisation, urbanisation, secularisation, and gay and women's liberations, have had a big impact on personal lives. The central argument of the individualisation thesis is that all of the above changes have contributed to detaching people from traditional roles and obligations. Individualisation refers to what Giddens calls 'structurally necessitated decision-making' or the process by which social categories such as gender, class, religion or status group no longer provide a clear biographical framework for people to follow. So the emphasis on the self is a necessary rather than a selfish focus. To Giddens (1991), 'How shall I live?' is a question fundamental to daily existence in late modernity. Decisions ranging from whom to love, how and for how long, how to behave, what to believe, what to eat and what to wear are more and more taken at the level of the individual rather than through traditional sources of guidance such as family, religion and shared mores attached to social class or status. This absence of guidance from older sources of knowledge and the need to create new guidelines and moral frameworks for living is discussed by Beck (1992) as a process of dis-embedding from the old and re-embedding new social codes or frameworks to live by.

There are several main implications of individualisation theory for family and intimate relationships. Because marriages and other kinds of family relationships may not be for life, individualisation theorists emphasise that new values, behaviours and a more negotiated and reflexive (or self-conscious) approach to relationships is coming into being. To keep pace with social change in gender, class and workforce certainties, it is claimed, law and policy-makers, and people living their daily lives, must often engage in a conscious process of re-thinking what it means to be moral, ethical and live well, because very little can be taken for granted. As Carol Smart has commented, 'it is the quality of decisions and actions that now demarcate the moral terrain, not obedience to a sedimented set of rules or conventions' (Smart 2000, p. 12).

Individualisation theory also asserts the relative fragility of intimate relationships, as many competing pressures on couples make it more difficult to sustain emotional commitments. Beck-Gernsheim (2002) has explored the implications of the normalisation of divorce and we will discuss this in Chapter 11. Beck-Gernsheim argues that we have moved to 'do-it-yourself' biographies, as the social and economic resources needed to sustain family relationships are under threat. The economic policies of flexibilisation and deregulation are having a marked impact on family life. The attributes that make people better for the job market (for example, willingness to work long hours or move cities at short notice) make them less likely to be able to form or maintain close or dependable long-term relationships.

> At work, more market, more competition, more speed, more change; in personal life, more community, more conciliation, more patience and more consideration for others. How is that supposed to happen? (Beck-Gernsheim 2002).

In their book *Individualization* (2002) Beck and Beck-Gernsheim argue that individualisation requires a 'staging of everyday life' because women and men need to do so much coordination and negotiation to keep their lives from falling apart. They emphasise the changes that are dividing couples and families, such as women's expectations of a 'life of their own' and the increasing demands for flexibility, long-hours and mobility of workers by employers, which often create tensions within couple relationships.

Critique of individualisation

ALTHOUGH THEORISTS WHOSE WORK COMES under the umbrella of individualisation are diverse, and not uniformly critiqued for their ideas, some of the broader tenets of the individualisation thesis as it applies to family life and relationships have been critiqued for a number of reasons.

In the first instance, Carol Smart (2007) comments that the individualisation thesis has become the latest 'big idea' in the sociology of family and relationships, without sufficient historical evidence or empirical social research to ground it. In other words, individualisation is often used as a 'grand narrative' or explanatory theory about how the world is today, without investigating its use or relevance to diverse social contexts. Smart is particularly critical of Beck and Beck-Gernsheim's reliance on appeals to the 'tradition' of the past biography versus the 'innovation' of the choice biography. She notes that the specific time period they are talking about is never discussed, and appears based more on speculation than close reference to historical family studies. The effect of this is to have us believe that up until a certain, vague point in recent history, people were slaves to class, rigid gender roles and religion, then suddenly, all this changed. Smart observes that this goes against an extensive body of social and historical research studies that have been conducted in the UK and other parts of Europe.

Carol Smart and Beccy Shipman (2004) have also argued that Beck and Beck-Gernsheim's work on love and gender relations under conditions of individualisation provides a 'monochrome' or one-dimensional and unnecessarily pessimistic view of families, which does not match the evident joys and successes of some aspects of contemporary relationships. Furthermore, the emphasis by Beck-Gernsheim on the 'fragility' of relationships perhaps undermines the sense of commitment people display to partners, children and other friends and family members when their lives are studied in context and in depth.

Giddens and 'the transformation of intimacy'

Giddens' (1992) work is consistent with the broad individualisation thesis, but is more optimistic than Beck and Beck-Gernsheim's when it comes to considering the contemporary state of interpersonal relationships. Giddens claims Western societies are experiencing a **'transformation of intimacy'**, by which he means intimate relationships are no less important, yet are judged by different criteria. For instance, the idea that marriage means a lifelong commitment to another person, even in the presence of conflict, unhappiness or the faltering of love, is no longer as prevalent as it once was. Giddens argues that the certainty, longevity and relatively fixed gender roles once taken for granted within marriage have given way to the relationship ideals based on the **'pure relationship'**. The basic idea of the pure relationship is that it is not a relationship modelled on duty or routine, or unequal power relations. It relies on the people in the relationship opening themselves up to each other emotionally, and is contingent on being desired by both parties who love each other and experience each other as equal partners in the relationship. It is:

> A situation where a social relationship is entered into for its own sake, for what can be derived by each person from a sustained association with another; and which is continued only insofar as it is thought by both parties to deliver enough satisfactions for each individual to stay within it (Giddens 1992, p. 58).

Giddens believes the model for this kind of relationship ideal came from the friendships women have historically tended to have with each other: that is, emotionally close and based on mutual disclosure of innermost thoughts and feelings. Because the pure relationship focuses on relationship quality, it is successful and only good for as long as those who are in it want to be in it. This constitutes its inbuilt paradox or contradiction. Because we value the quality of our relationships so highly, and because of their capacity to fulfil us emotionally, we are much more prepared to terminate them when they are not delivering the goods. So the pure relationship ideal brings with it an inherent instability.

Some sociologists have found Giddens' optimistic ideas about the democracy of contemporary relationship ideals very useful and generative, particularly researchers who are interested in new ideas about living together and relating, such as those often evident in the lesbian and gay communities (see Weeks, Heaphy & Donovan 2001; Roseneil & Budgeon 2004). The notion that contemporary relationships are open to more experimentation and negotiation because of the expectation of fulfilment is a useful one.

However, there have also been extensive critiques of Giddens' work on relationships. Sociologist David Morgan, for instance, has looked at how the much emphasised change in notions of marriage 'from an institution to a partnership' may be as much an ideological one as it is a real one. Jamieson (1998) argues that Giddens' portrayal of intimacy is a rather restrictive one, confined to the one main idea of mutual self-disclosure and is largely restricted to couple relationships. Jamieson, by contrast, suggests that intimacy is also intrinsically a part of mother—child and friendship relationships, and within these relationships there is considerable diversity in the form that intimacies take. Carol Smart and Bren Neale (1999) argue that the very important issue of caring for dependent children plays a very minor part in Giddens' work. Giddens is largely silent about how children factor into the pure relationship, particularly with regard to how ideals of commitment to relationships might change when children are involved (see Chapters 6, 9, 10 and 11 for more on the pure relationship).

Conclusion

ON EXAMINING THE RANGE OF theoretical perspectives with their competing and sometimes contradictory emphases, it can feel overwhelming to choose which theory to use to think about families and relationships. However it is still very important to use theory to contextualise our personal relationships and explore and explain the ways in which family life shapes and is shaped by wider social forces. Theoretical debate is an ongoing practice, so there will never be a single correct answer. Instead we should strive to use or develop theory that is most useful in illuminating the topic at hand.

One of our key arguments in this chapter is that theories are developed in their historical context and some have lasting influence while others do not. From the 1940s to 1960s, functionalism dominated sociology and politics. From the mid 1960s to the mid 1980s critical socialist and feminist theory gained ground and became dominant. Since the 1980s the so-called grand theorising characteristics of functionalism and classical Marxism have been rejected in favour of more nuanced accounts to do with family practices, and, since the late 1990s, individualisation developed and is gaining influence. Feminist theories are still influential in family studies but they are less inclined to generalise or to universalise women's experiences. In debates about domestic violence, sexual assault, domestic labour, parenting post-divorce and reproductive technology, feminist theory continues to be actively used. Some argue that functionalism is still influential but this is largely confined to political debate where it often has an unacknowledged influence on conservative commentators. In academia support for functionalism is rare.

Often the topic of inquiry suggests one theoretical approach over others. As families are complex and multi-faceted it is often useful to combine approaches to understand contemporary family life. The table below provides examples of appropriate living theories for different topic areas.

Table 4.1: Family research topics and compatible living theories

Topic or emphasis	Theoretical approach
Identity	Individualisation
	Micro sociology
New family forms	Individualisation
	Micro sociology
	Queer theory
Gender relations	Feminism
	Individualisation
Family processes and meanings	Micro sociology
	Systems theory
Wider social change	Individualisation
Resource distribution and inequality	Political economy
	Feminism

These examples are not the only ways of matching different theories with topic areas—various permutations and combinations are possible. Combining theories is often useful and necessary. For instance, Smart and Neale's work draws on feminism, in its keen attention to the manner in which gender significantly influences care relations. Yet in also drawing on individualisation theory, it is possible to see gendered inequities prevailing in social policy, while still accepting that new and negotiated approaches to working through family problems are required (Smart & Neale 1999).

The key to choosing a theoretical perspective is that it is appropriate for the scale of the topic area (for example examining some families versus most families in society) and that it matches the relative emphasis on structure or agency or material or cultural influences of your analysis. As we move through the topic chapters that follow we will further demonstrate the power of each of the living theoretical perspectives to explore and explain families and relationships.

Key concepts

Functionalism

Socialisation

Political economy perspective

Feminist theory/feminism

Liberal feminism

Socialist feminism

Radical feminism

Patriarchy

Symbolic interactionism

Family practices

Postmodernism

Individualisation

Pure relationship

Discussion questions

1   Why is it important to be aware of the various theoretical perspectives on families and relationships, in addition to looking at other sources of information, such as statistical trends?

2   Is feminist theory still relevant to the study of families?

3   What is individualisation? How is it connected to change in families and relationships?

4   What are some of the main criticisms of individualisation theories? Are you persuaded by them?

Recommended further reading

Brannen, J. & Nilsen, A. 2005, 'Individualisation, Choice and Structure: A Discussion of Current Trends in Sociological Analysis', *The Sociological Review*, vol. 53, no. 3, pp. 412–28.

Finch, J. 2007, 'Displaying Families', *Sociology*, vol. 41, no. 1, pp. 65–81.

Poole, M. 2005, 'Understanding the Family: Ideals and Realities', in M. Poole (ed.) *Family: Changing Families, Changing Times*, Allen & Unwin, Crows Nest.

Smart, C. 2004, 'Re-theorising Families', *Sociology*, vol. 38, no. 5, pp. 1043–8.

05 Young People, Relationships and Sexuality

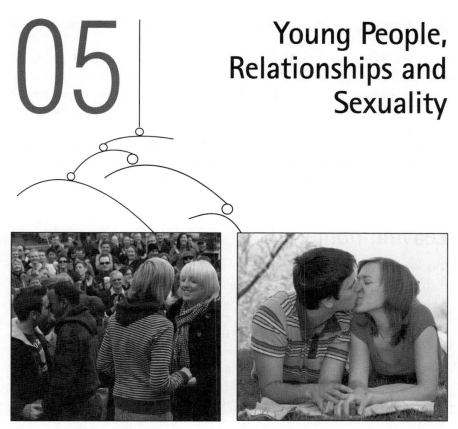

Figure 5.1: Friends and Relationships

Introduction

'I definitely want to get married when I'm older, maybe 30s. I wouldn't want it to be something that's rushed. I'd rather have a lot of adventurous years, travelling, trying things out.'

FIFTEEN-YEAR-OLD MELBOURNE RESIDENT Alex recounted this life plan to reporter Julie Szego, in a 2007 newspaper account of young Australians' life aspirations and relationships (Szego 2007, p. 5). Alex's comment gives insight into just how little significance marriage may have for young people these days as an event marking a clear transition from youth to adulthood. As we discussed in Chapter 2, in mid twentieth century Australia, getting married was taken for granted as a rite of passage from youthful dependence to adult independence. Most people married in their early to mid 20s, and this brought with it financial responsibilities, emotional commitment to a long-term partner, access to the only socially acceptable context in which to have sexual intercourse, and parenthood. Young men and women tended to live within their family of origin until they married, so marriage also marked the shift to setting up an independent household with one's husband or wife.

Fast-forward 50 or so years and young adults' sexual, financial, emotional and residential options look very different. First, sexual intercourse usually precedes marriage and parenthood by a number of years, as young people increasingly prioritise work and study over long-term relationship commitments. Second, financial dependence on parents may persist well into the 20s, either while living alone, in the family home or in households shared with an intimate partner or friends. As de Vaus (2004) comments, there is no longer a clear event, or set of events, marking the transition to adulthood.

Leaving home

THE EARLY 20S IS STILL the age when most Australian young people first leave the parental home, just as they did in the 1950s to 1970s (Qu & Soriano 2004). The majority of 18–19 year olds live with their parents (79 per cent), a statistic that drops to fewer than half (37 per cent) of 23–24 year olds, and only 19 per cent of young adults in their late 20s (ABS 2001 cited in de Vaus 2004). Leaving home to live with either a spouse or partner is now just one of the reasons young people leave the parental home. According to the 2001 Census, almost 5 per cent of 18–19 year olds, 16 per cent of 20–22 year olds and 33 per cent of 23–24 year olds were living with a partner. The proportion increased to over a half of 25–29 year olds (55 per cent) (de Vaus 2004).

Leaving the parental home does not necessarily mean leaving it for good. Moves in and out of the parental home throughout the 20s are common, particularly when young people leave home for reasons other than to get married. Such is the extent of this phenomenon that youth researchers Johanna Wyn and Rob White refer to the current generation of young Australian adults as the '**boomerang generation**' (Wyn & White 1997). The Australian Institute of Family Studies Young Adults' Aspirations Survey found that of young people in their 20s who had left home, 53 per cent had gone back to live with parents at least once before leaving the parental home for good (Kilmartin 2000). Reasons for returning home to live with parents include financial or emotional issues or problems encountered with rental or shared accommodation (Stone 1998).

Young people are also tending to stay at home with their parents longer than previous generations did. For instance, in 1981 only 13 per cent of young men in their late 20s were living with parents, as opposed to 20 per cent in 2001. The increase in young women living with their parents is even higher, with 26 per cent living with parents in 1981, rising to 34 per cent in 2001. The reasons for staying in the parental home include postponing entering the full-time workforce and the financial dependence on parents associated with this, delays in getting married, and a steep increase in the cost of home renting and buying in Australia in recent years (de Vaus 2004).

Staying at home with parents longer can also be explained by the prolonged amount of time young adults are now spending in tertiary education and the accompanying financial dependence this incurs. Young people in Australia are going on to further education and training after secondary school at rates never before seen in Australian history (Smart & Sanson 2005). Within the 15–19-year-old age group, tertiary education participation has gone up from 19 per cent in 1987 to 26 per cent in 2000. Among the 20–24-year-old group, the proportion undertaking tertiary education has almost doubled from around 18 per cent in 1987 to 36 per cent in 2000 (ABS 1999, 2002 cited in de Vaus 2004). The extended period of time spent in tertiary education, coupled with postponement of full-time work, is also associated with young adults' tendency to delay getting married or entering into a long-term cohabiting relationship.

Young people and partnering

De Vaus (2004) compiled ABS data on partnering patterns among young adults, and concluded that between 1986 and 2001 there had been an increase in the numbers of young men and women who remained without a cohabiting partner. Young men in their early 20s living without partners rose from 80 per cent in 1986 to 87 per cent in 2001, and the comparable figures for young women were 61 per cent (1986) and 76 per cent (2001). When it came to young adults in their late 20s living without partners, the respective figures were 47 per cent in 1986 rising to 59 per cent in 2001 for young men, and for young women 33 per cent in 1986 rising to 47 per cent in 2001.

However, this delay in setting up house with a partner does not mean that young adults today are less interested in long-term emotional commitments. The Australian Temperament Project, conducted by the Australian Institute of Family Studies, is a longitudinal study that has followed over 1000 young Australians resident in Victoria from early childhood. In 2000, 1250 17–18-year-olds in this study were asked about their intentions to get married and/or form a long-term relationship. The results indicated teenagers have strong intentions of making the commitment to a long-term relationship in the future, with 92 per cent of the group hoping to have a long-term relationship at some point. A relatively small percentage of the group had no desire for this kind of relationship (1 per cent) or said they had not really given it much thought (7 per cent) (Smart 2002).

However, living up to teenage aspirations with regard to the formation of long-term relationships appears difficult for the young adults of today. Research has found that the levels of partnering and marriage aspired to by teenagers are unlikely to be achieved. The Young Adults Survey conducted in 1998 by the Australian Institute of Family Studies asked a nationally representative sample of Australian young people aged between 20 and 29 years about their current relationship circumstances. Findings indicated that the proportion of young adults who are either living with a partner or married is lower than what teenagers hope to achieve by the time they enter their 20s. The Australian Temperament Project found that only 15 per cent of young men and 27 per cent of young women in their 20s were married or living with a partner, despite the fact that 80 per cent of teenagers wanted this. With regard to young adults in their late 20s, only 43 per cent of men and 64 per cent of women were cohabiting with a partner (Qu & Soriano 2004). The meaning of this gap between teenage aspirations and the realities of 'twenty-something' relationships is by no means clear cut. For some young adults, their more youthful relationship priorities shift as they enter their 20s, whereas others may find it more difficult than they anticipated as teenagers to enter or maintain long-term relationships.

When asked to explain why they are experiencing difficulty finding a partner, most of the respondents to the Young Adults Study emphasised personal constraints such as being choosy or cautious or lacking trust. Finding a socially and emotionally compatible partner is much more important than having a partner for financial or status reasons. This is consistent with Giddens' (1992) arguments about the contemporary importance of the **pure relationship** ideal (see Chapters 4 and 6). About one third of the group of young people believed they were very selective when it came to choosing a partner, and that they had high standards for compatibility, rather than a sense that being in a relationship for its own sake was the most important goal. Both young men and women emphasised the importance of shared life goals with a partner, and finding someone with whom they were 'on the same wavelength' (Qu & Soriano 2004). They also spoke to researchers of their 'fussiness' or 'high standards' when it came to relationships. Some young men and women also revealed they tended to take a cautious approach to relationships for fear of being hurt or because of their experiences of their parents' or siblings' divorces.

However, the influence of feminism on young women's expectations cannot be underestimated. Most young women now expect to work and achieve a measure of financial independence prior to marrying or starting a family. Yet they are also aware of the contemporary tensions between work and relationship commitments. Young women may be particularly attuned to the ongoing difficulties their mothers' generation face in juggling work and family life and stay single longer because of these. For instance, Naomi Rosh White (2003), in a study of young Australian adults' views about partnering and parenthood, observes the extent to which young women emphasise the difficulties they may encounter managing work and family in the future, and how this is crucial to prioritising career building and financial independence prior to marriage and children. Their changed expectations, together with knowledge that gendered inequities in household responsibilities still prevail, led some young women to doubt the wisdom of early partnering, as in the following quotation from one of White's participants:

> I think there are certain constraints brought about by being in a relationship. Less time to concentrate on work and personal goals … Often domestic arrangements completely destroy a relationship because all of a sudden someone has to do all the ironing, or the shopping or clean the bathroom … and often it's not the guy who does it (2003, p. 157).

Heath and Cleaver (2003) argue that for young people, friendships are increasingly important in the context of delaying 'serious' couple formation and first marriage. They contend that the heightened importance friendships can assume in young people's lives has often been viewed in quite a limited way, as part of the transition to fully mature adulthood. For instance, psychologists construct 'adolescence' as a developmental phase in which young people are very oriented towards their peers. Failure to develop friendships in this phase is often said to lead to poor or inadequate psychological development as an adult. However, there is also an expectation that reaching adulthood requires foregrounding long-term emotional commitment to a couple relationship and relegating friendships to the background. In this view, in order to achieve full adulthood, young people should transfer their attention and affections away from friends towards sexual partners, and ultimately the serious life partner with whom they will set up house and have children. When friendships retain greater significance than sexually intimate couple relationships, or completely replace them, this may be interpreted as delayed and inappropriate maturity. Heath and Cleaver (2003) argue that as long as youth researchers maintain this emphasis on young people as individuals in transition, rather than look in a more holistic way at the social context of young people's networks of intimacy and support, a rather limited outlook on the importance of young people's friendships will persist (see Chapter 7 for more on this theme).

Indications are that young people today have high emotional expectations of their long-term relationships, and view marriage as primarily an emotional commitment, rather than a symbol of independence from parents or a path to financial security.

Changing concepts of young adulthood

FOR SOME SOCIOLOGISTS, THE CONCEPT '**post-adolescence**' best evokes the dilemmas and experiences of contemporary young adulthood. Post-adolescence has been described by Manuella du Bois-Reymond (1998) as a time in which the youth phase and its characteristic freedom from responsibilities for children and a spouse is prolonged well into legal adulthood. It refers to the tendencies of young adults to defer having children and committing to a serious long-term relationship or marriage—'settling down'—in favour of prioritising careers, life experience and self-development. Post-adolescence, for du Bois Reymond, tends to reject notions of responsibility and the lack of spontaneity that goes along with this, although it is characterised by some degree of independent living. Independence, in this view, is constituted as conducting a life of one's own, having freedom to choose friendships and couple relationships, and having one's own work or study goals. Du Bois-Reymond (1998) notes that post-adolescence is more characteristic of young adults who can rely to some extent on their parents' financial, cultural and social support. It is more discernible among young people who are well-educated and have high expectations of their working lives.

Australian sociologists White and Wyn (2004), by contrast, challenge the notion that contemporary young adults are experiencing an extended period of youthful irresponsibility, as suggested by the concept of post-adolescence. Rather, these authors believe young adults are reframing notions of adult responsibilities and the relationship expectations that go along with them in light of historically unprecedented social and economic conditions, notably precarious housing and long-term job prospects. Similarly, Dwyer and colleagues (2003) argue that the insecurity of global labour markets and the constant de- and re-skilling characteristic of work has required young adults to become adult earlier than their parents' generation. In this view, because young people cannot take lifelong and secure employment for granted, they are forced to cultivate skills in personal development, self-sufficiency and multi-tasking, earlier and to a greater degree than their elders have ever had to.

It is apparent that young adults themselves are developing changing notions of what it means to be an adult. For instance, Arnett (1997) found that North American college students emphasised individual qualities and characteristics as signifying what it meant to be adult in preference to conventional transitional events such as finishing education, entering the labour force, marriage and parenthood. Accepting responsibility for one's own actions, making decisions about one's own beliefs and values independently to those held by parents, and the capacity to establish relationships with parents as equal adults were the qualities most emphasised as adult by Arnett's participants. Similarly, in a 1995 study, Jones' participants nominated freedom from parental control and economic self-reliance as key attributes of adulthood. As Natalier (2007) observes, such studies indicate that young people understand adulthood as judgments they make for themselves about what constitutes responsibility and independence, rather than rite-of-passage events or statuses conferred on them from outside.

Intimate relationships

ALTHOUGH YOUNG ADULTS ARE DEFERRING long-term emotional commitments, love, sex and relationships are no less important. As Allen (2004) comments, intimate couple relationships do occupy a central place in the lives of young people. However, the concept 'relationship' is quite a complex one. There is a tendency to take the term at face value rather than scrutinise what relationships mean and how they are constituted in young people's lives.

Allen notes there has been a tendency to discuss young people's relationships as if they are either 'short-term' or 'long-term'. On the contrary, Allen found in her study of 515 heterosexual New Zealand 17–19-year-olds that there was great variability within each of the four categories that young people themselves used to describe their relationships, that is, 'one-night stands', 'short-term relationships', 'casual dating' and 'going out'. The elements that made up and differentiated each type of relationship were as follows: how much time the partners spent together, how exclusive the sexual and emotional commitment was, the degree of emotional attachment to the person, the kinds of and frequency of sexual activity involved. Furthermore, Allen's study challenged the notion that young people's relationships are short, superficial and without strong emotional ties. Over half of the group of young people surveyed had been in a relationship that was more than six months long, and nearly 40 per cent of this group reported that the relationship in question had lasted between one and five years. Overall, the study provided evidence that youthful relationships often mirror those entered into later in life, with regard to their level of emotional seriousness and longevity.

In media commentary and sex education programs, young people's relationships are often problematised and discussed within a dominant framework that sees them 'at risk'; for example, from sexual coercion, sexually transmissible infections (STIs) and unwanted pregnancies (see White & Wyn 2004; Allen 2004). The current media fascination with young people and 'hooking up', or participating in short-term sexual encounters with multiple partners, often under the influence of alcohol, is a good example of this focus (see Szego 2007). Allen argues that although this negative focus has emphasised the importance of exploring young people's relationships for the benefit of their sexual and emotional health, it has also neglected some of the more positive dimensions of young people's intimate lives. For instance in Allen's study, although young people considered the sexual component of relationships important, they were also considered to offer other sources of pleasure more akin to intimacy in the sense of emotional and physical closeness to another person. Companionship, security and emotional support were important attributes of many of the relationships that Allen's participants discussed, as in the following interview excerpts:

[the best thing about relationships is] Mmm, the stuff you can do together I reckon. Like just not even sex and stuff. Maybe lying on the couch and watching TV (Rodney, 18 years) (Allen 2004, p. 476).

You go away like together and you do all this stuff together and then you can reminisce about it because there is someone there that you know. (Sharon, 18 years) (Allen 2004, p. 476).

Changing patterns of courtship in the USA

In *From Front Porch to Back Seat* (1989), Beth Bailey traces changes in the dominant conventions of heterosexual dating and courtship for young North Americans. Prior to the twentieth century, the dominant mode of courtship involved men 'calling' on the families of young women. Usually suitors would be received into the family parlour (good lounge room) and offered refreshments, meet the young woman's mother and perhaps listen to someone play the piano. This mode of courtship copied upper-class modes of socialising from the UK. Women had some say in courtship processes and could invite young men to call on them and could turn away an undesirable suitor by conveying the message that she was not 'at home'.

From the turn of the century to about the 1920s courtship began to evolve from 'calling' to 'dating'. Dates involved occasions where young women were taken out by men and entertained. In effect, courtship moved into the public realm, away from the supervision of immediate family. Young couples had new freedom but dating increasingly depended on men having the money to participate. Dating developed from working-class modes of socialising—because working-class women had no access to the parlours or pianos required for 'calling'. Dating became the dominant form of courtship from the 1920s to the 1960s. Access to cars helped couples escape from the front porch and surveillance of family and local community. However, sex was tightly controlled and a woman's value linked to her sexual morality.

Having sex has increasingly become an accepted part of contemporary courtship. Bailey argues that sex is the medium of contemporary courtship as 'technical' virginity has declined in importance. Arguably the link between a woman's value and her virtue has been broken. The dominant convention now is that sex is part of long-term relationships and a possibility on the first date.

Changes in courtship patterns have implications for gender relations and who takes the lead in initiating relationships. There is a need for more research on whether contemporary young women believe they can take the lead in asking someone out or whether they still tend to believe they have to wait to be asked.

Sexuality

PRIOR TO THE 1970S IN Australia, sex outside of marriage was still very much frowned upon. So-called shot-gun marriages were common among young adults, at a time when there was a complete absence of any welfare support for single parents, and poor legal access to safe abortion and reliable contraception (Gilding 1997). Up until the early 1970s, a **sexual double standard** was very much the norm. Young men were supposed to be sexually experienced but young women were supposed to stay virgins until they got married. Young women carried the burden of unwanted pregnancies and, if they were unable to marry the father, they were often faced with the prospect of giving their child up for adoption or having a dangerous and illegal abortion (Marshall & McDonald 2001). Under these conditions, having sex outside marriage was often fraught with difficulties.

Two decades later, the sexual arena for teenagers and young adults has changed considerably. Flood (2008) documents at least four shifts in the sexual lives of young people. First, children in Western countries are entering puberty earlier than they used to, most likely due to improved nutrition. Second, the average age of first sexual intercourse has declined slightly, particularly for women. For instance, for people now in their 50s, the median age of first sexual intercourse was 18 for men and 19 for women, often taking place for women on their wedding night. For young people now aged between 16 and 19 the age of first intercourse for those who have experienced it has dropped to 16 for both men and women—though it is important to bear in mind that a large proportion of 16–19-year-olds have not yet experienced intercourse (40 per cent of men and 43 per cent of women) so the average age may not be substantially lower than for previous generations (Richters & Rissel 2005). Third, young people's sexual styles are distinctive in that they engage in a range of sexual behaviours, such as oral sex and anal intercourse, which are not as common among older people. Fourth, young people today tend to have more sexual partners than their parents' generation had. Young people—men and women—usually expect to have had several sexual partners and/or relationships before they commit to a long-term relationship.

Intimate relationships and sex among urban heterosexual Vietnamese young people

Sexuality and relationships among young adults are greatly influenced by the social and cultural context in which they occur. Vietnam, in contrast with Australia, is a country with a relatively youthful population: 70 per cent of the population is under 30, and the 15–30-year-old age group accounts for about 30 per cent of the entire population of 80 million people (Nguyen 2007). It is also a country that has witnessed a great deal of political, social and economic upheaval and reform in the past two decades; notably, the fall of a totalitarian socialist government in the mid 1980s and the switch to a capitalist free market economy.

Up until the mid twentieth century, Confucianism largely guided the conduct of sexual and gender relations in Vietnam, and sex before marriage was very strongly condemned. Women, in particular, were subject to the dictates of Confucian sexual ethics, and a young woman's pre-marital chastity and marital fidelity were considered the foundation of her own and her family's dignity and reputation. Although male chastity was considered virtuous, it was never policed in reality, and the practice of taking of multiple wives and adultery were tolerated (Marr 1981). Under the socialist regime that came to power in 1954, pregnancy outside of marriage, and adultery, remained practices that could incur punishment. The state took a strong interest in ensuring men and women chose suitable marital partners, and also in monitoring their pre-marital relationships (Nguyen 2007). For instance, Nguyen reports that when a woman and man were interested in dating, they were required to inform their work units of the fact that they wanted to have a relationship. This led to the creation of the phrase *bao cao to chuc*, or 'reporting to the organisation', which Nguyen notes is still used in a joking manner by young people in Vietnam today to refer to 'going public' with one's relationship.

Nguyen (2007) argues that a number of major social and cultural transformations in Vietnam since the mid 1980s have accompanied economic and political reform, and have led to more relaxed sexual mores for young men and women. These include the easing of stringent political controls on individual behaviour and on access to Western media and communications, increased access to work that allows independence from family support, and greater possibilities for travel and Western-style recreational activities among young people. Nguyen conducted interviews in Hanoi between 1999 and 2004 with 100 unmarried young Vietnamese men and women aged between 20 and 30, from various walks of life. She found that urban Vietnam now offers young men and women a number of avenues through which to explore their sexuality, including relatively affordable access to the internet and its wealth of chat rooms, erotic literature and pornography, and also venues specifically set up for sexual recreation and prostitution. Premarital sex, unmarried cohabitation with an intimate partner and dating multiple partners were largely socially accepted by the young people interviewed. The young men and women Nguyen spoke to defined premarital sex broadly to include not only sexual relationships with girlfriends and boyfriends, but also casual encounters. However, in keeping with the traditional sexual double standard, young men reported more casual encounters and many were open about having sex with prostitutes. Nguyen noted that young men and women spoke about their sexual experiences and relationships, for the most part, in an open and comfortable fashion. Few of the young women she spoke to regarded chastity as a marital requirement. Parents and older relatives increasingly knew about and accepted (sometimes reluctantly) their children's sexual activities.

The fact that sex has become a normalised part of dating experiences for young people (see Bailey 1989) has both positive and negative implications. On the positive side, young people today enjoy considerable sexual freedom in both dating and long-term relationships. Levels of safe-sex knowledge and expertise are high and the stigma surrounding unmarried sex has receded for a large proportion of the youth population. For perhaps the first time in history the possibility of sexual experimentation with a number of partners is open to young women as well as young men.

However, the tight link between dating and sex may lead to newer social pressures both young men and young women are aware of. For instance, staying a virgin beyond a certain age can now be source of social stigma, leading young people of both genders to feel a sense of obligation to have sex, perhaps before they would choose to. Feeling pressured into having sex or feeling like you can't say no to sex is something that happens to both sexes. A national study of Australian secondary school students conducted in the late 1990s found that 28 per cent of sexually active young women and 23 per cent of sexually active young men in Years 11 and 12 had experienced unwanted sex at some time (Lindsay et al. 1997). Some said they were too drunk to say no and others said they had felt under pressure from partners. Different sexual behaviours and demeanours continue to be considered appropriate for young men, as opposed to young women, and continue to influence the way in which young heterosexual people's relationships are represented and expressed. For instance, there is a view that men have stronger biological urges to have sex than women. This indicates that the sexual double standard that was very prominent before the 1970s still prevails to some extent.

Lindsay (2002) argues that the sexual double standard is more complex than it used to be. Young women are increasingly encouraged towards sexual expertise in the advice columns of magazines such as *Cleo* and *Cosmopolitan*, an expertise aimed at pleasing men rather than themselves when it comes to sex. Firminger (2006) contends that in magazines aimed at teenage girls, life success—including success in heterosexual love—is depicted as girls' responsibility, linked to their ability to choose men well and present themselves to men in the appropriate manner. Yet at the same time, young women are in danger of developing a reputation as a 'slut' if they appear too sexually available and experienced. In other words, contemporary young women get very mixed messages about how to conduct their sexual lives.

Anita Harris (1999) also notes that young women are increasingly encouraged to relate to their bodies as objects for the sexual pleasure of others, particularly with regard to the appearance of their bodies. This is not necessarily linked to their own sexual pleasure or fulfilment. Levy (2005) describes this phenomenon as part of the rise of 'raunch culture', in which the imagery of pornography and prostitution is commonplace in the expression of sexuality by young women, and there is an expectation that women will display their bodies and present themselves as sex objects. A recent article in Melbourne newspaper *The Age,* considering how American socialite Paris Hilton is a sexual role model for young women, illustrates this tendency (Cunningham 2007). In the article, Hilton reflects on her sexual image and explains that her boyfriends see her as 'sexy' rather than 'sexual'. The journalist, Sophie Cunningham, discussing Hilton's observation of herself, supports the arguments made by Lindsay (2002) and Harris (1999). Hilton's own comments on her sexuality draw attention to the importance of looking sexy for the benefit of others rather than feeling sexual and acting in accordance with her own needs and desires. In this way Hilton embodies the newer version of the sexual double standard for young women. Look and be sexy, have sex, and be good at it, but not necessarily because you enjoy it.

To take a more optimistic view of young heterosexual sexuality, there is also evidence that young people's sexual subjectivities are shifting in the sense that girls these days are more able to openly articulate a desire for sex, and boys a desire for love. Allen (2003) found that a significant minority of the 17–19-year-old young women she interviewed were able to resist dominant meanings about appropriately feminine sexuality either some or all of the time. For instance, in the following quotation 'Anna' formulates her own desire and sexual activities as reasonable and resists being labelled a 'slut': 'I was called a slut when I cheated on someone … but a slut is supposed to be someone who sleeps around. I don't sleep around' (p. 223). Furthermore, other young couples who participated in Allen's research were able to openly discuss, in focus groups or couple interviews, the female partner's more active interest in sex than the male's. Young women overall felt they had more control than young men over the kinds of sexual activity they took part in, and over contraception decisions and how often to have sex; and young men were able to openly express the view that love, commitment, honesty and care were more important than sex in relationships.

Same-sex-attracted young people, coming out and family support

Writing Themselves In (Hillier et al. 1998) was the first national study in Australia of same-sex-attracted young people. The term '**same-sex-attracted-youth**' (SSAY) was used in preference to lesbian, gay or bisexual, in order not to pre-empt the complex relationship between sexual behaviour, sexual attraction and sexual identity. Indeed, the survey came about due to findings from two previous national surveys that revealed between 9 and 11 per cent of young people did not regard themselves as exclusively heterosexual, and was aimed at any young person aged between 14 and 21 who had ever felt sexually attracted to a member of their own sex. Recruitment to the study was through youth magazines *Dolly* and *Smash Hits* and a number of mainstream and queer-specific websites. Young people were asked questions about their sexual attractions, identities and practices, levels of safe sex and drug use, sexual health information sources, experiences of verbal and physical abuse and quality of life overall. Importantly, they were invited to tell their stories about disclosing their same-sex attractions or experiences, that is, 'coming out' to friends and family.

One fifth of the group had never come out to anyone and were struggling with fear of rejection should they tell someone about their sexual feelings or practices. Friends were generally the people turned to for support. Although female friends were more often chosen as confidantes than male friends, around three quarters of male and female friends were found to be supportive when confided in. It was quite uncommon for young people to seek support from professional helpers such as doctors, youth workers, teachers, counsellors or student welfare coordinators. Mothers and sisters were more likely to be chosen as confidantes than fathers or brothers, and this was true for both young men and women. About one in three participants overall had spoken to their mother and two thirds of this group found Mum supportive. About a fifth of participants had confided in their father and half of this group found their father to be supportive. Overall, sisters proved to be the most supportive family members.

The study results also indicated significant gender differences with regard to patterns of sexual attraction, behaviour and identity. For the young men in the study, there was more congruence between feelings of gender a-typicality, same-sex attractions and same-sex behaviours, and young men were also more likely than young women to identify as gay. Overall, young women displayed more fluidity with regard to their sexual feelings, behaviours and identities. They were more likely to be experiencing lesbian desires or fantasies, while only having heterosexual sex and relationships. Young women were also grappling with limited and emotionally fraught opportunities for sex with other girls who were already known to them as friends, whereas young men appeared to have more access to sexual networks outside their friendship networks. The relative invisibility of lesbianism as an identity or practice led to confusion among young women about what their feelings of attraction to other women or girls meant in the context of their sexual futures (see Dempsey, Hillier & Harrison 2001).

Despite a number of positive coming out experiences and stories, many young people sent in stories emphasising their fears about bringing shame on their family or being rejected by their family if they came out. Young people from non-English-speaking backgrounds were less likely to have told their parents about their sexuality and also less likely to have received any information about lesbian, gay or heterosexual sex from family members. Indeed, many of the fears and triumphs expressed about coming out hinged on perceived or actual reactions of family members. When young people felt largely negative about their sexuality, it was often because they had met with a hostile response from family members. Where participants told more optimistic stories, there had generally been some support offered or an encouraging response from family members.

Writing Themselves In Again was conducted in 2004, six years after the original survey (Hillier, Turner & Mitchell 2005). In the intervening years, there had been a great increase in awareness-raising about same-sex-attracted young people and many more support groups and community programs set up around Australia, due largely to the original research findings. The main differences were encouraging. By 2004, there had been a shift to more young people feeling positive about being lesbian, gay or bisexual, with 76 per cent feeling 'great' or 'good' about their sexuality as opposed to 60 per cent in 1998. There was a greater tendency to come out to fathers as well as mothers, and to parents before sisters and brothers, indicating parents are becoming more accepting of same-sex relationships and practices. One discouraging finding was that in 2004, schools and family members were still providing young people with very little information about lesbian and gay sex (including safe sex) or relationships, and were the sources young people were least likely to turn to for this information.

Conclusion

THE SOCIOLOGICAL RESEARCH ON YOUNG people and relationships paints a complex picture. Available evidence indicates that the relatively linear 1950s and 1960s pattern of dating then leaving home to get married has changed considerably. Instead, today's young adults are freer to take a number of paths and back-track and start again if these do not work out. At the same time, young people are constrained by increasingly precarious labour markets and the greater imperative to gain higher education credentials before entering the full-time labour market. The delay in economic independence from families caused by a longer time in education has flow-on effects and delays partnering and parenting. One of the major changes that has occurred in relationship formation is the normalisation of sex in both dating and long-term relationships. Despite newer and more complex permutations of the sexual double standard, it is also true that unmarried people of this generation, both heterosexual and same-sex-attracted, can engage in sexual intimacy with less fear of the stigma and shame that previously accompanied any form of sex outside of marriage.

Nonetheless, marriage still manages to maintain its allure as a life goal for young people, exemplified by Alex's quote at the beginning of the chapter. In the following chapter we examine the social institution of marriage.

Key concepts

Boomerang generation

Pure relationship

Post-adolescence

Sexual double standard

Same-sex-attracted youth (SSAY)

Discussion questions

1   Do you agree that young people today are experiencing an extended period of adolescence that is relatively free from responsibility? Or are you more persuaded by the idea that young adulthood responsibilities are being reformulated due to the different set of social and economic pressures facing young people?

2   What defines adulthood today? Are key events such as marriage and becoming a parent still relevant?

3   Does the sexual double standard still exist? What is the evidence?

Recommended further reading

Allen, L. 2003, 'Girls Want Sex, Boys Want Love: Resisting Dominant Discourses of (Hetero)sexuality', *Sexualities*, vol. 6, no. 2, pp. 215–36.

Dempsey, D., Hillier, L. & Harrison, L. 2001, 'Gendered (S)explorations Among Same-sex Attracted Young People in Australia', *Journal of Adolescence*, vol. 24, issue 1, pp. 67–81.

Heath, S. & Cleaver, E. 2003, *Young, Free and Single: Twenty-somethings and Household Change*, Palgrave Macmillan, Basingstoke, Chapter 3 'Risk, Individualization and the Single Life'.

White, N. R. 2003, 'Changing Conceptions: Young People's Views of Partnering and Parenting', *Journal of Sociology*, vol. 39, no. 2, pp. 149–64.

06 | Love, Commitment and Marriage

Figure 6.1: Prince Frederik and Princess Mary; Elton John and David Furnish

Introduction

SOME SOCIOLOGISTS ARGUE THAT MARRIAGE has been 'deinstitutionalised' in the sense that it is no longer a taken-for-granted adult role (Cherlin 2004). So does this mean marriage has become irrelevant for people in Western societies? The photos above illustrate two high-profile weddings. The first is from the Royal Wedding of Crown Prince Frederik and Crown Princess Mary of Denmark in 2004 and draws on traditional symbols of heterosexual marriage. The second photo, from the same year, is the civil partnership ceremony between Sir Elton John and his long-term partner David Furnish. The image marks the beginning of a new tradition—the legal recognition of same-sex relationships in the UK. At the beginning of the twenty-first century, marriage remains a popular aspiration but instead of being a taken-for-granted adult status, marriage now represents one lifestyle choice among others. Unmarried **cohabitation** and non-cohabiting same-sex and heterosexual intimate relationships continue to grow in popularity. In Australia, for the first time since white settlement, fewer than half—49.6 per cent—of the adult population aged 15 and over is officially married and one third has never married (ABS 2007e).

In this chapter we begin by discussing love and romance and then explore changing understandings of couple relationships, including marriage. We look at overall patterns, demographic trends and legislative or policy controversies with regard to forming intimate relationships and getting married. We also consider the meanings of love and intimacy for women and men in the context of marriage, same-sex partnerships and cohabiting heterosexual partnerships. We discuss the different meanings of **commitment** involved with regard to cohabiting as opposed to marriage relationships, and some of the implications of this.

Love and romance

CONTEMPORARY WESTERN FAMILIAL RELATIONSHIPS ARE underpinned by an ethos of love and intimacy. Marriage and cohabiting couple relationships are generally presumed to be the outcome of romantic love and are considered to be the antithesis of commoditised or work relationships. Intimacy, in the form of a very particular kind of knowing, loving and being close to one's partner (Jamieson 1998), is presumed to be at the core of a meaningful personal and familial life.

Love is a notoriously difficult concept to define. According to a number of theories, and in numerous literary traditions, it has been portrayed as sexual passion, romantic idealisation, affection, companionship, dependence, attachment and shared experiences (Coltrane 1998). Love has often been ignored by sociologists. This is possibly because even sociologists have tended to think of love as an intense feeling or one of our most personal, mysterious and fundamental emotions. We often think of emotions as natural or pre-social. However, in the last few decades, a sociology of the emotions has developed and a recognition that emotions such as love are socially constructed and subject to cultural influence and historical change.

Modern romantic love developed alongside the modern family form (as discussed in Chapter 2). As industrialisation developed, women became domestic specialists and were also seen as the specialists in romance. There was a new association between love and marriage that had not existed before. Beck-Gernsheim argues that there was a shift in marriage from a 'team' sharing work in pre-modern times, to a couple sharing emotions in modern and late modern times. Emotional life and marriages became intensified (Beck-Gernsheim 2002).

Contemporary romance has two elements: first, the quest to find a partner—where you fasten on and idealise the other—and second, that this attachment should be the basis for future development into a long-term relationship. Giddens (1992) contends that the late eighteenth century marked the beginning of the kind of love we associate with modern romantic love.

This kind of love incorporated elements of courtly and passionate love, while distinguishing itself from both. For Giddens, the main difference between romantic love and its earlier manifestations is that it introduced the idea of a plot or storyline. The story attached to romantic love was one of freedom and self-realisation through love. It promised finding oneself through love with a special other who represents 'the one' who will make life complete. Although passion may accompany romantic love, the superior qualities that pick the loved one out as special or unique tend to be emphasised over and above sexual passion. Giddens argues that romantic love is characterised by its future orientation; it is predicated on imagining a long-term future life with the partner.

Being 'in love' and love as long-term affection

ACCORDING TO STEVI JACKSON (1993), contemporary romantic love is usually separated into two phases of experience: being in love or falling in love as the more overwhelming, irrational sexual phase, as distinct from a more companionate kind of love that mellows out over time and is associated with shared history and experiences, and long-term affection. The first phase of romantic love is seen by Jackson in a similar light to how Giddens describes passionate love throughout history. The notion of being in love is presumed to precede the development of a more long-term love, in which the passions die down to be replaced by a different quality of love. Some commentators have seen a functional relationship between the two phases of love. The intense sexual phase compels the choice of partner, whereas the mellower, companionate phase maintains the relationship. Yet there is also a fundamental contradiction or paradox implied here. The very kind of love that impels us to form monogamous relationships is the source of their potential undoing, as the desire to experience that initial exciting phase of love all over again can actually threaten relationship stability over time.

Feminist critiques of love

> 'It starts when you sink into his arms and ends with your arms in his sink.'

THIS SLOGAN, ACCORDING TO STEVI JACKSON (1993), sums up the cynicism inherent to many second wave feminist critiques of romantic love. Feminists argued that love is an ideology that masks women's oppression and makes marriage attractive. Early second wave feminists such as Simone de Beauvoir and Shulamith Firestone believed love was an ideology that perpetuated men's power over women and legitimated women's inequality. Firestone, writing in 1970, went as far as to say that love was the absolute linchpin of women's oppression.

De Beauvoir's emphasis was on how women in love were dangerous to themselves because they became so preoccupied with it. Love not only reinforced subordination, but led to women seeing themselves as constituted by subordination. Despite quite different approaches, de Beauvoir and Firestone agreed that women invest far more in love than men do, and get far little in return from men for the amount that they invest. This made them more vulnerable to exploitation and also to being hurt. Some women's liberation era feminists were remarkably cynical about gender relations in the extent to which they emphasised the doomed nature of marriage and indeed all intimate liaisons between women and men.

These ideas about the inherently exploitative nature of love were not confined to women's liberation-era feminism and its precursors. Christine Delphy and Diana Leonard published their book *Familiar Exploitation* in 1992, in which they asserted that the ideology of love and women's emotional role in marriage and heterosexual relationships is always a dimension of men's exploitation of women's unpaid labour. So, for instance, when women claim that preparing meals or doing housework is an expression of love for their husband, they saw this as evidence of women's false consciousness. In other words, there is no room in Delphy and Leonard's work for love or a sense of emotional connectedness to men in marriage to be in any way genuine or expressive of women's active engagement and desire.

These kinds of feminist ideas about love as oppressive ideology have been very valuable in looking at the power inequities justified in the name of love, but they often don't really give women much credit for having any power at all in relationships. Some research within cultural studies on women's readings of romance highlights the theme of transformation that dominates romantic fiction. In many romance novels women have power over men and are able to transform them (Radway 1984). Perhaps by being interested in romance women are yearning for a different organisation of gender roles and society?

Sociologists have often neglected collecting data about how love is manifest or conceptualised in relationships and instead focused on concepts such as labour, care or most recently on commitment (Smart 2007). It seems likely that our emotional expectations and experiences have changed as relationship patterns change.

Government-assisted love: The social development unit in Singapore

In the face of declining marriage and fertility rates the Singaporean Government established the social development unit (SDU) to encourage young graduates in particular to marry and have children. The latest version of the website has a home page entitled 'LoveByte' <http://www.lovebyte.org.sg/web/host_p_1main.asp>, which offers a variety of opportunities including dating services and events for singles to meet with the aim of developing relationships. Anecdotally, there is some stigma among young Singaporeans using this government service, illustrated by the joke that SDU stands for 'Single, Desperate and Ugly'. Perhaps this is why the 'LoveByte' title is now given greater prominence—the website has a funky look, targeting a technologically savvy youth audience. The following quotation from the website outlines the government's aims for the program:

LoveByte's formula for romance
We aim to help you in your quest for new friends and potential partners. To that end, we've come up with the following recipe to help us, help you:
- We want to create awareness amongst you, our eligible graduates, on the importance of marriage and family, and the need to start early.
- Having the LoveByte café, MatchBox and our activities and services to create opportunities for eligible graduates like you to meet.
- Through our empowerment (aka public education) programmes, we hope to help you set your expectations right in the search for a life-partner.
- Ultimately, we hope you would be looking forward to an enriching marriage and a fulfilling family (LoveByte 2008).

Feminist critiques of marriage

LOVE MAY HAVE BEEN NEGLECTED by sociologists but marriage has certainly not. As outlined in Chapter 4, in the 1950s functionalists such as Talcott Parsons described what they saw as the necessary and complementary roles played with husbands and wives within families. Family sociologists after World War II argued that marriages were becoming more companionate and women and men were enjoying symmetrical if distinct roles (Cherlin 2004).

By contrast, second-wave feminists strongly disagreed with this line of theorising and identified marriage as central to women's oppression. Feminists argued that marriage, historically, denied women equal status and recognition as citizens and was a central mechanism for controlling women's sexuality and establishing paternity of offspring. Socialist feminists identified the unequal labour relationship involved in marriage that supported capitalism. Radical feminists highlighted that the privacy around marriage and expectations of monogamy operated to hide domestic violence toward wives and children. For example, Delphy and Leonard argued that men get '57 varieties of unpaid service from marriage' (Delphy & Leonard, 1992, p. 260).

In the late 1980s Carole Pateman outlined the inherent inequalities involved in the sexual contract of marriage (Pateman 1988). She argued that the whole notion of contract was based on and reinforced patriarchal power. Men's conjugal or sexual right over women was central to their political power:

A (house)wife does not contract out her labour power to her husband. She is not paid a wage—there is no token of free exchange—because her husband has command over the use of her labour by virtue of the fact that he is a man. The marriage contract is a labour contract in a very different sense from the employment contract. The marriage contract is about *women's* labour, the employment contract is about men's work (Pateman 1988, p. 136, original italics).

Over a decade earlier, Jessie Barnard, an American sociologist, developed the influential argument that there were two distinct versions of marriage within every conjugal relationship—'the husband's marriage' and 'the wife's marriage' (Barnard 1982). Barnard outlined evidence that marriage was good for men; married men had better mental health and enjoyed better career and income earning prospects than those held by their unmarried counterparts. By contrast the wife's marriage was shown to have a very negative impact on women's psychological health. In research on marriage, women were substantially more likely to report problems and disappointments within their marriage than men (Barnard 1982). Barnard was particularly scathing about the housewife's role:

> Dwindling into a housewife takes time. It involves a redefinition of the self and an active shaping of the personality to conform to the wishes or needs or demands of husbands (Barnard 1982, p. 39).

Johnson and Lloyd (2004) argue that this type of rejection of the housewife role, illustrated by Barnard's comment, was central to the development of second-wave feminism. Lesley Johnson and Justine Lloyd have charted the troubled relationship that feminism has had with the role of the housewife over the last 60 years. Second-wave feminism depended largely on rejecting the domestic sphere, as represented by the housewife, and valorising the world of paid work for women. The downside of this is that the domestic sphere as a site for developing meaning and maintaining humane and communal values has been neglected in subsequent feminist analysis (Johnson & Lloyd 2004). We take up this line of analysis again in Chapter 10 when we discuss domestic labour. It is clear that the second-wave feminist critique of marriage changed the ideological landscape profoundly and, coupled with rising divorce rates, operated to make people question the desirability of marriage.

Changing relationship patterns

THERE IS LITTLE DOUBT THAT beliefs about and experiences of intimate relationships have changed significantly over the past 30 to 40 years. This is reflected in four pronounced trends in Australia that are echoed in other Western countries. Lower rates of marriage and delayed marriage, higher rates of divorce, more cohabitation, or living together in a couple relationship without being married, and larger numbers of people staying single longer are all trends very characteristic of contemporary times. In the section below, we discuss broad trends in relation to marriage and cohabitation.

Marriage patterns in Australia

MOST AUSTRALIANS DO EVENTUALLY MARRY at some point in their adult life, with the latest figures suggesting this applies to 72 per cent of men and 77 per cent of women (de Vaus 2004). However, there has been a downturn in marriage rates since the 1980s, and people are choosing to marry at a later age than in the postwar era.

Marriage rates have fluctuated since 1901 and have broadly followed economic and social conditions. The crude marriage rate has fallen in times of depression (the 1930s), increased during times of war and declined substantially since the 1980s and has remained stable since 2002 (ABS 2007c). If we look at the postwar era in Australia, between 1940 and 1970 there was what demographers call a '**marriage boom**'. This was apparent in two ways. First, there was a tendency between these years for people to get married at a relatively early age, for example, in their late teens or early 20s. Second, there were large numbers of first marriages. Gilding (1997) notes that over 90 per cent of Australian women of marriageable age got married in the 1950s and 1960s. According to de Vaus, Qu and Weston (2003), the social factors that appeared to foster this marriage boom were the improved economic conditions prevailing after World War II. Marriage rates, like fertility rates, have historically tended to go up when the economy is doing well. Furthermore, after the war, there was a great deal of social encouragement provided in the media for getting married and raising a family.

The marriage boom reached its pinnacle in the early 1970s. Lyn Richards conducted research on marriage and parenthood at the time and sketched out a very different landscape to the one young people inhabit in the twenty-first century. In the 1970s young people 'settled down' in their early 20s and marriage was almost universal. Few of the men or women Richards interviewed had considered the possibility of remaining single. 'For almost all the only question was, not whether, but when they would marry and whom' (Richards 1985, p. 78).

During the marriage boom years, there was continuing stigma attached to sex outside of marriage and unmarried mothers, which meant that many people did not have sex for the first time until after they were married, or did not have sex unless they were intending to marry. The contraceptive pill became available in the early 1960s, but was not widely used by unmarried women until the late 1960s and early 1970s when social mores about sexual behaviour began to relax. So-called 'shot-gun weddings', in which young men were coerced into marrying the young women they got pregnant, were still very common in the 1950s and

1960s. According to McDonald (1995), they still accounted for a quarter of all first-time marriages during the 1960s. Until 1973 there was no social security benefit paid in Australia to unmarried women with children. Single parenthood was largely unacceptable and couples who became pregnant 'had to get married' to avoid social stigma (Richards 1985). The prevalence of shot-gun weddings throughout the 1950s and 1960s no doubt has bearing on why so many people were keen to make use of the new 'no fault' divorce laws that came into being in Australia in 1975. Before that time, it had to be proved that one party was responsible for the failure of the marriage before it could be legally dissolved.

From the late 1970s, changing sexual and contraceptive behaviour and the rising age of marriage began to be documented. This era is sometimes referred to as the beginning of the **'marriage bust'** (Bittman & Pixley 1997). For instance, a 1977 survey of young Australian adults documented changing sexual and contraceptive behaviour and beliefs. In this survey of 18–25-year-olds, over 80 per cent approved of sex before marriage and over two thirds of women and men were sexually experienced. The researcher working on this study, Stefania Siedlecky, concluded that the prevailing pattern among her respondents was to have sexual intercourse and use contraception well before marriage, and that contraception delayed not only the birth of children, but also the perceived need to get married at an early age.

Marriage remains a major aspiration for many people but attitudes have changed and marriage has lost its social importance. The crude marriage rate has been in decline since the 1980s as illustrated in Figure 6.2. It is now possible and increasingly acceptable to live independently, have a sexual life, or move in with a partner without marriage. The rise in divorce over the last two decades has made many wary of marriage. In 1971 the mean age of brides and bridegrooms, at first marriage, was 21 and 23 respectively. Over two decades later, people are marrying when they are considerably older. In 2006 the median age of marriage was 28 for women and 30 for men (ABS 2007c).

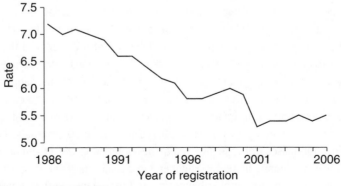

Figure 6.2: Marriage Rate

Source: ABS 2006c, *Marriages Australia*, cat. no. 3306.0.55.001

Marriage and partner choice

THERE ARE STRONG SOCIAL PATTERNS in how people fall in love and who they fall in love with, which supports the argument that love is a social construction. As Baker (2001) comments, when we fall in love, the tendency is to conform to strong cultural ideas about appropriate partners. Partners are usually about the same age. Women are seldom more than three years older than their partners, but men are occasionally much older than their partners. When men are substantially younger than their partners, the expression 'toy boy' is used, which suggests that this is a short-term sexual relationship rather than a serious partnership.

In partner selection other gender stereotypes are reinforced. In personal advertising for relationships, men continue to search for younger women who are slim and attractive while women continue to focus on a man's occupational status as well as his older age and appearance (Baker 2001). It is also the case that partners tend to come from similar racial, cultural, religious and socio-economic backgrounds, which is known as **homogamy**. Research has consistently found most heterosexual partners meet through friends or family, and most other partners meet through school or work. By contrast, **hypergamy** or the phenomenon of marrying higher up the social ladder is relatively rare. Where hypergamy does occur, it tends to be women who marry up, although the practice is weakening as women increasingly have careers and financial wealth of their own. Some women still use marriage as a path to financial security and upward mobility, the theory being they are able to trade youth and beauty for social status.

'The Deinstitutionalization of American Marriage'—Andrew Cherlin

Andrew Cherlin traces historical change in North American marriages (2004). The period 1850–1960 was a period of 'institutional marriage', where marriage was the only acceptable way to have a sexual relationship and raise children and was a ticket to a 'full family life'. Following World War II until the 1960s, the 'companionate marriage' began to emerge. Marriage was increasingly important to young people; the marriage rate rose and the age of marriage declined. At this time there was a strict division between breadwinners and homemakers but new expectations of intimacy, that partners would be 'friends and lovers', began to emerge. According to Cherlin (2004), since the 1960s marriage has become desinstitutionalised through five major developments; the changing division of labour in the home, increased childbearing outside marriage, a steep rise in the divorce rate, the growth of cohabitation and most recently the growth in same-sex marriage. Cherlin (2004) argues that 'individualised marriage' is now the norm.

People look beyond the satisfaction gained through building a family and playing the roles of spouse and parent and aim for personal growth and deep intimacy within their marriages. According to Cherlin (2004) the practical importance of marriage has declined but its symbolic importance has remained high. Marriage is now a marker of prestige and personal achievement. Young people in the USA see marriage as a status to 'build up to' by achieving a stable job and a committed relationship and, increasingly, by having children first (2004).

Unmarried cohabitation

WHILE THERE HAS BEEN A DECLINE in marriage rates overall, the proportion of couples who cohabit has increased progressively (from 6 per cent in 1986 to 12 per cent in 2001). This means that marriage rates are becoming less useful as an indicator of relationship rates (Weston & Qu 2007). Cohabiting remains more common among people in their 20s and 30s than in older people, whether as a prelude to marriage or an alternative to marriage.

In the 1980s, there was a growing tendency for young people to begin living together or cohabiting as couples without being married. It's important to emphasise how much of a novelty this still was in the early 1980s, and it was still common to hear older people talk of cohabiting couples as 'living in sin'. The first Australian sociological study of cohabiting couples was conducted by Sotirios Sarantakos in 1983 and he describes living together as 'an experiment' or an alternative to marriage (Sarantakos 1984). Other research conducted at that time indicates that cohabitation was still subject to considerable parental disapproval and religious objections. However, Gilding (1997) reports that by the late 1980s, less than 10 per cent of cohabiting women participating in a national Australian study indicated they were worried about social disapproval.

For heterosexual couples unmarried cohabitation is increasingly likely to be part of their relationship histories. Unmarried cohabitation is becoming more common in all age groups but particularly for those in their 20s. In 2006 in the 20–24 age group 12 per cent of men were in cohabiting relationships and 4 per cent were married, while 18 per cent of women were cohabiting and 10 per cent were married. Among 25–29-year-olds 21 per cent of men and women were in cohabiting relationships and 25 per cent of men and 36 per cent of women were married (Heard 2008). The majority of this generation will cohabit sometime in their lives and cohabitation before marriage is now the norm with 76 per cent of couples marrying in 2005 having cohabited prior to marriage (ABS 2007c). By contrast, 30 years earlier in 1975 only 16 per cent of people marrying had cohabited beforehand (ABS 2007c).

However, cohabiting couples are not homogenous and, like others, this lifestyle choice is socially shaped (Dempsey & de Vaus 2004). A variety of people cohabit for a variety of reasons. Cohabiting is more common among the young than the middle-aged or older members of the community. Divorcees are more likely to cohabit than never-marrieds. Religion has an impact; cohabiters are much less likely than other people to have a religious affiliation. Cohabiting is less common among affiliates of Islam, Orthodox and fundamentalist Christian Churches, such as the Pentecostalists, and sects, such as the Mormons and Jehovah's Witnesses, than it is among those people nominating affiliation with mainstream churches including Catholics, Anglicans, Presbyterians and the Uniting Church (Dempsey & de Vaus 2004).

Ethnic background also has an influence on choosing to cohabit with a partner. Men and women born in Southern Europe, North Africa, the Middle East and certain Asian nations, including China, are far less likely to cohabit than people of Australian birth. Among members of most of these ethnic groups the cohabiting rates of younger people are moving in the direction of those of Australians who have been residing here for at least three generations. The lower rates of cohabiting among people of non-Anglo background appear to be linked to such factors as higher levels of religious affiliation, a strong emphasis on female virginity, less emphasis on individual freedom and more emphasis on group obligations (Dempsey & de Vaus 2004).

Cohabitation as an ambiguous commitment

Jo Lindsay conducted research in the early 1990s on young unmarried heterosexual couples living together and found that moving in to a cohabiting relationship was an ambiguous transition that was profoundly different to beginning a married relationship (Lindsay 2000). The cohabiting men and women played down the moving in transition and most described it as a pragmatic rather than a romantic event.

Some saw it as 'the next step' in their relationship (fewer than a quarter) and a third saw it as something that 'just happened' or something they 'went along with'.

Jo: Was it something you always expected to do, to move in together?

Neil: I didn't.

Nicole: No, not really, I don't know, it was just like a situation that you just got put in.

Neil: Yeah.

Nicole: And that was it. I didn't particularly want to move back home with my mum and I didn't really have any other options of where to go, and I don't think we even discussed it.

Neil: No, it wasn't a real conscious thing.

Nicole: Yeah, it just happened and that was it.

The majority moved in for pragmatic reasons (23/30 cohabiters); for 'convenience'; or because cohabitation was a practical solution to housing problems, or a way to save on rent money. Most were spending time at each others places anyway, some said they were 'virtually living together anyway'. These pragmatic reasons for moving in are quite different to what married couples would regard as their motivations. It is generally not acceptable to say publicly that one married because it was 'convenient' or 'to save on rent'. Only two of the 30 cohabiters mentioned love as a reason for moving in (Lindsay 2000).

In contrast to marriage, beginning a cohabiting relationship is socially ambiguous, it is informal and private and there is a striking absence of social ritual and symbolism. By 'keeping it quiet' the transition is downplayed and obscured. If there are no decisions or promises then neither partner has to accept responsibility if the relationship doesn't work. A lack of ritual also prevents others (such as friends and family) from attaching shared meanings to the relationship (Lindsay 2000).

None of the couples in Lindsay's study made an announcement about moving in. They did tell their parents and some friends but they all had friends or relatives who 'assumed', 'guessed' or 'found out on the grapevine'. When they did make their cohabiting public, most received low-key responses such as 'that's good' or no comment. Five of the 30 received negative responses and two women had not told their parents for fear of the negative reaction they would receive.

The cohabiters downplayed the transition but most did change their lives dramatically. They reshaped their social lives and increasingly developed integrated social networks, moving from 'singles' to 'couples' socialising. Many cohabiters were increasingly incorporated into each other's families, many taking up traditional son-in-law or daughter-in-law positions (Lindsay 2000).

The day-to-day lives of married couples and cohabiters may be similar in many respects but there are three major differences between marriage and cohabitation. First, the ambiguous beginning of cohabiting relationships is one major difference. On moving in, a commitment to stay together in the future has not necessarily been made. The organisation of money is a second major difference. Singh and Lindsay (1996) compared the ways in which married couples and cohabiting couples organised their domestic finances and found a sharp distinction in money management styles. The dominant way of organising finances for middle-income Anglo couples was by common pot pooling (Singh 1997). The joint bank account was a particularly strong example of commitment and trust. By contrast the dominant way of organising money for cohabiting couples was having separate accounts and purposive pooling—'going half and half' for expenses (Singh & Lindsay 1996).

One final important distinction between unmarried cohabitation and marriage is that marriage is linked more strongly to childbearing than cohabitation. Almost all married women have had a child by their early 40s whereas almost a quarter of cohabiters aged 40–44 had no children (Birrell et al. 2004). Nevertheless the proportion of children being born outside marriage continues to increase: in 2005 33 per cent of births were to unmarried parents in comparison to 17 per cent in 1986 (ABS 2007b).

Commitment and equality

INFLUENTIAL SOCIOLOGISTS SUCH AS GIDDENS and Beck-Gernsheim describe how the process of individualisation is changing our commitment to relationships and marriage. Giddens' (1992) concept of the pure relationship where individuals only stay in relationships that provide personal satisfaction is highly relevant here. Duty and inequality have given way to negotiation. Moreover, second-wave feminism has fostered new expectations that marriages should be egalitarian.

There have been a number of criticisms of Giddens' work on the pure relationship, including that it does not take into account how responsibilities for children influence adults' commitments to their marriage or couple relationships (see Jamieson 1999). However, it is persuasive to the degree that a notion of equal partnership is clearly an ideal guiding the contemporary Western view of couple relationships. With more relaxed sexual mores, and the movement of women into the workforce, there are fewer economic reasons propelling women or men into early marriage or commitments to a long-term partner, so the scene is set for the pure relationship to become a cultural ideal.

Social researchers have also documented the increased importance of partnership in marriage in surveys and qualitative research studies conducted among Australian men and women. Gilding (1997) notes, that from the early 1970s, women's workforce participation and feminism gave rise to increased interest by sociologists in marriage and the roles assumed by men and women in marriage. Between the early 1970s and mid to late 1980s, there were big shifts noted with regard to attitudes to marriage and marital roles. Whereas in 1971, a researcher called Helen Glezer found that 44 per cent of married women aged 18–34 agreed with the statement that 'important decisions should be made by the husband', by 1991 only 8 per cent of women agreed with this statement (Glezer 1971 cited in Gilding 1997). By the late 1980s, married respondents concluded overall that a good marriage is first and foremost an enduring companionship, with a good sexual relationship coming in second in importance. Satisfaction with one's spouse as a breadwinner or performer of household duties was not significantly related to overall marital satisfaction.

The wedding ceremony and Christian ritual

SO WHAT DOES THE CONTEMPORARY wedding, as the ritual enacting marriage, represent in the era of high divorce rates and socially acceptable cohabitation? According to Andrew Cherlin, the symbolic significance of marriage as a marker of prestige and personal achievement has remained high even though the practical importance of marriage has declined (Cherlin 2004). The purpose of ritual is to make a social relationship 'real' or meaningful and solid and to dispense with ambiguity and uncertainty. As Moore and Meyerhoff (1977) argue, 'ritual can assert that what is culturally created is as undoubtable as physical reality'. Rituals encourage an emotional and perceptual transformation in those who participate. Traditionally, marriage involves both the church and the state and the crucial element of traditional wedding ceremonies is that they take place under the scrutiny of friends and family who witness the commitment being made during the ceremony.

The wedding ceremony traditionally reinforces a social order affirming heterosexuality, patriarchal control, monogamy and lifelong commitment. In a traditional church wedding the bride wears white and a veil to symbolise her purity and virginity. Brides are 'given away' by their father to their husband during the ceremony which symbolises that brides are dependent on their husbands rather than fathers. The throwing of confetti or rice are fertility symbols and emphasise that the central purpose of marriage is reproduction.

Feminist writer Dale Spender published a book called *Weddings and Wives* in 1994. She found that many young women still very much wanted to have a wedding, but very much distinguished becoming a bride from becoming a wife. According to Spender, the ideology of partnership and companionate marriage was highly valued by her respondents. Many of the women Spender interviewed made comments such as 'I'll be a partner, an equal, a friend' but never a wife. So in this regard, the ideals of partnership reject the rigid gender roles associated with the older terminology of 'husbands' and 'wives'. And these days you often hear people under 50 saying my partner, rather than my husband or my wife, even when the people concerned are married.

The shift to valorising a notion of equitable partnership in marriage has became apparent in the growing tendency for the bride's traditional promise 'to love, honour and obey' her husband to be dropped even from church-based marriage vows. This notion was certainly well entrenched by the 1980s, a point well demonstrated by the media controversy over Sarah Ferguson's decision to promise to obey Prince Andrew in her 1986 wedding ceremony, in contrast to Princess Diana's decision not to vow obedience to Prince Charles in their ceremony 5 years earlier.

Wedding vows

Traditional wedding vows emphasise that marriage is a commitment until death.

I, (Bride/Groom), take you (Groom/Bride), to be my (wife/husband), to have and to hold from this day forward, for better or for worse, for richer, for poorer, in sickness and in health, to love and to cherish; from this day forward until death do us part.

From the King James Bible

Contemporary wedding vows are more likely to emphasise friendship, emotional support and personal growth.

I, _____, give myself to you, _____, in marriage.
I will love you openly and completely,
Not possessively but with passion.

I promise to care for you and be cared for by you,
To always talk honestly and deeply and freely,
To laugh and play and cry with you.
To dream a future and build it together.

I will take the time and make the place to be with you.
I love you and accept you as you are now,
and I will love and accept you as you grow and change
through the rest of your life.

Reproduced with kind permission from
Brigid Philip and Tim Campbell

In contemporary Australia, most couples prefer to personalise their wedding ceremonies. New values of gender equality and female independence mean that many reject the content of traditional church weddings. Civil celebrants are an expanding professional group and in this century more couples are choosing to be married by celebrants than by church representatives. In 2006 61 per cent of marriages were conducted by civil celebrants and 39 per cent were conducted by ministers of religion (ABS 2007c). Writing your own vows or mixing traditional and contemporary sentiments is an example of people reflexively engaging in shaping the wedding ceremony. A brief scan of wedding websites or magazines shows that contemporary vows now include promises of friendship, supporting goals and unconditional love (see 'Wedding vows' text box above).

Despite these opportunities for individualising ceremonies, the Federal Government intervened in 2006 to ensure that marriage celebrants were using the monitom from the *Marriage Act* and the words 'husband' and 'wife' in the ceremony instead of 'partner', emphasising that the state only recognises heterosexuals.

… Marriage is the voluntary commitment of a man to a woman, and a woman to a man. It is entered into with the desire, the hope, and the firm intention, that it will endure the challenges which you will surely face as a married couple (extract from the *Marriage Act 1961*).

The content of vows is just one of the many choices and decisions to be made for a contemporary wedding. Weddings are now extremely commodified and commercial events and the wedding industry is active in increasing perceptions of wedding needs (Boden 2003). The average cost of a wedding in Australia is about $28,000 and contemporary couples are highly reflexive about wedding consumption decisions. According to Glenn Findlay, managing director of Australian Bridal Service, in recent years there is a shift in where the money is being spent and couples are taking steps to economise (Lee 2005). Older brides are less traditional and are having smaller numbers of attendants and leaving extended relatives and distant friends off the invitation list. It is now more common for the bride and groom to pay for the wedding and this has an impact on the decisions they make (Boden 2003; Lee 2005).

The marriage squeeze

THE PERSISTENCE OF GENDER STEREOTYPES in partner selection alongside rapid demographic change and the entry of women into higher education and employment has created a problem known as the **marriage squeeze**. Basically women aim to marry men with higher educational and occupational status than themselves, and vice versa, but for some groups this is increasingly difficult to achieve. Older women with higher levels of education and younger men on lower incomes are disadvantaged in the marriage market and find it difficult to meet suitable partners.

The *Men and Women Apart: Partnering in Australia* report (Birrell et al. 2004) found that Australia has experienced a sharp decline in levels of partnering, particularly married partnering, among young people in their late 20s and 30s. By 2001, 41 per cent of males and 34 per cent of females aged 30–34 were not partnered. Most of the decline in partnering has occurred among men and women who do not hold tertiary degrees. Contrary to much of the literature on the subject, partnering rates among degree-qualified men and women have stabilised. Men without post-school qualifications are the biggest losers (Birrell et al. 2004).

The marriage squeeze and decline in marriage rates have implications for understanding fertility rates. There is a strong connection between marriage and fertility so that almost all married women will give birth, bar medical infertility, by the time they reach their early 40s. As Birrell and colleagues summarise:

The problem is the drastic decline in the proportion of young women who are married. The decline in partnering is also linked to the rise in the number of lone parent households. They now account for more than one in five households with young children. Amongst men, the main losers are those on low incomes. Their partnering rates are low and their marital breakdown rates are high leaving very large proportions living alone, in group households or at home with their parents.

This statistical analysis is supported by qualitative research from Australia and the USA (Warr 2001). Financial security is commonly seen as a prerequisite for marriage. In Warr's research of disadvantaged young people in Melbourne many felt that they could not even think about marriage or children in their current circumstances (Warr 2001). Lack of financial stability was found to be a major barrier to marriage among low-income parents in the USA (Gibson-Davis et al. 2005).

Arranged and assisted marriage in Australian and British Indian communities

Counter to the privileging of romantic love and individual choice as the basis for marriage relationships, in many parts of the world parents and other extended family members continue to arrange marriages for young people (see also Chapter 3). In the Middle East, Muslim Africa, India and Indonesia, **arranged marriages** are common, in keeping with collectivist rather than individualistic assumptions about family relationships. Parents may assume it is their responsibility to organise a good match for their children, even after migrating to a Western country.

Gopalkrishnan and Babacan (2007) researched attitudes to marriage and partner choice among 17–24-year-old Muslim and Hindu young people in Queensland, Victoria and New South Wales, whose parents had migrated to Australia from mainland India. These authors contend that the context of the Indian **diaspora** (the dispersed migrant population) greatly influences marriage practices and partner choice. Young people's sense of identity, as fashioned through communities of religion, caste, race, imagined connections to an Indian homeland or family members and geographical location were important in marriage decision-making processes. Marriage was viewed as a means of retaining cultural heritage. This could cause tension in families if children chose to marry outside their geographic or religious community, as in the following quotations from the study:

> We are Muslims and I am expected to marry within the faith if not within the community (young woman, family from Uttar Pradesh, p. 513).

> My parents will never allow me to marry a boy who is not a Nair (young woman, family from Kerala, p. 513).

However, Gopalkrishnan and Babacan (2007) also found evidence of shared values about choice of marriage partners between the older and younger generations:

> I think the modern arranged marriage is a much better process. It enables me a lot more choices of proposed partners but also I can have a say on who I marry (young woman, p. 519).

> Arranged marriages can work, one has to be reasonable with parents. It is good to have the best of both worlds (young man, p. 519).

As the authors explain: 'A picture emerged of young people negotiating tensions between obligation and independence, belonging or exclusion, and constraints or new opportunities of being' (p. 511).

Despite possible tensions between the generations with regard to marriage decisions, nowadays it is customary in British and Australian Indian communities for the son or daughter getting married to have some say in the decision, with parents and other relatives choosing the field of eligible contenders (see Wood & Guerin 2006; Goodwin & Cramer 2000). Goodwin and Cramer (2000) see this as evidence that marriage decision-making within immigrant Indian communities is coming to reflect an integrationist strategy, whereby some traditional cultural practices are retained along with the social preferences more characteristic of the Western cultural setting. Among Indian Hindus in Australia, potential partners are often introduced to each other rather than the marriage being fully arranged, and this was also the majority pattern in a Hindu Indian community in Leicester, UK (Goodwin & Cramer 2000), where most of the seventy couples of all ages described their marriages as 'partly arranged'. Gopalkrishnan and Babacan (2007) call this **'assisted marriage'**. Determining candidates for a suitable match is generally based on factors such as economic status, caste, social reputation and religion, and advertisements to find suitable partners are often placed in local newspapers (Mullati 1995). Criteria in these advertisements may be quite exacting, as in the following example from the Australian *Bharat Times*:

> brilliant engineer (B.Tech.Hons, doing M.E), Australian citizen … seeks girl from (State in India and Caste) high status family, pretty, slim, tall, homely, very fair, within 22 years, with Indian values. (reprinted in Gopalkrishnan & Babacan 2007, p. 517)

Gay marriage and commitment ceremonies

CHEAL (2002) NOTES THAT THE ideology of companionate marriage, so central to contemporary heterosexual partnerships, has been adapted by same-sex couples, where ideals of love, friendship, communication, sharing and negotiation may be specially valued. In the context of cultural ideals, emphasising marriage as a partnership, rather than an institution characterised by rigid gender roles, there is increasing interest among some gay men and lesbians in having the right to marry. A growing number of same-sex couples are pledging their love to each other in commitment ceremonies, and weddings in those countries where this is legal.

Gay marriage is now legal in some parts of the world, including Denmark and several states of the USA, including Vermont and California. It is currently a very controversial issue in Australia. Changes to the *Marriage Act 1961* (Cth) by the Howard Government in 2004 added the words 'man' and 'woman' to a previously gender-neutral clause. This constituted a pre-emptive move designed to make it more difficult for discrimination-based challenges to the legislation by gay and lesbian activists and has no doubt provoked renewed interest among activists in the marriage issue. This occurred also despite the recognition in state law of rights and responsibilities of partners in domestic relationships for the purposes of over forty pieces of state legislation.

The gay and lesbian rights movement continues to fight successfully for recognition of same-sex relationships and equal rights to heterosexuals in a range of social policy areas including family law, access to IVF, adoption, superannuation and taxation. Broad social acceptance of same-sex unions has increased substantially in the last few decades. Elton John's civil union pictured at the beginning of this chapter was celebrated in the media by celebrities and fans. Under the *Civil Partnership Act 2004* in the UK, the first gay 'marriages' were conducted on 21 December 2004. Elton John and David Furnish's ceremony was one of 700 ceremonies conducted on that day. The recognition of same-sex unions is very recent history. Northern European countries including Denmark (1989), Norway, Sweden and Iceland (1996) were the first to recognise same-sex unions. France introduced a civil contact in 1999 and other countries have followed with law reform since 2000, including Finland, Spain, Germany, Britain, New Zealand, Canada and Argentina. In the USA, there has been heated debate about law reform but some states including Vermont, Connecticut, California, Massachusetts and Oregon have introduced their own legislation (BBC 2005).

Although Australia is not on the list of countries recognising same-sex unions, celebrants do offer commitment ceremonies that are not recognised by law. An extract from the Queensland-based Light Hearted Services (2007) website states;

> A commitment ceremony has the similar format to a wedding ceremony but without the associated legal status ... Your love doesn't have to wait for the law to change. Your love continues to grow and having a commitment ceremony is a joyous public celebration for you and your beloved, your friends and family.

In summary, state support for same-sex unions is growing but it is an area of law that is controversial and the gay rights movement has suffered opposition and setbacks as well as considerable success.

Gay and lesbian critiques of marriage

THE NEW CIVIL RIGHTS MOVEMENT on the part of gay men and lesbians for access to marriage has rekindled debate about whose interests marriage serves. Catherine Donovan (2004) is against same-sex marriage for two main reasons. First, she argues that marriage is a privileged legal and economic contract that reinforces inequalities between married relationships and all other relationship statuses. Second, she argues that the model of love presented by marriage with its privacy and focus on one person at the exclusion of all others is troubling and constrains other possibilities for 'loving in egalitarian and non-violent ways' (Donovan 2004, p. 28). Others have argued that marriage will benefit 'straight acting gays', those who are most like heterosexual married couples and further marginalise non-normative relationships. Abraham has argued that conservative marriage advocates want marriage to change queers, not queers to change marriage (Josephson 2005).

Conclusion

To SUM UP THE RECENT shifts in Australian patterns of partnering, formal marriage is by no means the only way in which to partner these days, although most people still marry at some point in their lives. Many people, if not most, live in cohabiting relationships before they marry. However, de Vaus, Qu and Weston (2003) comment that it's important not to exaggerate the changes in partnering patterns over recent years. There is a good degree of continuity. First, the fact that many same-sex couples aspire to marriage rights indicates the ongoing appeal of public recognition and sense of stability it affords. Second, the vast majority of men and women form a long-term cohabiting heterosexual relationship at some point in their lives. Third, while more people are unpartnered now than in the postwar marriage boom, this can be attributed to divorce or separation rather than never having found a partner. Fourth, taking into account greater likelihood of cohabitation rather than marriage with regard to first significant relationships, men and women are still entering into intimate live-in relationships by their mid 20s, around the same time as they did in the earlier part of the twentieth century before the post-war early marriage boom. As Heath and Cleaver (2003) note, for many young adults, cohabiting relationships followed by marriage are equated with 'settling down', after having first experienced a degree of independence from families of origin.

In terms of couple relationships there are substantial differences as well as similarities between marriage and cohabitation. Marriage can be described as a defined narrative that begins with the wedding ceremony. There is a proper path of 'getting set up' becoming financially secure and 'settling down' (Richards 1985). There are different ways of being husbands and wives but marriage is perceived as a significant transition and commitment to a shared future. They lived 'happily every after' is the desired ending, even if this cannot be achieved by many at this point in history. By contrast, unmarried cohabitation—whether between 'straight' or 'gay' couples—is a more open narrative that begins with the ambiguous transition of moving in. It is a commitment to live publicly as a couple for the present but future plans remain obscure and unarticulated. It is not the fairytale but a 'choose your own adventure' story offering a range of possible paths and endings.

Key concepts

Commitment

Marriage boom

Marriage bust

Homogamy

Hypergamy

Arranged marriage

Assisted marriage

Diaspora

Cohabitation

Marriage squeeze

Discussion questions

1 Is marriage becoming irrelevant? Consider the evidence for and against this proposition.

2 What does Giddens mean by the 'pure relationship'? To what extent does this concept shed light on changing patterns of partnering?

3 Would you expect arranged marriages to have lower divorce rates than marriages entered into 'by choice'? If so, why?

4 Some lesbians and gay men are not in favour of marriage. Why might this be?

Recommended further reading

Dempsey, K. 2002, 'Who gets the best deal from marriage: women or men?', *Journal of Sociology*, vol. 38, no. 2, pp. 91–110.

Lindsay, J. 2000, 'An ambiguous commitment: Moving in to a cohabiting relationship', *Journal of Family Studies*, vol. 6, no. 1, pp. 120–34.

Smart, C. 2007, *Personal Life*, Polity, Cambridge, Chapter 3, 'Emotions, love and the problem of commitment'.

07 | Relating Beyond the Cohabiting Couple Household

Figure 7.1: Friends and Housemates from *Love My Way*

Introduction

IN THE PAST DECADE, A NUMBER of North American, British and Australian TV shows such as *Sex and the City*, *Friends*, *This Life* and *Love My Way* have portrayed heterosexual, lesbian and gay adults living independent, fulfilling and socially connected lives in the context of sole person and **shared/group households**. The mainstream popularity of these shows indicates the extent to which being **single** or living for long periods of time outside a cohabiting couple relationship has become a socially acceptable and viable way of life. Despite the visibility in the popular media of these young–mid adult lifestyles and relationships, Sasha Roseneil and Shelley Budgeon (2004) comment that sociologists have been, until recently, relatively neglectful in researching the social and emotional dimensions of non-couple-based relationships and/or households among adults. Elsewhere, Roseneil (2000a) contends that this is consistent with the prevailing tendency to infantilise or subordinate adult interpersonal relationships that are not structured around a cohabiting heterosexual couple.

Unpartnered adults of all ages and sexualities, and those who live separately from intimate sexual partners, to varying degrees, maintain connected lives that provide them with love, care and companionship. The conceptual and material dimensions of their relationships are the focus of this chapter. We begin with a general discussion of the claim that sociologists should devote more attention to 'non-standard intimacies'. Then, we take a closer look at the significance of **friendship** to contemporary adults. Finally, we examine three very contemporary ways in which adult personal lives are lived beyond the cohabiting couple, considering the relational lives of single adults, shared householders, and adults in committed couple relationships who, either through the circumstances of work or personal choice, find themselves '**living apart together**'.

Beyond heterorelationality

As we discussed in Chapter 3, lesbians and gay men have long treated the heterosexual nuclear family model with a degree of scepticism and may fashion their most sustaining networks of support and intimacy from friendship ties. Particularly among gay men, there may be less interest in equating commitment with monogamy or sexual exclusivity, along with reluctance to set up house with the one, long-term sexual partner (see Weeks, Heaphy & Donovan 2001; Stacey 2004). Budgeon and Roseneil (2004) contend that increasing numbers of heterosexuals and 'non-heterosexuals' alike know a considerable number of people who are either divorced, single, gay or lesbian, and also live their lives in circumstances where relationships with family of origin and sexual partners are less important than friendships in providing the kind of daily support, intimacy and care, often associated with family or couple relationships. For these authors, privileging **heterorelationality**, or the cohabiting, monogamous sexual relationship, as the primary relationship in a fulfilling, socially connected personal life is becoming less important and/or feasible for a wider range of people than ever before:

> ... a range of personal relationships—non-co-residential intimate partnerships, friendships, household communities—are important in providing intimacy, care and companionship in an individualising world, and ... these relationships are central to people's core values (Budgeon & Roseneil 2004, p. 128).

The contemporary social transformations that are undermining the dominance of couple-based households and relationships among heterosexuals include the changing expectations of young women (notably with regard to their education and career goals), the changing conditions of work and the high divorce rate. All of these structural circumstances of people's lives may give rise to a situation where there is greater reliance on friends for love, care and companionship, along with reduced daily or regular involvement with intimate partners and family of origin. The high divorce rate has particularly served to challenge the predominance and desirability of the household based on a cohabiting heterosexual couple. Divorced people may consciously choose not to re-enter a cohabiting relationship due to the emotional resonance of the relationship break-up, or the possible negative impact this could have on their children's domestic or emotional lives. Divorced men and women may also find it difficult to re-partner, meaning friends increasingly share the time and activities that were once engaged in with the cohabiting partner. As Allan (2008) notes, there may be a number of voluntary and involuntary situations in which separation or divorce leads to domestic and familial lives assuming less importance than the solidarity, emotional and social support shared with friends.

Friendship

FRIENDSHIP IS A COMPLEX CONCEPT that can describe a broad range of close or distant personal relationships. The ancient Greek philosopher Aristotle made a distinction between three kinds of friends: those useful to us for social advancement; those we seek out because of the sheer pleasure we take in their company; and those whose values we share. For Aristotle, it was the last of these kinds of friendships that was of the highest moral value and which truly established a meaningful relationship between two people (see Pahl 2000).

In contemporary as in ancient times, people may refer to acquaintances they hardly know or see as 'friends' for reasons of social expediency or status. Conversely, the word 'friend' may describe an emotionally close and committed relationship, characterised by frequent contact, various exchanges of social support and care, and disclosure of innermost thoughts and feelings. Pahl (2000) coined the term 'fossil friends' to refer to relationships with very old friends that are more active in our imaginations and memories than our social calendars. Despite this diversity, friendships are widely considered to be informal and highly individualised, in the sense that they begin and end by virtue of personal choice. Generally too, there are no legal obligations or commitments that govern them (see Pahl 2000). As Allan (2008, p. 4) summarises: 'How friends define their relationship, what they do with each other and what expectations they have are matters for them to determine'.

Early to mid twentieth century social theorists considered friendship to be of marginal importance in modern Western societies (Pahl 2000). In the first decades of the twentieth century, Georg Simmel wrote about friendship asserting that modernity is not conducive to close friendship because social relations are so individualised, specialised and competitive. Simmel believed that the notion of friendship as a self-disclosing, trusting relationship was too threatening for modern people, and that it was more likely that we would have fairly superficial relationships with separate friends geared towards specific activities (for example, those we play sport with, those we go dancing with or those who help us out with the children on occasion). For Simmel, this specialisation made it less likely that friends could know too much about our lives and thus gain too much control (see Ritzer & Goodman 2004).

Anthropologist David Schneider, in his influential 1960s book *American Kinship*, made a clear distinction between friendship and **kinship** in American culture. For Schneider (1980, p. 49), kinship represented 'diffuse, enduring solidarity'. By 'diffuse', he meant that kinship is not an instrumental relationship, but encompasses many dimensions of social life; 'enduring' refers to the unlimited lasting power of the relationships; 'solidarity' means the relationships are seen as providing significant help, social support and cooperation. For Schneider, friendship differed from kinship primarily on the grounds that it may be diffuse and solid but cannot be considered enduring. In other words, friendship is chosen and terminable in comparison with the ties of love, blood and law that define kinship.

From a more twenty-first century perspective, Ray Pahl (2000, p. 1) suggests that friendship can now be seen as an important kind of 'social glue' for adults of all ages throughout the life course. Pahl believes there are two distinctive processes at work with regard to friendship in contemporary societies. In the first instance, one indication is that friends may be increasingly relied on to perform the kinds of social support tasks that were once the domain of kinship ties, particularly when family members are not available or geographically close by. For example, friends' help may be sought in picking up sick children in the absence of geographically proximate relatives, particularly in an era of working mothers and grandmothers, and dual earner families. Friends may also take on many of the care and support roles conventionally associated with family relationships in the face of rejection from family of origin, as has been well documented historically in the context of gay and lesbian communities (Weston 1991; Weeks, Heaphy & Donovan 2001). In the second instance, Pahl believes the social meaning of friendship is changing in the sense that we have increasing expectations of the emotional quality it should offer us, in keeping with Giddens' idea of the pure relationship (see Chapter 6). Central to this ideal of relationship quality, is a privileging of emotional satisfaction, openness and trust, as the basis for deciding whether there will be ongoing commitment to keeping the friendship active. Indeed, Pahl and Giddens express similar ideas in suggesting late modern people largely seek to achieve happiness and social connectedness through the quality of their interpersonal ties with others, rather than membership of a broader social category or group.

Beck and Beck-Gernsheim (1995) suggest that friendship is particularly important these days because of the highly individualised lives many of us are leading—a position that seems to directly counter Simmel's early twentieth century perspective. For Beck and Beck-Gernsheim, friendships may be relatively non-threatening because they enable a degree of intimacy, social support and meaningful interaction without necessarily compromising independent life decision-making. We do not usually expect to have to take our friends' wishes into account when we make life-changing decisions yet we may certainly value and appreciate their opinions. For instance, in committed couple relationships, where both partners have some expectations of fulfilling their own life goals, considerable negotiation with a partner is required before making significant life changes such as moving house, changing jobs, returning to study or deciding to travel overseas. This may lead to relationship break ups or cause considerable tension within marriages or cohabiting relationships, as one partner's opportunities may represent the other's threats or worst fears. Under these circumstances, friends may provide a particularly valued source of continuity, guidance and connection.

A question of some interest to sociologists is the extent to which friendship ties can be considered to substitute for married or marriage-like couple relationships within late modern societies (see Allan 2008; Pahl 2000). Pahl and Pevalin (2005) contend that meaning and substance of friendship in an individual person's life can differ quite dramatically at different time periods in their life course, and that the presence or absence of a committed cohabiting partnership may be an important factor in this. Graham Allan (2008) emphasises that while friends are important to most adults to varying degrees, research indicates that privileging friendship over other kinds of intimate and committed relationships in any individual's life course tends to be time-limited. For instance, young adults who are establishing independent lives from family of origin may display a greater reliance on friends than on parents or committed partners, but most will move on to one or more marriage-like relationships. After divorce, friendships with other unpartnered adults may be key to re-establishing a sense of identity beyond the marital and family relationships, but again, this may only be the case until a new cohabiting partner is found.

Allan (2008) contends that friendships are ill-suited for sustaining ongoing intensive needs for physical care or emotional support because they are predicated on different assumptions about reciprocity or exchange than kin or committed couple relationships. Allan points out that solidarity between friends tends to rely on the equality that comes from both parties coming from similar social backgrounds and is maintained on a basis of implicit, yet carefully monitored equivalent social exchanges. Because of this basis for equality, each party is attentive to not becoming too indebted to the other, and if the balance of social and emotional favours gets too out of balance, the friendship is likely to be threatened. By contrast, in family or committed couple relationships, there tends to be less ongoing attentiveness to balance in social and emotional exchanges. In other words, family and committed couple relationships usually assume less self-monitoring of the balance of social supports, and can thus sustain situations where one party needs a lot more care and emotional support than the other for longer periods of time.

Somewhat contrary to this view of friendship, Roseneil and Budgeon (2004) emphasise the capacity friendship has to take on long-term and daily relationships of physical care and nurture, particularly in the lives of the unpartnered. These authors argue that friendship can present itself as a more stable basis for household organisation, emotional support and the meeting of children's daily support needs when certain social conditions are met. The heterosexual, lesbian and gay participants in Roseneil and Budgeon's study (conducted in northern England) largely organised their social and emotional lives around supportive communities of friends, which included extended periods of shared household living and care at times of severe illness or distress. The various life situations featured in their study demonstrate the extent to which friendship ties can sometimes present as a more stable basis on which to found household life and emotional support than conventional family or couple relationships (see the section on group households later in this chapter).

Researchers continue to find that never marrying or staying single for prolonged periods of time after divorce still constitutes a stigmatised or 'deficit identity' (see McVarish 2006; Reynolds, Wetherell & Taylor 2007; Sandfield 2006). Despite the evidence for some enmeshment between family and friendship ties in late-modernity, such stigmatisation suggests that friendship remains less culturally salient as a relationship that can substitute for the intimacy and support of a long-term couple relationship. In the next section we discuss the social and emotional dimensions of living life without a cohabiting partner.

The single life

'SINGLE' IS AN AMBIGUOUS CONCEPT that has historically been defined in reference to marriage. It can mean 'never married', 'separated', 'divorced' or 'widowed'. These days, defining single people as never married also stands to include many who are living in cohabiting relationships. For this reason, in everyday speech and some official definitions, single is being redefined to mean 'unpartnered' in the sense of not being in a cohabiting or committed intimate relationship.

Many single people live alone. The proportion of people living alone in Australia increased from 7 per cent in 1986 to 9 per cent in 2001 (ABS 2006b). This makes the lone person household the fastest growing household form in Australia, with the number of people living alone expected to increase from 1.8 million in 2001, to between 2.8 and 3.7 million in 2026. This projected increase relates to the ageing of the population, the tendency to delay marriage and the high rate of divorce and separation. About 55 per cent of the people living alone are women, which reflects the fact that women tend to live longer than men and are over-represented in the older, widowed group of sole householders (ABS 2006b).

As McVarish (2006) notes, contemporary popular representations of life as a single person are often positive and tend to emphasise freedom from responsibility to domesticity, a partner or family as a benefit, and the state of being single as a personal choice. Mundane, daily pleasures are played up in accounts of single lifestyles, such as having enough 'personal space' and no one to fight with over the TV remote control. Rather than emphasising loneliness or the solitary nature of single life, there is a tendency to represent single people as living life to the full with many friends and varied social activities. A recent Australian feature article on life as a single person featured interviews with women and men of all ages—never married, separated, divorced and widowed—and all were depicted as leading very busy and rewarding lives. For instance, 42-year-old never-married tax lawyer Errol's weekly activities included kayaking, kite flying, barbecues with friends and interstate travel to see friends: 'Life is very full, very dynamic', he explained to the reporter. 'What part of my life would I give up so I would have space for a girlfriend?' (Schmidt 2006, p. 12).

Many of the existing research studies of never-married singles have been conducted with women, which indicates researchers perceive singlehood as a potentially more problematic state for women than for men. Never-married fictional heroine Bridget Jones' oft-quoted fear of dying alone and being 'found three weeks later eaten by Alsatians' (Fielding 1999), illustrates a common perception that older single women are all sick, lonely and uncared for. Although psychologists and healthcare researchers consistently find that never-married older single women often enjoy good social and emotional health (see Cwikel, Gramotnev & Lee 2006) singlehood has been viewed as a particularly problematic identity for women. Historically it has been perceived to defy the feminine norms of marriage and motherhood. Older single women have been found to believe they are perceived as unwomanly because of their never-married state (Byrne 2003), although research suggests this is changing for younger single women (Reynolds & Wetherell 2003; McVarish 2006). Researchers have also found that unmarried, childless women are perceived as selfish, lonely and neglectful of their duties to society (Lees 1999).

In comparing the historic term for never-married women, 'spinster', with 'bachelor', the comparable term for never-married men, the gendered distinction is apparent. The idea of a spinster conveys a bitter, undesirable and pitiable woman, who has not been 'chosen' by a man (Reynolds & Wetherell 2003). By contrast, 'bachelors' tend to be viewed in more value-neutral terms, or as lucky, attractive men who can continue to choose many rather than one woman and 'play the field' well into their old age. Although some researchers have sought to reclaim the term spinster as a positive and empowering identity for women (see Simpson 2003), research conducted with single women themselves indicates few are interested in describing themselves as spinsters (McVarish 2006; Reynolds, Wetherell & Taylor 2007).

For young adult never-married women, living alone and/or being single during the 20s and early 30s is largely experienced as a positive demonstration of financial and emotional independence, in keeping with feminist expectations of self-reliance. For instance, a report conducted by Lewis (2005) on young women sole householders in the UK found that being single and living alone was presumed to be a temporary stage in life. Living alone was regarded as a transitional period between leaving the parental home and 'settling down' with a long-term partner. As such, it presented an opportunity for self-discovery and to achieve a sense of independence from parents, before becoming seriously committed to a partner. The women in Lewis' study largely drew satisfaction and pride from living alone, and also believed it enhanced their self-esteem.

However, studies with older, never-married, childless women, aged from their mid 30s to 50s, tend to reveal more ambivalence about being single, and some scepticism about the upbeat tone of much contemporary media commentary on the single life. McVarish (2006) found that the women she interviewed were quite familiar with the more positive representations of the single life such as the choice to have freedom from responsibilities, yet found it difficult to embrace their single status wholeheartedly. Particularly for women who wanted to have children, and had already fulfilled significant work and travel goals, singlehood did not hold much appeal in the face of the prospect of remaining childless or unpartnered permanently. One woman in McVarish's study expressed her ambivalence thus:

> Sometimes I'm so glad to come home at the end of the day, shut my door and think I do not have to deal with another human being if I don't want to. And that is actually a luxury. Especially when I've spent a weekend with friends with children and I think, my god, what a struggle, constant noise, constant demands ... But then I think I wouldn't have any regrets if a child took up all my time because I've done the travelling ... and I've got a career ... so I'm ready, you know, to be that person. (McVarish 2006, p. 4).

Reynolds, Wetherell and Taylor (2007) conducted interviews with 30 women aged between 30 and 60, asking them to reflect on their relationships and the reasons they were single. 19 of these women had never married and 11 were single again following divorce, separation or the death of a partner. The authors found that the women's responses were often contradictory, drawing sometimes on the idea that they had made a choice to remain single (for example, perhaps they didn't want that kind of partnership), and at other times on ideas of chance (they hadn't met the right person, the timing wasn't right). The authors came to the conclusion that the complexity and contradictory nature of the women's accounts of being single was indicative of the still stigmatised yet changing cultural expectations with regard to singlehood. On the one hand, women are expected to have power and agency in the decisions they make about their life and the women drew on notions of choice and freedom to accentuate this. Yet on the other, they also wanted to emphasise their desire for relationships in the future. Declaring a desire for permanent singlehood as a personal choice did not appear to be a feasible position for interviewees to take up. At the same time, the desired future relationship presented itself to the women as something over which they perceived little control. Reynolds, Wetherell and Taylor (2007) discerned that many of the women interviewed believed women still have less power to choose men than the other way around, and a number of women struggled with wanting to feel 'chosen' by the right kind of man.

The discussion above indicates that the appeal of staying single as a permanent and entirely chosen option should not be over-stated. For instance, many single householders in Australia are widowed or divorced women who are living alone as a result of circumstances rather than choice (de Vaus 2004). The fact that the sole person household is Australia's fastest growing household type does not mean that more people are happy being single or want to be so for the long term. And that some singles would much rather be partnered is indicated by the endless dating advice columns, self-help books and introduction agencies that now abound. Although more needs to be known about how the growing numbers of Australian sole householders are maintaining social connections and social lives, and indeed their relationship statuses and aspirations, it is also evident that long-term partnership, whether or not it involves marriage, remains a strong ideal.

The emotional and social significance of group households

> A rat died in the living room at King Street and we didn't know. There was at least six inches of compacted rubbish between our feet and the floor. Old Ratty must have crawled in there and died of pleasure. A visitor uncovered him while groping about for a beer!
>
> John Birmingham, *He Died with a Felafel in his Hand and Other Stories*

SHARE OR GROUP HOUSEHOLDS ARE a social phenomenon in Australia, the UK and the USA that until recently attracted little attention among researchers (Natalier 2007). That said, popular stereotypes of group households as squalid, alcohol- and drug-addled and populated by slack students or psychopaths also abound. In Australia, this is thanks in no small measure to writer John Birmingham's published recollections. Birmingham's focus was the unrelenting seediness of shared households having lived, for over a decade or so of his adult life, with 89—invariably weird—housemates.

The 2006 Australian Census reveals that nearly 4 per cent of Australian households are group households shared by unrelated adults, a slight increase on 2001 figures (ABS 2007e). Figures derived from the 2001 Census show that 9 per cent of Australian young people aged between 15 and 24 and 8 per cent of those aged between 25 and 34 live in group households (de Vaus 2004). Of 20–24-year-old Australians who do not live with their parents, 39 per cent live with peers in group households or about the same proportion as those who live with a partner (Burke, Pinkey & Ewing 2002). Group households are usually based on either pre-existing friendships or those that develop out of the intimacy of day-to-day domesticity. They raise questions about the importance and nature of support networks beyond family of origin and coupledom, and how friends are family, like family or become family, at different points in young and older adults' lives.

In their study of young British students and workers choosing to live in group households, Heath and Cleaver (2003) explored to what extent there is potential for housemates to take on some of the supportive roles that might otherwise be fulfilled by partners or parents and siblings. What they found was that the friendships that developed between housemates were often of lasting significance. For two thirds of the 81 young people involved in their UK-based research, their lives were closely enmeshed with their housemates' lives, with regard to time spent together and emotional support. It was also common for the relationships with housemates to continue well beyond the life of the household. As a result of living together for the first time, many had developed very interdependent housing histories.

Kenyon and Heath (2001), in their study of young people in professional and managerial jobs who chose to live in group households, emphasised that economic constraints are only part of the rationale for opting into this way of living. The company of friends was often considered to be a strong advantage that far outweighed some constraints on privacy. Kenyon and Heath noted that most of their participants believed living alone was an unattractive prospect and equated it with being lonely, isolated, bored and insecure. Sharing allowed the study participants to have economic independence from parents within a context that also enabled them to maintain a desirable single lifestyle with unrelated friends, perhaps in conjunction with an intimate sexual relationship with a non-live-in partner.

In her Australian study, Natalier (2007, p. 70) described the importance of friendship in single and dual sex group households, noting the extent to which it is a 'key discourse'. The sense of friendship and mutual support experienced by residents was crucial to them understanding these environments as home. McNamara and Connell (2007) also found that notions of home among Sydney-resident young people living in group households were heavily reliant on the ideology of friendship, despite the fact that economic necessity was often part of the initial decision to live communally. These authors found that housemates provided each other with practical support such as sharing books and music, care when sick, and exchange of domestic advice and skills. Many of the household members also went out together socially, and organised group events to do with the house, such as parties and garage sales. Over three quarters of the participants in the study considered the group household to be home, and related this to the sense of freedom to express their identities without feeling constrained. As one young woman explained why her group household was home:

> I guess knowing I can be myself. I think when you walk outside … you know you have to be socially accepted. I feel your home is where I have no feelings of restraint, like none (Natalier 2007, p. 83)

De Vaus (2004) argues that group households tend to be a transitional housing arrangement rather than a household form that is stable over the life course. Or in other words, when young people do decide to move in with friends or acquaintances this usually comes between moving out of the parental or family of origin home and moving in with a spouse or serious partner. It is certainly true that Australian group households are largely populated by young adults, with 68 per cent of the people living in them aged between 15 and 34 (McNamara & Connell 2007). However, all of the above studies challenge the conclusion that relationships developed and maintained in group households are necessarily transitional, trivial, or even destructive as in Birmingham's popular account. Although the households often dissolve over time, the friendships formed within them may be enduring and potentially lifelong.

So too, it is not only young adults who appreciate the social and emotional as well as economic benefits of sharing a household with unrelated friends or acquaintances. Most of the 51 participants in Roseneil and Budgeon's (2004) UK-based study of cultures of intimacy and care beyond the family were aged between 30 and 50, and many of them had made the conscious decision to share their lives with others in the context of group households. As the authors illustrate through several diverse case studies, group household life for older adults can actually provide considerable stability, ongoing care and emotional support that these adults do not believe can be found as easily in the context of cohabiting couple relationships.

For instance, 'Karen' and 'Polly' were two of Roseneil and Budgeon's participants, both mothers in their late 30s and long-term friends, and their life stories illustrate how stable and considerably interdependent relationships of reciprocal care and exchange can be maintained between friends in shared households. Karen has two children from a marriage that ended badly, and Polly is an unpartnered sole parent who adopted her daughter through an inter-country adoption program. The two women decided to buy a house together to live in and raise their daughters. They are not and have never been in a sexual relationship, although sometimes people they meet think they are a lesbian couple because of the way they have organised their domestic lives. As an example of the levels of support the women extended to each other, Karen had been able to accept work overseas for a three-month interval, and leave her daughters and the running of the household in Polly's hands while she did so. Their decision reflected a need for mutual support in the rearing of their children, but was also part of a conscious decision to expose their children to other ways of living in the world that countered what they called 'typical, middle-class values' (Roseneil & Budgeon 2004, p. 149). Karen explained how she saw stability for Polly, herself and the children in the context of this arrangement as opposed to cohabiting coupledom:

> We've been separated for three years now so I've been on and off single. I've had a variety of boyfriends and it's been fantastic … I don't want to tie myself up totally to anybody … it can wait, it doesn't have to happen now. This is more important here. My security for my girls … I'm really enjoying this moment and I enjoy finding somebody new that comes along for a short term but I … try not to involve them too much with what's here (Roseneil & Budgeon 2004, p. 151).

It is apparent in the quotation above that the perceived risks of cohabiting coupledom (as a parent) outweigh the perceived benefits at a time when Karen has found an arrangement in which her children are settled and happy, and she has the flexibility of a friend she can rely on for ongoing support. Karen's reflections on hers and Polly's arrangement hint at its time-limited rather than 'forever' dimensions and thus do not refute Allan's argument, outlined earlier in the chapter, that relying on friendships for ongoing support and care tends to be temporary in the context of the adult life course. However, in an era in which many marriages may well be as short-lived as group households, this and the other case studies discussed by Roseneil and Budgeon certainly challenge those who would trivialise or minimise the importance and stability of households shared by friends.

Living apart together (LAT)

THE LAST SCENARIO WE CONSIDER in this chapter is the 'living apart together' or LAT phenomenon. LAT relationships can be defined as those in which couples maintain separate residences, while still considering themselves to be in a committed couple relationship. LAT couples include same-sex and heterosexual couples. LAT relationships are included in this chapter because they undermine one key assumption of heterorelationality: that ongoing commitment to an intimate couple relationship also requires cohabitation.

French philosophers Simone de Beauvoir and Jean-Paul Sartre may well be the most famous historic example of the lifelong LAT relationship. De Beauvoir and Sartre met as students at the Sorbonne University in Paris in the 1920s and maintained a committed emotional, yet non-monogamous, relationship from separate residences for the duration of their adult lives. This was consistent with the tenets of existential philosophy and their political beliefs about gender relations, and was a consciously bohemian or anti-Establishment decision to make in their historical context. There are other more mainstream historical precedents for contemporary LAT relationships in the sense that it is not entirely new for one member of the couple to spend periods of time not residing with other family members. For instance, men have gone to war leaving wives and children behind, or taken seasonal jobs involving relocation such as those on oil rigs or in the fishing industry. The difference between these distance relationships and the contemporary LAT context is the tendency for women's as well as men's career interests to be relevant in the decision to live apart, and for separate households to be maintained by both parties (Levin 2004).

This relatively new social phenomenon has become increasingly popular under conditions of a high divorce rate and an increasingly globalised, mobile workforce. LAT relationships are often between divorced people with children, who have a number of pragmatic and more emotional reasons for not wanting to reorganise their lives into cohabiting coupledom. Where parties have been divorced, and live in relative geographic proximity, the decision to live apart is often a voluntary one (see Levin 2004). LAT relationships are also conducted as distance relationships, where couples must live separately by necessity because both want to maintain careers, but their workplaces are in different cities, towns, states, or even countries. When work gives rise to the decision to conduct an LAT relationship, the decision is often a more reluctant or ambivalent one in the sense that, ideally, the couple would cohabit if work circumstances allowed. The research conducted thus far with this group indicates dual-career, highly skilled professional couples, notably academics, are those most often involved in long-distance LAT relationships (Gerstel & Gross 1984; Holmes 2004).

Two Versions of LAT Life

'Susan' and 'Simon', who participated in Irene Levin's study, illustrate the perceived benefits of LAT life for those who voluntarily choose it (Levin 2004). Susan and Simon are in a committed couple relationship and have been for the past 10 years. They each have children from previous marriages, and maintain separate households and finances. Susan lives with her children in one town, and Simon lives alone in the neighbouring town in which his ex-wife and children also live. Susan and Simon both feel they benefit from the arrangement because it enables them to be a couple, yet maintain the domestic and social needs of their respective children and ex-partners. By conducting their relationship from separate towns and residences, Simon is able to regularly see his children, and Susan and her children do not have to relocate their respective workplace, school or friendship networks (see Levin 2004, p. 223).

'Margaret' and 'Joe', who participated in Mary Holmes' study of LAT couples in distance relationships, are fairly typical of the more reluctant distance relationship pattern (Holmes 2004). They have been in a dual-earner relationship for 10 years and have lived apart for three, with a brief hiatus during which Margaret took maternity leave after the birth of their first child. They are both academics who were not able to find positions in the same geographical locale. Margaret works in the north of England and Joe in the south-east, a journey of two to three hours. Margaret would prefer to work in the same town as Joe, although this is unlikely to happen in the near future. Joe and Margaret see each other every weekend, usually in the town where Joe works, and keep in touch by phone every day during the week.

From one perspective, LAT living arrangements offer a new kind of autonomy in relationships, particularly for women, as they enable both members of a couple to maintain independent identities, and other important relationships while still maintaining the intimacy and companionship of a long-term sexual partnership. Women living with male partners often find themselves subsumed with domesticity, and their own paid work and leisure needs are compromised. Relating from separate households can provide women with a sense that they are valued as people who have interests and identities beyond their relationship or family. For instance, one of the divorced women in Levin's study blamed the break up of her marriage on the fact that she became a less interesting person once she married. This woman believed that her own desire to immerse herself in the housewife role and take care of her husband once she lived with him had ultimately obliterated other valued aspects of herself as a person. She feared that this could easily happen again if she moved in with her new partner, and avoided cohabitation as a result. Other women in Levin's study emphasised that separate households allowed them to avoid men's rather than their own gendered assumptions about housework. Another woman commented she liked to join colleagues for a drink after work occasionally, and by living separately from her partner, there were no expectations that she was home every night of the week 'to boil the potatoes' (see Levin 2004, p. 234).

Levin (2004) also found that older couples who form relationships after divorce or widowhood and retirement may be quite reluctant to live together for a range of practical and emotional reasons. When both have long established households, perhaps those in which their children grew up, the decision to merge a lifetime of possessions into the one household may prove less than appealing. As Levin points out, things are connected to lots of memories about the past, and people with many years of accumulated possessions may not be so keen to rationalise these reminders of the other people to whom they are connected.

Maintaining relationships with separate grandchildren may also be perceived as easier from separate homes, particularly if there is an established care routine.

Holmes (2004) comments that distance LAT relationships challenge the common assumption that real intimacy has to involve constant geographic proximity. She notes the extent to which 'close' has often appeared to be synonymous with 'intimate' and that literal closeness is believed necessary in order to sustain a notion of commitment to another person. Distance relating provides new and different opportunities for intimate connection with partners, in the sense that it detracts from the more mundane features of cohabiting domesticity. Partners in distance relationships report that they come to appreciate each other's qualities more because they don't take them for granted and that distance can make it possible to keep novelty and a sense of romance alive in the relationship (see Gerstel & Gross 1984).

However, distance LAT relationships also bring with them particular challenges, especially in a heteronormative culture that continues to consider cohabiting coupledom as the relational benchmark all people should strive for. Holmes (2004) contends that the kind of autonomy distance relationships offer continues to be a gendered phenomenon, in that women may continue to assume a disproportionate responsibility for the work involved in maintaining intimacy from a distance, such as explaining and defending the unusual arrangement to other family members, particularly the reason why the woman does not join her partner in his town or city. Maintaining the relationship is a responsibility that conventionally falls on women's shoulders, and the following exchange between Holmes' participants 'Meg' and 'Ben' indicates the extent to which Ben is oblivious to the 'behind the scenes' queries family and friends have of Meg about their arrangement:

> Meg: I mean people are always asking me when am I going to get a job down here [in the town where Ben works]. Do people ever ask you when you're going to get a job [where I work]?

> Ben: No, that's true, people don't ever ask me.

Despite these drawbacks, LAT relationships are evidently a workable compromise for some contemporary couples. Given women's and men's increasing expectations of some independence and autonomy in relationships, the number of couples negotiating LAT relationships is likely to increase as we live longer, the divorce rate remains high and the labour market encourages job mobility and specialisation (Levin 2004).

Conclusion

HETERORELATIONALITY, ACCORDING TO ROSENEIL, ASSUMES a normative sequence of events in adulthood, the pinnacle of which is the committed cohabiting long-term relationship. In this chapter we have emphasised that many contemporary adults cannot or choose not to live their lives according to this model of relating, in considering the lifestyles, relationships and experiences of unpartnered adults of all ages and sexualities, and those who live separately from intimate sexual partners.

In an era in which many people are not marrying, and the marriages that do occur are often temporary, it makes sense that more and more people are looking to creative solutions to the need for care and social connectedness through maintaining friendships, group households and long-distance relating. It is important to heed Roseneil and Budgeon's challenge to those who would trivialise or minimise the importance of 'non-standard' intimacies. In years to come, the social and emotional arrangements discussed in this chapter may well be far more commonplace than they are today, as economic and social opportunities for work, care and partnering continue to evolve.

However, the discussion in this chapter has equally emphasised the difficulties associated with maintaining a sense of emotional stability and security long-term, in the absence of a cohabiting couple relationship. A long-term, loving partnership whether or not it involves marriage, remains a strong cultural and social ideal.

Key concepts

Heterorelationality

Friendship

Kinship

Single

Group/shared households

Living apart together

Discussion questions

1   What is heterorelationality? What evidence do you see of its influence in contemporary social life?

2   To what extent can friendships substitute for the social support and care often exchanged in couple relationships? Do you agree with Allan (2008) that the norms of reciprocity in friendship make it unsuitable for sustaining long-term relationships of daily social support and/or care?

3   Do you agree that singlehood is stigmatised in contemporary societies? Is this more of a problem for women than men? What is the evidence?

Recommended further reading

Allan, G. 2008, 'Flexibility, Friendship and Family', *Personal Relationships*, vol. 15, pp. 1–16.

Heath, S. 2004, 'Peer-shared Households, Quasi-Communes and Neo-Tribes', *Current Sociology*, vol. 52, no. 2, pp. 161–79.

Roseneil, S. & Budgeon, S. 2004, 'Cultures of Intimacy and Care beyond "The Family": Personal Life and Social Change in the Early 21st Century', *Current Sociology*, vol. 52, no. 2, pp. 135–59.

08 | Fertility, Technology and Family Change

Figure 8.1: Two Contemporary Political Controversies Over Reproduction: Same-sex Parents and Abortion

Introduction

WOMEN MAY SOON BE ABLE to produce their own sperm. Or, at least, that was the claim in the first sentence of a recent English newspaper article (Connor 2007). Scientists in the UK are perfecting the technique of creating sperm cells from bone marrow tissue that may be used to assist infertile men father their own children. The technology is particularly newsworthy because it could also facilitate sperm production from a woman's bone marrow tissue. This would enable lesbian couples and single heterosexual women to have babies without any involvement whatsoever from men.

Reports about these kinds of experimental **assisted reproductive technologies (ART)** always make great news because they challenge the age-old relationship between having children and sexual intercourse. The 1960s and 1970s ushered in considerable technological advances such as the pill, and safe, medically induced abortions, which greatly facilitated women's ability to control the relationship between sexuality and reproduction. Throughout the 1970s and 1980s, the development of ART such as in vitro fertilisation (IVF), sperm cryo-preservation or freezing and IVF surrogacy made it increasingly possible for doctors to assist infertile heterosexual couples to have their own biological children. The existence of these technologies has, over time, facilitated newer controversial trends such as increased demand for clinical donor insemination and IVF by unpartnered heterosexual women and lesbians.

Contraceptive technologies also continue to be controversial because they have enabled heterosexual women and men to have unprecedented control over the timing and spacing of their children, and indeed the number of children they will have. Along with this, most developed countries have experienced declining **fertility rates**. European, North American and Australian women, and women in the industrialised Asian nations, are having fewer children than they were just one generation ago. Many countries now have birth rates well below replacement level, meaning there are not enough new babies being born to make up for the people who die. Many governments, including the Australian government, are becoming concerned about low levels of fertility as they signal a diminishing workforce and taxation base to maintain the ageing population.

This chapter considers changing fertility patterns and trends in Australia and abroad, outlining competing explanations for and controversies about fertility control throughout the developed Western world. It unpacks the relationship between technologies, sexuality, and changing notions of what constitutes a family, posing the question of how central biological relationships are to Western notions of family and kinship.

Fertility trends

FERTILITY DECISIONS ARE COMPLEX AND multifaceted—they are shaped by economics, paid and unpaid labour, geographic location, socialised expectations and choice. Demographers tend to measure fertility with reference to the following key terms: **total fertility rate** (TFR) and **replacement fertility level.** The Australian Bureau of Statistics defines the TFR as the number of children a woman would have during her lifetime if she experienced current age-specific fertility rates at each age of her reproductive life (ABS 2007b). Replacement Fertility Level is the estimate of the number of children a woman would need to have in her lifetime to replace herself and her partner. This level varies between countries because it depends on the rates of survival of babies to reproductive age (de Vaus 2004).

During 2006 there were 265,900 births registered in Australia to 261,600 mothers. This represents a 2.4 per cent increase on 2005 figures, and was the highest number of births recorded in Australia since 1971. In 2006 Australia's TFR was 1.81 babies per woman, which is still below the

Australian replacement fertility level of 2.1. Fertility levels have also fallen below replacement level in a number of other developed countries. With the exception of the USA, all member countries of the OECD (Organisation for Economic Cooperation and Development), with the addition of Hong Kong and Singapore, have below replacement fertility. Italy and Spain had the lowest fertility levels followed by Greece, Hong Kong, Austria and Germany, Japan and then Singapore. This means that although Australia's fertility rate is below replacement level, it is actually higher than that of a number of other developed countries (de Vaus 2004).

Table 8.1: International Total Fertility Rates: 1965–2010

	1965–1970	1970–1975	1975–1980	1980–1985	1985–1990	1990–1995	1995–2000	2000–2005	2005–2010
Afghanistan	7.7	7.7	7.7	7.8	7.9	8.0	8.0	7.5	7.1
Australia	2.9	2.5	2.0	1.9	1.9	1.9	1.8	1.8	1.8
Canada	2.6	2.0	1.7	1.6	1.6	1.7	1.6	1.5	1.5
China	6.1	4.9	3.3	2.6	2.5	1.9	1.8	1.7	1.7
East Timor	6.2	6.2	4.3	5.4	5.2	5.7	7.0	7.0	6.5
France	2.6	2.3	1.9	1.9	1.8	1.7	1.8	1.9	1.9
Germany	2.3	1.6	1.5	1.5	1.4	1.3	1.3	1.4	1.4
Greece	2.4	2.3	2.3	2.0	1.5	1.4	1.3	1.3	1.3
Hong Kong	4.0	2.9	2.3	1.8	1.3	1.3	1.1	0.9	1.0
India	5.6	5.3	4.9	4.5	4.2	3.9	3.5	3.1	2.8
Indonesia	5.6	5.3	4.7	4.1	3.4	2.9	2.6	2.4	2.2
Italy	2.5	2.3	1.9	1.5	1.4	1.3	1.2	1.3	1.4
Japan	2.0	2.1	1.8	1.8	1.7	1.5	1.4	1.3	1.3
Korea, Republic of	4.7	4.3	2.9	2.2	1.6	1.7	1.5	1.2	1.2
Malaysia	5.9	5.2	4.2	4.2	4.0	3.5	3.1	2.9	2.6
New Zealand	3.4	2.8	2.2	2.0	2.1	2.1	2.0	2.0	2.0
Niger	8.1	8.1	8.1	8.1	8.0	7.8	7.7	7.5	7.2
Papua New Guinea	6.2	6.1	5.9	5.5	5.0	4.7	4.6	4.3	3.8
Singapore	3.5	2.6	1.9	1.7	1.7	1.8	1.6	1.4	1.3
Somalia	7.3	7.3	7.3	7.2	7.0	6.6	6.8	6.4	6.0

(continued)

Table 8.1: (*Continued*)

	1965–1970	1970–1975	1975–1980	1980–1985	1985–1990	1990–1995	1995–2000	2000–2005	2005–2010
Spain	2.9	2.9	2.6	1.9	1.5	1.3	1.2	1.3	1.4
Sweden	2.2	1.9	1.7	1.7	1.9	2.0	1.6	1.7	1.8
Uganda	7.1	7.1	7.1	7.1	7.1	7.1	7.0	6.8	6.5
United Kingdom	2.5	2.0	1.7	1.8	1.8	1.8	1.7	1.7	1.8
United States of America	2.6	2.0	1.8	1.8	1.9	2.0	2.0	2.0	2.1
Vietnam	7.3	6.7	5.9	4.5	4.0	3.3	2.5	2.3	2.1
Yemen	8.6	8.7	8.7	8.7	8.4	7.7	6.7	6.0	5.5
World	4.9	4.5	3.9	3.6	3.4	3.1	2.8	2.7	2.6

Source: *Population Division of the Department of Economic and Social Affairs of the United Nations Secretariat, World Population Prospects: The 2006 Revision, Medium variant* <http://esa.un.org/unpp>

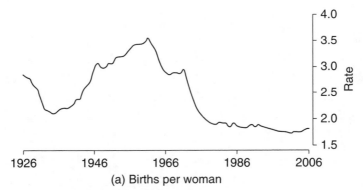

(a) Births per woman

Figure 8.2: Total Fertility Rate (a) Australia

Source: ABS 2007b, *Births Australia 2006*, cat. no. 3301.0, p. 11

In 2001, Australia recorded the lowest fertility rate on record, but it has been rising each year since then. There have been considerable fluctuations in the fertility rate over the past century. There was a sharp dip from almost three to two children per woman between 1920 and the Depression (early to mid 1930s). An economic boom followed World War II and between this time and 1960, the fertility rate climbed to 3.5 children per woman. The early 1960s marked economic recession and the invention of the female contraceptive pill. This was the beginning of another period of steep fertility decline. Finally, increases in the workforce participation of women begin to be noted around the commencement of the 1980s and the birth rate has remained low and flattened out with a declining trend until 2004 (de Vaus 2004). In 2005 and 2006, an upward trend in the fertility rate began for the first time in many years.

The total birth rate can only tell us about average fertility. This in itself cannot tell us very much about what the different aspects of fertility decline are. For instance, are women remaining childless, or avoiding large families or do they prefer single child families? Part of the reason for the fertility decline is that Australian women are giving birth to their first child at a later age than ever before. The age of marriage and the age at which women first gave birth dropped after World War II, and then rose from the early 1970s until 2002. The average age of Australian mothers when giving birth is 30.2 years which is higher than at any previous time in the twentieth century. Recent trends also show that there has been a gradual decline in births to Australian teenage mothers (de Vaus 2004). In 2006 women aged 30–34 years had the highest fertility of all age groups in all states and territories with the exception of Tasmania and the Northern Territory, where women aged 25–29 years recorded the highest level of fertility. Between 2005 and 2006, all states and territories recorded increases in fertility of women aged 30–34 years (ABS 2007b).

If we want to look at whether women in Australia are having fewer children, the best way to do this is through looking at the family size of women who are beyond their childbearing years (de Vaus 2004). The most dramatic change is in the shrinking tendency to have a large family when we compare women in their 40s with women in their 60s. We also know that a woman's educational status has strong bearing on family size. There are two main features of the link between education and fertility: the more highly educated a woman is, the more likely it is that she will not have any children and the less likely it is that she will have more than three children. Overall, women in professional jobs have higher levels of childlessness than those in blue collar or sales jobs. We also know that ethnicity has a bearing on family size. The highest fertility rates among Australian resident women are among those born in North Africa and the Middle East, where the average number of children is 2.7. Indigenous women have fertility rates of 2.19 children per woman compared to 1.75 for other women (de Vaus 2004).

Childlessness

JUST AS FERTILITY IS DECLINING, childlessness is increasing. If we look at twentieth century patterns in the proportion of women in Australia who remained childless at age 45–49 years the highest levels of childlessness were experienced by women born at the turn of the century, 30 per cent of whom never had children. These women lost many boyfriends, fiancés and husbands in World War I. Those who had husbands were in their childbearing years during the Great Depression in the 1930s, a time when economic difficulties greatly influenced the low birthrate. This is a telling reminder for people who like to hark back to the days of 'traditional Australian families' with high fertility. By 'traditional', they are actually referring to the relatively recent baby boom after World War II. Childlessness steadily declined for women born between 1905–25, levelled out to 10 per cent for those born between 1931 and 1945, then began to rise again in the 1950s. Current projections estimate that rates of childlessness among women will return to those characteristic of the 1930s within the next decade or so. Current levels of childlessness among Australian women aged 45–49 are estimated at about 20 per cent and the Australian Bureau of Statistics projects that about one quarter of all women in their reproductive years now will remain childless throughout their lifetime (de Vaus 2004).

Social consequences of falling fertility rates

IT IS WIDELY AGREED THAT the falling fertility rate has social consequences, although differences of opinion exist about how these should be dealt with. Some environmentalists argue that smaller family sizes should be encouraged on the grounds of environmental sustainability. Well-known scientist and 2006 Australian of the Year Tim Flannery argued in his 2003 *Quarterly Essay* that we should aim for a more egalitarian and proactive migration policy and a smaller Australian population. However, politicians and policy-makers are more likely to view falling fertility rates as a social problem, and now focus their attention on developing policies aimed at boosting family size. Former federal treasurer Peter Costello's oft-quoted advice to Australian families during the 2004 to 2006 Budget presentations was that they should have three children—one for Mum, one for Dad and one for the country. A 'baby bonus' policy providing a one-off payment of several thousand dollars to parents for each child coincides with the upturn in the birthrate although it is a source of some debate as to whether this alone can explain the increase.

A low fertility rate is of great concern to governments because it has a number of detrimental consequences for social planning and the economy. First, declining fertility and an ageing population increases the likelihood of labour market shortages in the future. Second, population ageing and a smaller workforce also means a decrease in the available taxation base necessary to fund social expenditure such as income support or benefits and the health care system. Some social commentators argue that decreased fertility will lead to increasing intergenerational resentment in the future, as increasing taxes will be required of the working population in order to support social services for large numbers of elderly people (Encel 2003).

Explanations for fertility decline

THE PATTERNS IN AUSTRALIAN WOMEN's fertility discussed earlier make it difficult to ignore that there is some relationship between economic conditions, technological change, women's workforce participation and the birth rate. However, there are a number of competing explanations for discernible fertility patterns, particularly why the fertility rate is so low and why childlessness is on the rise, which we explore in the section below.

Mitchell and Grey (2007) contend there are two main schools of thought when it comes to explanations for fertility decline. The first tends to emphasise a range of systemic factors such as improved knowledge of and access to contraceptive technologies, the changing structure of work, changes in gender role expectations, global economic changes and a decrease in social welfare payments to families. The second emphasises changing life expectations, attitudes to parenting and the value of children that work in favour of low fertility. In this latter view, the social values characteristic of late modern society are said to hold the most sway over fertility decision-making. It is likely that structural factors and social values are interrelated and that each influences the low birthrate.

Contraception

CASTLES (2002) ARGUES THAT IT is the spread of the contraceptive pill that best explains consistency in fertility decline across a number of developed countries. According to this point of view, the technology is responsible for driving social change. For instance in Greece, Portugal, Spain and Ireland, steep fertility declines were evident in the 1980s and 90s, which coincides with the later ready availability of the pill in these countries. In Australia, there was a sharp then gradual decline in fertility beginning in the early 1960s that is consistent with increasing rates of usage of the contraceptive pill (de Vaus 2004).

Marshall (2005) contends it is flawed to believe one piece of technology causes fertility decline although she does not entirely reject the view that technologies influence fertility rates. For instance, pregnancy testing kits may influence women's willingness to consider abortion as they can now find out very soon whether or not they are pregnant and opt for early and safe termination without having to wait weeks or even months like they used to, or eventually going through with the pregnancy. Marshall also points out that contraceptives and associated technologies such as pregnancy testing kits do not become popular unless there is a market for them. In this regard technologies follow rather than drive change in social mores and attitudes. In other words, the pill is as much an effect as the cause of changed perspectives on fertility and the lower fertility rate. Supporting this view, we can also look back to the earlier discussion of historical patterns of low fertility and recall the steep declines in Australian women's fertility rates long before the introduction of the pill in the 1960s.

The economy

LIKE MARRIAGE RATES, FERTILITY RATES used to have a positive relationship to the economy—in good times the rates went up and in bad times the rates went down. However since the 1980s the relationship is less clear-cut. Women's employment and educational aspirations have increased and childbearing has been delayed. We have higher expectations of living standards and it is more difficult to achieve the financial security often seen as necessary for having children. For example, in Australia home ownership is a primary aspiration and prerequisite for starting a family. Lyn Richards calls this 'getting set up' before 'settling down' (Richards 1990). At the same time, housing affordability in Australia is at a low point. This means tertiary educated young people repaying university loans are likely to delay childbearing even longer in years to come.

Some writers link fertility delay and decline among young adults with the globalisation of the economy and related changes in the structure of work over recent decades (see Heath & Cleaver 2003; Kohler, Billari & Ortega 2004). In Australia, there are now very few low-skilled and well paid jobs for school leavers, meaning young people tend to stay in the education system until well into adulthood. This results in delayed marriage and, in turn, delayed fertility. Additionally, the current era is characterised by job insecurity rather than a notion of 'jobs for life'. Many industries are now dominated by contract and casual labour, providing young people with limited economic security (McDonald 2000).

Local economic conditions also have an impact. For example, it is more costly to raise children in urban areas, accommodation and food are more expensive and women are more likely to engage in paid work, so childcare costs are a further consideration in the timing and number of children.

Gender regime explanations

THE GENDER REGIME PERSPECTIVE ON fertility decision-making is advanced by McDonald (2000) among others. This perspective explains decreased fertility with reference to gendered expectations, the structure of work and family institutions and how these mesh with government policies and cultural values in society. In this view, it is inappropriate to isolate one factor such as gender relations, technology or economics and use this to explain fertility decline. The basic idea is that if the institution of the family and the government policies that affect families do not mesh with the labour market in a way that makes it easy for women to be full-time workers, then the fertility rate will be low. McDonald argues that the mismatch between high gender equity in education and the workplace and low equity in the domestic sphere, means that having children carries a particularly high cost for women.

We do know that generous family-friendly government policies can have some impact on fertility rates. For instance, Nordic countries with increasing fertility rates have generous family leave provisions including incentives for men to take parental leave. By contrast, progress in implementing family-friendly policies in Australia has been identified as partial and patchy, with differing industries and sectors offering extremely varied opportunities for work/life integration. Australia is one of the few OECD countries that does not have a paid maternity leave policy.

However, other developed countries facing fertility decline have turned towards policy measures with less encouraging results. As de Vaus (2004) comments, there are some barriers to fertility that are not within the domain of policy-makers to influence. For instance, there is little policy-makers can do to encourage men and women to either want a partner or to find a suitable partner, or to prevent them from feeling parenting is an overwhelming commitment and responsibility. People's choices about whether and when to have children will always to some degree be independent of government enticements and barriers. It has also been said that making policies about fertility is difficult for democratic governments because of the tension between what is good for the country and the sometimes competing need to respect individual liberties (de Vaus 2004).

The problem of partnering

ANOTHER STRUCTURAL ISSUE INFLUENCING FERTILITY rates is the contemporary marriage squeeze discussed in Chapter 6. Bob Birrell and colleagues (2004) argue that the decline in the fertility rate is strongly related to finding partners and marriage. At this point in time, because of the rapid entry of women into education and employment alongside the traditional preference for women to marry men with higher levels of income, tertiary educated women and low earning men are disadvantaged in the marriage market. Leslie Cannold's research provides some support for this perspective. It seems that there is a growing proportion of women who will not find partners in time to reproduce. Cannold (2005) conducted interviews throughout the 1990s with childless women in the USA and Australia and documented a very contemporary social phenomenon called '**circumstantial childlessness**'. Circumstantial childlessness, according to Cannold, is a situation women find themselves in when they are either without a partner when nearing the end of their reproductive years, or with a partner who does not want or does not feel ready for children at that time. Mary's story is characteristic of the circumstantially childless women Cannold interviewed:

> I always thought I would have children … I would have loved to have had a child when I was 25 or 26. I talked about it with my husband … and he said, 'Why don't we keep working? We'll just pay off the house first' … Then we got to the point where [he said] 'you only have one more year and then you get long service leave. Why would you throw that away?' He was never really as keen to have children as I was … We started to argue all the time ('Mary' quoted in Cannold 2005, p. 179).

Cannold also argues that it is high time researchers paid more attention to men's role in the declining fertility rate, rather than always look to women for the explanation.

Cultural beliefs about parenting

FINALLY, MARSHALL (1993) EMPHASISES SHARED cultural ideologies of parenthood that are prevalent at any given time as a reason for delayed childbearing, increased childlessness and smaller family size. She contends that these ideologies are perpetuated through the media and other social institutions, notably through dissemination of information from experts who give advice to parents about being parents. Contemporary psychologists, have enormous social power to tell people how to become parents and to foster the view that there are right and wrong ways to parent. Think of the range of self-help parenting books on the market these days. Or the popularity of the reality TV show *SuperNanny*, where expert Nanny Jo goes into desperate parents' homes to help them control their unruly youngsters. For Marshall, these ideologies about parenthood are not all powerful and all dominant, but they consist of interlocking and sometimes contradictory ideas about what a parent is and what it should be.

Marshall emphasises two main aspects of current parenting ideology. The first component is the notion that being a parent is an almost overwhelming commitment. According to Marshall, people these days view parenthood as a great responsibility and many consider it irresponsible to go into parenting without being fully prepared and financially secure. The second component of the dominant parenthood ideology is that being a parent demands great sacrifices. According to Marshall, it is very much believed that parenting demands private sacrifices of time and other resources that are privately rewarded. This tends to apply to women more than men.

Marshall explains these two cultural ideologies of parenthood as significant factors in both fertility delay and decline because they encourage would-be parents to plan parenthood very carefully and assume a certain standard of living and maturity is required before people become parents. Beck and Beck-Gernsheim (1995), echoing Marshall's observations, make the ironic observation that increasingly, in Western countries, we remain childless for the love of children. People put off having children until they feel up to the level of commitment and sacrifice required, however, the delay may lead to never having children at all or having fewer children than we would like. The relationship may never feel up to what is required of a good parent, or fertility may have diminished by the time the required level of financial security is achieved.

Childfree by choice

CHILDLESSNESS CAN BE VOLUNTARY AND involuntary and sometimes it is difficult to know the difference. About 7 per cent of heterosexual couples of reproductive age are infertile, which accounts for some involuntary childlessness (de Vaus 2004). The Fertility Decision Making Project conducted in 2004 by the Australian Institute of Family Studies indicated that most men and women currently in their 20s or 30s want to have at least two children (Weston & Qu 2004). Despite this, the ABS estimates that about 25 per cent of women now in their childbearing years will not have any children at all (ABS 2001). These figures reveal that medical reproductive disorders are, at best, a partial explanation for why many women who intend to have children will end up childless.

With such a large proportion of people remaining childless it is now much less stigmatised to be childless by choice, or 'childfree' using a different set of assumptions. The cultural environment has changed to support this lifestyle choice. Only a generation ago the childfree were viewed as selfish, maladjusted and lonely but it is apparent that these attitudes are changing.

Abortion in Australia

The use of abortion to control fertility has become increasingly available to Australian women since the early 1970s, although it remains a controversial issue. Fifty-eight per cent of Australians said they supported abortion on request in the 2001 Australian Electoral Survey and only four per cent thought it was always wrong (de Vaus 2004). In 2004, the then federal Health Minister Tony Abbott— devout Catholic and anti-abortionist—made the claim that Australia was in the grip of an abortion epidemic. This was in response to his reading of Australian Institute of Health and Welfare figures indicating between 75,000 and 100,000 abortions are performed in Australia each year. Abbott's claim reignited debate in Australia about whether abortions were too readily available as a means of fertility control, although abortions are to some extent decriminalised in every State and Territory of Australia. The abortion issue again became front page news in early 2006 when federal parliamentarians were permitted to exercise a conscience vote to support a private members' bill that removed the former Health Minister's authority to decide a doctor's or patient's access to the abortion drug RU486.

A prominent slogan of the 1970s Women's Movement was that 'abortion is a woman's right to choose'. The argument was that women should have the ability to control their fertility through safe and affordable contraception, and also through access to safe and affordable abortions if these were needed. The success of campaigns hinged on the threat to women's health posed by 'backyard' abortions. The feminist 'pro-choice' position is still contested by the 'pro-life' movement, particularly in the USA where right to life protests outside clinics known to perform abortions have ended in violence and even death (Albury 1999).

Although few feminists supported Tony Abbott's position on abortion, a point well illustrated by the t-shirt worn in Parliament by then Greens Senator Kerry Nettle (see picture at the beginning of this chapter), some now question whether notions of women's 'right to choose' abortion help resolve the abortion debate. Feminist ethicist and social researcher Leslie Cannold (1998) argues that basing the abortion debate on notions of women's right to choose has impoverished the discussion because it requires that women's rights are placed in competition with the rights of foetuses. In order to argue that the rights of women are paramount, feminists have had to argue that the rights of foetuses are irrelevant. Cannold contends that looking at complex issues of morality are more important than asserting rights and chose to do this through a social research study into how women themselves understand the choice of whether or not to have an abortion.

Cannold interviewed forty-five women with a range of views about abortion, basing her interviews on difficult ethical scenarios that may confront a pregnant woman. The ethical scenarios posed were: 'Would you have an abortion if you knew the child could be adopted? What if we had the technology for the foetus to be brought to term in an artificial womb? Is it morally OK to abort for a personal reason, such as if you were offered an all expenses paid trip to the Olympics?' She discovered that 'pro-choice' women tended to discuss motives rather than rights when it came to considering these scenarios and their own reasons for having had an abortion were about relationships rather than rights. No one represented in the study made reference to women having an absolute right to have an abortion under any circumstances. Those women who either would have or had had an abortion considered it to be an ethical form of family planning. By 'family planning' they meant that they wanted their children to come into a family that was ready for them. They wanted the children to be loved and cared for well. Some considered that giving a child up for adoption was to deny responsibility for a problem they had created. All of the women in the study believed that abortions kill and that the foetus is alive. But the fact that abortion kills, according to Cannold, does not assist women or society to evaluate whether or not abortion is a feasible method of fertility control.

Assisted reproductive technologies and family change

THERE IS A STRONG ASSOCIATION between parental age and infertility, and increasingly, fertility specialists warn women against delaying pregnancy until they are in their late 30s or early 40s. This brings us to the topic of assisted reproductive technology (ART), which account for about two per cent of births in Australia (de Vaus 2004). ART are distinctive because they are conceptive technologies that assist in the creation of new life. They were developed in order to assist infertile heterosexual couples to have children, and allow the infertility of intending parents to be bypassed in two major ways. First, they enable medical intervention into the process of fertilisation, whereby the eggs and sperm of the intended parents are brought together in a medical laboratory rather than inside the woman's body. Second, ART may require the use of donated gametes. Gametes are the reproductive cells that contain human genetic material, the egg and the sperm. When the intended parents do not have fertile eggs or sperm, donated gametes can be used, meaning a third party provides the genetic material.

Types of ART

ART include donor insemination, in vitro fertilisation (IVF), and gestational surrogacy, among others. Donor insemination is the process by which sperm from a (usually anonymous) man is placed in a woman's vagina using a needle-free syringe, generally because her male partner is infertile. In recent years, increasing numbers of single women and lesbians worldwide have begun using this process in order to become pregnant (see Agigian 2004; Hertz & Ferguson 1997). Many lesbians use a process that has become known as self- or home-insemination, whereby they ask a man they know, often a friend, to provide the semen, and the insemination occurs at home without any medical intervention (see Agigian 2004; Donovan 2000; Dempsey 2002). Donor insemination and self-insemination do not require nearly as much medical expertise as other ART and rely largely on making sure the man is fertile and the semen is inserted at the right time of the month. Although as a technique it is known to be at least 200 years old and had been practiced for at least 30 years in Australia by the time IVF was invented, donor insemination did not become more widely practised until the 1970s when social mores surrounding human intervention in reproduction became more relaxed. In the 1970s, more technologically sophisticated medical procedures such as ovum extraction and embryo transfer were developed, which are both required in IVF. In an IVF procedure, sperm and ovum are placed together in a culture dish in the laboratory in the hope that fertilisation will occur.

Social acceptance of ART

The first IVF baby in the world, Louise Brown, was born to immense controversy and fanfare in England on 25 July 1978. The world's fifth IVF baby, Candice Reed, was born in Melbourne in 1980, which indicates that Australian doctors were at the forefront of development of these technologies. When news of the first IVF baby was made public, reactions were very mixed. People spoke of 'test tube babies', as if the entire process of gestation and not only fertilisation took place external to the woman's body. Some people were deeply opposed to and distrusting of the technology, seeing it as 'unnatural' or evidence of 'playing

God' or human intervention in God given, mysterious and unseen processes. Many very religious people, particularly Catholics, still disapprove of IVF. For instance, some hospitals run by the Catholic Church will still not perform some IVF procedures because these require the fertilisation of the egg by the sperm outside of a woman's body.

Generally speaking, attitudes to married couples using IVF have become more favourable over the years. This is probably related to the fact that the success rates of IVF keep increasing, up from 13 per cent 'take home' babies in 1992, to 21 per cent in 2001. Fourteen Australia-wide interview surveys that included questions relating to IVF were carried out between July 1981 and November 2001 as part of regular polls of community attitudes on various topics. Support for IVF to help infertile married couples increased from 77 per cent in 1981 to 86 per cent in 2001 (de Vaus 2004).

However, there is generally low community approval of extending eligibility criteria for IVF and donor insemination to women without male partners. We know this from the level of media debate often generated by these issues and also from values surveys conducted. In 1995–97 The World Values Survey found that over half of 2014 Australian respondents disapproved when asked the following question: 'If a woman wants to have a child as a single parent, but she doesn't want to have a stable relationship with a man, do you approve or disapprove?' Age is an important factor in this disapproval. While only 37 per cent of people in their 20s disapprove, almost three quarters of people in their 70s disapprove.

Controversy over lesbians' and single women's eligibility for ART

Many years of psychological research studies with children of lesbian mothers have demonstrated that these children do very well socially and emotionally in fatherless families (see McNair 2004 for a comprehensive review). However, media debates about who should be eligible for IVF and clinical donor insemination bring into the public spotlight dominant beliefs about family relationships and the extent to

Figure 8.3: Leesa Meldrum: A Single Woman Wanting Motherhood

which some people believe the conventional nuclear family should not change.

A prolonged media debate occurred in July/August 2000 after Leesa Meldrum (pictured above), a single heterosexual woman, gained the right to join the IVF program in Victoria. Leesa's doctor, John McBain, took legal action on her behalf due to his belief that the state legislation was causing him to break federal anti-discrimination laws. Subsequently, Justice Sundberg of the Federal Court found that the *Infertility Treatment Act 1995* (Vic), contravened the federal *Sex Discrimination Act 1984* (Cth) in denying some women access to assisted reproduction on the grounds of their relationship status. This legal decision became very controversial because the then Australian Prime Minister John Howard intervened and declared his intention to repeal the relevant sections of the *Sex Discrimination Act 1984*. Howard was quoted in bold print on the front page of every major newspaper in the country: 'This issue involves overwhelmingly the right of children to have the reasonable expectation of the affection and care of both a mother and a father'. The debate soon turned to whether lesbian couples should be eligible for ART. Such was the tenor of the debate over lesbian motherhood, it subsequently became the topic of an art installation by activist artists Deborah Kelly and Tina Fiveash, which appeared all over Sydney bus shelters as part of the Sydney Gay and Lesbian Mardi Gras Arts Festival in 2001 (see Figure 8.1).

Dempsey (2006a) argues that the Australian media debate following the McBain case emphasised a number of very different concerns about family relationships, including strong beliefs that the nuclear family is natural, and distaste at the idea that children could grow up not knowing who their sperm donor father is. The former Prime Minister's claim that children need a mother and a father was certainly one of the more prominent themes in the debate, as in public resistance to lesbian, gay or single motherhood by choice in the USA and UK (see Stacey 2004; Donovan 2000). Evidently, many Australian newspaper columnists and concerned members of the public supported John Howard's views. A vast array of feature articles and opinion pieces on the importance of contemporary father/child relationships appeared in Melbourne newspapers *The Age* and the *Herald Sun,* and national broadsheet *The Australian,* for several weeks after the McBain decision was reported. Some commentators proposed the lack of a social father inevitably harms children's development, making them more susceptible to delinquency and emotional problems. Others were more concerned with accentuating the specific care-giving benefits to children of live-in fathers. 'Active' fathering—resident, attentive and responsible caring at each stage of a growing child's life—garnered considerable attention at this time. Dempsey (2006a) contends the attention given to active fathering in this debate revealed fears among some heterosexual men about losing valued relationships with children, at a time when so many Australian marriages end in divorce and most divorced men become non-custodial parents (see de Vaus 2004). The debate also reflected the strength of the ideal that contemporary Australian heterosexual parenting relationships should be egalitarian, with mothers and fathers both providing substantial care and guidance to children, even though this is more of an ideal than a reality.

The significance of biology to family relationships

IN USING ART, THE IMPORTANCE of biological relationships between parents and children may be accentuated or downplayed, depending on who the intended parents are. This emphasises the extent to which the significance of biological relationships for family relationships is very much socially constructed. For example, if the male partner in a heterosexual couple has no sperm, donor sperm can be used, which means the biological father will not be the child's social father. The sperm donor relinquishes all legal rights to paternity and the social father's name is on the child's birth certificate. Since technologies facilitating ovum retrieval and IVF became available, it has been possible for a woman to donate an egg to enable another woman to gestate and give birth to a child she wants to raise, without the genetic mother being legally or socially positioned as the child's parent. In a reversal of this, a gestational mother or surrogate may have a legally and socially ambiguous relationship to social parenthood when the genetic mother is the intended parent of the child (see Thompson 2005).

Although the clinical practices now taken for granted in assisted reproduction clinics show flexibility in deciding how biological relatedness is relevant to social parenthood, these practices remain controversial. According to anthropologist Marilyn Strathern (1992), this is because through notions of shared biological substance—whether blood or genes—a cultural logic of inheritance is sustained in the developed West. During the 1980s, not long after the development of IVF using donated gametes, a public debate about **genealogical bewilderment** emerged in Australia, the UK and USA. The concept arose initially in the context of the rights of adopted children (Marshall & McDonald 2001) and was first used to describe children born of what was then known as 'artificial' insemination by Sants (1964). Sants believed that a genealogically bewildered child could be found in any family where one of the 'natural' (that is, biological) parents was unknown. Many donors of ovum and semen to reproductive medicine clinics worldwide do so on the condition they remain anonymous. However, there is growing tide of opinion against this practice. The argument against anonymity for donors of ova or sperm is based on the premise that a child's sense of who they are is inextricably linked to making sense of whence they came, or, their 'origins', as symbolised in the meeting of egg and sperm. Various commentators since Sants maintain that children born of assisted reproductive procedures should have the right to access identifying information about the women and men from whose gametes they were created (see McWhinnie 2001).

The Human Genome Project has also done much to emphasise the importance of genetic inheritance. As Cussins (1998) notes genes now serve as the 'definitive mark of individuality (the DNA fingerprint) which is passed down … from a mother's and father's individual contribution' (p. 57). Diagnosing or determining the probability that a baby will be born with a genetic defect is now made possible through procedures such as ovum and sperm analysis, pre-implantation embryo diagnosis, gene therapy and amniocentesis. Biomedical science continues to propose and provide the public with evidence that genetic histories hold the key to predicting an individual's future health and well-being. With this, it becomes harder to ignore that knowing as much as possible about a child's biogenetic constitution is a responsible decision made in the interests of that child's future health.

Kaja Finkler (2000) contends that genetic science is changing the way all Westerners think about family relationships because it is leading to the medicalisation or geneticisation of kinship. Finkler's argument is illustrated by preoccupations evident in a recently published story by a young woman who was conceived through anonymous donor insemination, who worries about the health conditions she may have inherited yet will never know about:

> At the optician or general practitioner, I am asked about my family history, yet I know only half of it ... in my more paranoid moments I ruminate over those rare familial conditions I might have inherited. Am I safe taking the Pill? Should I have my cholesterol measured? Should I be screened for colonic polyps? (Anonymous 2002, p. 2)

In a similar vein, Smart (2007) argues that the genetic and biological bases for relatedness underlying much use of ART has led to a more impoverished understanding of family connections, because adoptive parents now think of adoption as a means to acquire another person's child rather than their 'own' child. In other words, genes and other forms of biological relatedness are reinforced as the 'real' forms of relatedness by these technologies. This sits uneasily with the equally strong contemporary notion that families are increasingly based on principles of care and choice (see Chapters 3 and 7), and it is often difficult to reconcile these two points of view.

As more lesbians and gay men use donated gametes to have children, their preoccupations about the meaning of biological relatedness prove quite similar to those aired in the literature on heterosexual couples and their donor gamete children. McNair and colleagues (2002) surveyed Australian lesbian mothers and found that many preferred the idea of an identifiable sperm donor due to concern about children's 'right to know' their biological origins. Dempsey (2005) found in her qualitative research with Australian lesbian couples and single mothers that lesbian mothers often prefer their children to have the option of a social relationship with the biological father—without him having the rights or responsibilities of conventional fatherhood— and also support being open with children about the circumstances of their donor insemination conception. Many would also rather approach a man they know and ask him to be the biological father of their child, rather than be inseminated with sperm from a donor who would always remain anonymous. This was due to concerns about a perceived link between biological relatedness and identity. Karen's story was typical:

> The experience of adoption has taught us that people's identity or sense of themselves is about origins. Lots of children or adults who were adopted have talked about feeling like there's this hole in their lives because they don't know who their mother or their father is. They feel like something

is missing. I didn't want that experience for my child. I wanted my child to be able to have a full picture of who they were, where they had come from and why and I felt really strongly about that (Dempsey 2005, p. 192).

Conclusion

THE SEPARATION OF SEX FROM reproduction is one of the most profound changes to reshape relationships and families in living memory. The first part of the revolution was the possibility of sex without reproduction and the second part was the possibility of reproduction without sex. Rather than a taken-for-granted consequence of marriage, having children is now a 'choice' and a difficult one at that. Fertility decisions are sometimes influenced by the availability of technologies yet equally depend on social forces such as the economy, the gendered division of labour, material aspirations and beliefs about parenthood, opportunity and individual preference. Cultural ideologies of parenthood generally emphasise having children as a big social and economic responsibility and thus can be linked to fertility decline and delay.

Although ARTs such as IVF, surrogacy and donor insemination came into being as a way of helping infertile heterosexual couples have a 'normal' nuclear family, the existence of these technologies has also enabled newer family forms such as sole parents 'by choice', lesbian-parented families, and families headed by two gay male parents with the aid of a surrogate mother. Although there is increasing legal recognition and social support for these families, public opinion still tends to disapprove of newer family configurations that include children. The vexed question of how important it is to be biologically related to our parents, as opposed to related to them by virtue of daily nurture and care will continue to be posed, as newer and hitherto unimagined technologies, and social uses for them come into being. We can expect many more years of sustained reflection and debate on these issues.

Key concepts

Assisted reproductive technologies

Contraceptive technologies

Fertility rate

Total fertility rate

Replacement fertility level

Gender regime perspective

Circumstantial childlessness

Genealogical bewilderment

Discussion questions

1   Which explanations for the declining fertility rate do you find most convincing? Can we blame it on the pill?

2   What are the problems and/or benefits of a falling fertility rate in Australia? What policy issues does falling fertility raise?

3   Why are single mothers by choice and lesbian mothers so controversial? On what basis should law and policy-makers decide who is eligible for procedures such as donor insemination and in vitro fertilisation?

4   How have ARTs such as donor insemination, surrogacy and IVF challenged taken-for-granted notions of the link between biological relatedness and parenthood?

5   There has been renewed interest in the abortion debate in Australia in recent years. Should abortion be every woman's personal choice or should society intervene to control the number of legal abortions performed?

Recommended further reading

Cannold, L. 2005, *What, No Baby?*, Curtin University Books, Fremantle.

Dempsey, D. 2006, 'Active fathers, natural families and children's origins: Dominant themes in the Australian political debate over eligibility for assisted reproduction', *Australian Journal of Emerging Technologies and Society*, vol. 4, no. 1.

Mitchell, D. & Gray, E. 2007, 'Declining fertility: Intentions, attitudes and aspirations', *Journal of Sociology*, 43, pp. 23–44.

09 | Parenting, Children and Childcare

Figure 9.1: Bindi Irwin

Introduction

BINDI IRWIN, DAUGHTER OF THE late 'Crocodile Hunter' Steve, has a very busy life. At the age of 10 she has her own TV show, a kids' fitness DVD, a fashion label and a magazine column, not to mention a substantial public relations and performance role at the family business, Australia Zoo. When Bindi's father was killed unexpectedly by a stingray barb in September 2006, she gave a moving eulogy several days later at his televised memorial service, vowing to continue her father's conservation work, with fans from all over the world looking on. Since the death of Steve Irwin, media debates about Bindi have been polarised. On the one hand she is lauded as a happy, active and talented child, whose greatest joy is to be in the public eye, continuing on in her father's footsteps. On the other, critics lament her lost innocence and presume she was given inadequate time to grieve before being thrust into the spotlight, accusing her mother and minders of using her to further their own economic ends.

The substance of the concerns about Bindi reveal the extent of social expectations that childhood should be a special time quite different from adulthood. In critics' views of Bindi's plight, the assumption was that children should be free from adult responsibilities such as work and also from having to display the emotional resilience expected of adults such as putting on a brave public face after the loss of a loved one. Against this set of assumptions about how childhood should be, popular debate often paints a very grim picture. Contemporary childhood is seen as 'toxic' or 'hurried'. Children are seen as at risk of obesity, exploitation by advertisers and sexual assault by pedophiles on the streets and on the internet. Childhood innocence and freedom is interrupted by overprotective parents, the commodification of playtime and the omnipresence of television. Children are purported to be damaged by long day care and corrupted by being sexualised at an early age by advertisers and marketers.

The media debate about Bindi also taps into dominant societal views about parents, particularly mothers, and how they should behave in relation to their children. In allowing Bindi to resume a taxing show business schedule in the weeks following her father's death, Terri Irwin was castigated for not looking after her daughter's emotional health, and thus violating normative expectations of mothers. Social expectations of parenthood are equally emotive to those of childhood. Contemporary parents and parenting practices are blamed for a variety of social problems including raising children with psychological problems, behavioural issues, eating disorders, substance abuse problems or problems with the law. Clearly there is high anxiety around parenting practices yet parenthood remains a major aspiration for most people even though the fertility rate is in decline. Parenting remains a deeply gendered practice and the expectations of responsible parenting are very different for mothers than for fathers. Much of the literature points to stresses and strains in undertaking parenting in the contemporary context—in Australia parents are said to suffer a 'work/life collision' (Pocock 2003). Mothers struggle with the 'mother wars' (Pocock 2003) and an 'epidemic of guilt' (Buttrose & Adams 2005) while fathers struggle to be 'more than breadwinners' (Singleton 2005).

In this chapter we chart the changing contours of childhood and parenthood in terms of both social expectations and experience, exploring the question: 'Is childhood really any less safe or enjoyable for contemporary children than for previous generations?' We argue that a sociological perspective drawing on both cultural and historical comparisons enables us to see how the experience of childhood and parenthood very much depends on the social context they are located within. Like social change in other domains of family life, changes in the experience of childhood are often contradictory—some things are better for this generation of children and some things are worse.

Childhood and historical change in Western countries

OUR UNDERSTANDINGS OF CHILDHOOD AS a life stage have varied over time. In Western history prior to industrialisation, children were viewed as miniature adults who made an economic contribution to the family and household. As industrialisation became established, middle-class families pioneered a new way of thinking about childhood as a distinct phase in the life course. Children were viewed as innocent and in need of socialisation and education before participating in society as full citizens. In the post-industrial world we now inhabit, childhood is seen as a risky life stage where children need to be protected from a range of threats and carefully managed and nurtured by parents.

The changing value of children is key to understanding historical change in Western countries such as Australia. Children have lost their economic value to families as they are no longer expected to work and support the family. In fact they are now an economic burden rather than a resource. Children are now valued for their emotional contribution to individual families. Viviana Zelizer (1994) argues that contemporary children are viewed as economically worthless but emotionally priceless. However, running alongside the value of children for individual families is the recognition on the part of governments that children are a national resource that are necessary to fill projected labour market shortages and support an ageing population.

Prior to the nineteenth century, children were viewed as the property of parents and protected by neither churches nor governments. Historians argue that there was not a strong differentiation between childhood and other life stages (Aries 1962). Throughout the nineteenth century, working-class children were expected to help support the family and childhood continued to be not much different from adult life. By contrast wealthy families in the nineteenth century could afford to pamper their children and idealise them as symbols of innocence. As industrialisation developed it seems that children were increasingly viewed as innocent and in need of protection. Bourgeois families (the newly formed middle class) were able to create an idyllic private sphere for children to inhabit and these families would eventually go on to change not only what people do with children but also what they think and feel about children.

In the twentieth century, with industrialisation and the introduction of compulsory education children were no longer an economic resource but a financial burden for individual families. This notion is underlined by the cost of children figures that are calculated in many Western countries and publicised in the popular media. For example in 2006 the cost of raising a child from infancy to 18 years of age was estimated to be $250,000 (Bradbury 2004). According to Zelizer the emotional worth of children has increased just as substantially as their economic worth has decreased (Zelizer 1994). Children are seen to provide love, companionship and enjoyment and offer fulfilment and contribution to identity for parents.

Beryl Langer argues that childhood is now seen as a short but precious time of dependence, and vulnerability in which children should be free to grow, learn and play under the protective gaze of nurturing adults (Langer 2005). However we would extend this argument further to state that contemporary childhood is now viewed as a pressured and risky life stage to be carefully managed and negotiated by parents (Elkind 2007; Lumby & Fine 2006).

Cultural differences in childhood

THE CULTURAL VARIATION IN CHILDHOOD experience both within societies and between societies is substantial. In contemporary industrialised Western societies children rarely participate in paid labour whereas in many developing countries children make an important economic contribution to both their family and wider economy.

Cindi Katz's (2004) ethnography of childhood experiences in Howa, a village in the Sudan, paints a complex picture where children combine work and play. The children in the village were involved in animal husbandry, fetching water, procuring fire wood, agriculture and collecting wild food and other resources from the surrounding environment. They were also substantially involved in household domestic labour such as childcare, cooking, cleaning and running errands and other chores in addition to attending school. Often play and work was intertwined:

> Much work was playful, especially that which took the children on journeys outside the village, and a lot of play activities were 'workfull', such as Talal's kitchen project or other boys' bird-snaring. Still other forms of play—such as the endless dramatic games of 'fields'—rehearsed work activities that the children engaged in at other times, while some play involved toying with likely future work activities, such as the girls' games of 'house' (Katz 2004, p. 67)

Expectations of appropriate activities for children to engage in vary widely according to context and range from childhood seen as a time of innocence and protection from adult life, to preparation for adult life. Children are born into a set of expectations about what it means to be a child and ideas about what children can and cannot do at particular ages (Langer 2005). The boundaries between child, youth and adult shift according to historical and cultural context. In industrialised countries such as Australia, the child phase is shortening and the youth (or adolescence) phase is beginning at an earlier age and extending for longer, as young people are dependent on their parents for longer periods. Interestingly, even biological markers of adulthood such as puberty have changed over time (by up to four years in some parts of Europe) in response to social conditions (Brannen 2002). Legal classifications of the boundaries between childhood and adulthood are also variable, context-specific and gendered. For example, think about the varying ages at which young people can drink alcohol, earn money, consent to sexual intercourse, or join the armed forces. Variations such as these are equally evident between different countries and cultures, which illustrates that childhood is socially constructed (Holloway & Valentine 2003).

Changing research perspectives on childhood

As we outlined in Chapter 4, sociological perspectives adapt to historical and political change within society. From the 1950s to the 1970s, the dominant mode of understanding childhood was via the concept of socialisation, which was an essential part of the functionalist framework. From this perspective, children were seen as developing individuals with a dependent status within the family. The psychology of child development in particular has dominated the research field and there has been a heavy emphasis on appropriate ages and stages, regardless of social factors such as gender, class, ethnicity and so on. Under the influence of psychoanalysis, attachment to the mother has been seen as a major influence on children's development (Brannen 2002).

A second perspective examines children's social interaction in other contexts. In this perspective, socialisation is not simply a given but there is a focus on the ways in which children learn, develop and interact with adults who care for them in schools and other institutions. This perspective follows the constructivist theoretical tradition and allows children some agency (as social actors) but there is also an emphasis on the ways in which children are regulated by social institutions (Jenks 2005).

The third and most recent perspective sees children as social agents acting in their own right. In this view children are a permanent social category rather than a transitory social group and as such should be allowed independent rights. Sociological research from this framework is conducted for children as active members of families and the wider society rather than on children as passive family members (Brannen 2002; Mayall 2002; Jenks 2005). A discussion of research from this perspective appears later in this chapter in the section on children's agency in contemporary society.

Children and consumer society

LIKE OTHER SOCIAL INSTITUTIONS, THE nature of childhood is changing rapidly in contemporary society and the development of consumer capitalism and new communication technologies is reshaping the way we think and feel about children and no doubt the ways in which they think about themselves.

Beryl Langer has argued that under consumer capitalism we have changed from a 'culture of making do to a culture of having more' and we are conditioned into continuous consumption to keep the capitalist system going even when our basic needs have been met (Langer 2005). Children are increasingly targeted as consumers by multinational companies from toy and food industries—among others—and consumption is now central to the way contemporary children are socialised (Langer 2005). Langer (2005) outlines how generic toys that have been the mainstay of childhood play for the last century such as a doll, train set, or blocks have been replaced by 'commoditoys'. Commoditoys are branded toys such as 'Barbie, Bratz or ninja turtles' and are subject to fashion cycles and marketing. Often these toys are linked to a range so each purchase stimulates desire for another toy. The emerging health issue of childhood obesity can be in large part attributed to the entertainment product cycle where companies utilise character licensing of foods such as cereals and snack foods and toy collectables to promote fast food (Langer 2005).

Our perceived expectations about children's needs have expanded. In terms of housing, expectations about internal space have expanded and at the same time the size of backyards have reduced. It is now commonly assumed that children need their own rooms, toys and, increasingly, computers and mobile phones. Child-friendly neighbourhoods where children play in the street have diminished and instead children are ferried to sports and other activities or play/watch TV inside their houses (Langer 2005). According to the ABS the most frequent leisure activity of children is watching TV, DVDs or videos (ABS 2006e).

To look at consumption from a slightly different angle, children themselves have become objects of consumer choice in the adult lifestyle market (Langer 2005). Recently the 'child free' movement has emerged where children are seen as a consumer choice and parents are 'users' who should pay for them. From this perspective, state support for children through the tax system or through family friendly politics is defined as discriminatory to people without children. Langer describes the perspective of 'Mike' on an ABC online forum on maternity leave. He argued that children today are more of a lifestyle choice than the responsibility of society as a whole and compared maternity leave to giving people 'paid holidays to enjoy a new boat or car they have purchased' (Langer 2005, p. 166). Clearly, this perspective is quite a dramatic change from having a child as taken for granted and central part of adult life.

Children, TV and technology

THE RELATIONSHIP CHILDREN HAVE TO TV raises an enormous amount of anxiety among parents, public commentators and child experts. Lumby and Fine (2006) argue that there has been a 'moral panic' about TV and its effect on 'passive' children.

According to Lumby and Fine (2006), the moral panic about the negative effects of TV on children means that a number of myths have gained currency. The first is that children do not use their imaginations when they watch TV. However, watching TV requires viewers to 'interpret fast-paced edits, narrative twists and turns and shifts between fantasy and reality' (Lumby & Fine 2006, p. 94). A number of studies have shown that children take characters from TV and incorporate them into their games (Lumby & Fine 2006). A second myth is that TV is the cause of obesity. However, there is no direct link between children's physical activity, food consumption and TV watching (Lumby & Fine 2006). A third dominant myth is that advertisers have incredible power over vulnerable children. However, according to Lumby and Fine, 'The best studies show that preschool children are unlikely to recall ads or associate them with products and that school-age children are very aware of advertising and quickly become cynical about false claims' (Lumby & Fine 2006, p. 176).

Despite the high anxieties around it watching TV is clearly an enjoyable pastime for the majority of Australian children. Nevertheless, TV operates to reinforce gender stereotypes and it organises and distorts the way gender difference is presented. Boys' programming focuses on action, objects and conflict while girls' programming privileges relationships, beauty and harmony (Kenway & Bullen 2001). Female characters are offered a narrower range of roles in comparison to male characters and advertising in particular offers stereotypical gendered scripts to the audience with advertisements targeting boys containing more 'cuts, loud music and boisterous activity' whereas advertisements targeting girls contain 'more fades, soft music and quiet play' (Kenway & Bullen 2001, p. 52). However other media studies academics such as Meyrowitz argue that through TV, children have access to both male and female role models and a new androgynous style of behaviour is emerging (Kenway & Bullen 2001).

The positive and negative effects of TV and other forms of technology such as the internet are debated but it is clear that contemporary children inhabit a landscape that is fundamentally shaped by new information and communication technologies. These require new competencies in terms of processing information and understanding 'the differences between data, information, knowledge, education, entertainment and advertising', which is a new challenge for parents, schools and children themselves (Kenway & Bullen 2001, p. 188).

Children's use of the internet

Figure 9.2: A Dangerous Activity?

Contemporary children often display greater skill and knowledge about computers and the internet than their teachers and parents. However children's safety online is seen to be the responsibility of parents, which raises adult anxieties. These anxieties can only have been heightened by the Australian government intervention 'NetAlert—Protecting Australian Families Online', offering internet screening software to all Australian households. A quotation from the message from the former minister of communication gives a flavour of the campaign:

> The internet is a window on the world that has simply transformed the way we communicate. Properly harnessed, it has enormous potential as a tool for education, entertainment, interaction and global engagement. Just like the real world, however, there is a lot on the internet that you wouldn't want your children to see and things aren't always as they seem.
>
> Tackling the dangerous side of the internet poses two main challenges: the content available online and, most concerning, the contact by online predators with unsuspecting children <http://www.netalert.gov.au/news_and_events. html, accessed 23 October 2007>. According to radio reports, within days of its release a 14-year-old had found a way of immobilising the software. In contrast to the government approach, Lumby and Fine argue that providing information to children about their bodies and sexuality, and telling them that it is their right to say 'no' to someone wanting to touch them or talk to them, and telling them where to go for help will be more effective than building 'technological fences' around them (Lumby & Fine 2006).

The research findings from an in-depth study of children in the UK and their use of computers support the argument that the moral panic about children and computers is misplaced.

Our research demonstrates the other popular fears about children's use of computers in general, and the Internet in particular, are also unfounded. Children are not spending excessive amounts of time indoors and in front of the computer screen instead of playing outdoors, and ICT use does not encourage social isolation or the breakdown of family relations and friendships. Rather, young people appear to use technology in balanced and sophisticated ways to develop and enhance both on-and off-line social relationships which can open their minds to a wider, if Americanised, world (Holloway & Valentine 2003, p. 155).

The sexualisation of children

ANOTHER AREA OF HIGH ANXIETY about the changing nature of childhood is 'sexualisation' or the idea that children, and girls in particular, are being encouraged to present themselves in sexualised ways through fashion and beauty. Ariel Levy's book *Female Chauvinist Pigs: Women and the Rise of Raunch Culture* describes the wider context of changing modes of femininity and expression of sexuality. There are great fears that children are being subject to pressures to participate in this raunch culture from an early age.

This debate is particularly polarised. On the one hand we have reports such as *Corporate Paedophilia: Sexualisation of Children in Australia* (Rush & La Nauze 2006), which paints an extreme picture of advertising and marketing abusing both children and public morality. Rush and La Nauze argue that there is increased pressure for children to adopt a sexualised appearance and behaviour. Key examples are girls posing as sexy models in advertisements and being encouraged to adopt sexualised behaviour by TV programs and music video-clips in particular.

New ways of marketing products to young girls have exacerbated fears about the premature sexualisation of girls. The introduction of girls' magazines on the Australian market such as *Barbie Magazine, Total Girl* and *Disney Girl* contain a large amount of material related to beauty, fashion and celebrities (Rush & La Nauze 2006). Apart from offending the morality of some adults, Rush and La Nauze (2006) argue that there are three major risks posed by premature sexualisation. The first is dissatisfaction with body image and the increasing incidences of eating disorders. The second relates to lowering the age of intercourse and the third is that a sexualising media may play a role in making young girls more vulnerable to paedophiles.

By contrast, writers such as Lumby and Fine (2006) argue that there is nothing new about moral panics about teenage girls being made precociously sexual by shocking new forms of music, fashion or media—they cite Elvis, the 'bodgies' and 'widgies' and punk fashion and music as examples. They counter many of the arguments presented by writers such as Rush and La Nauze by arguing instead that children have always played at being grown-ups and that 'Little girls were running around in bikinis in the 1970s. They've been dressing up in their mum's high heels and playing with her make-up for generations' (Lumby & Fine 2006, p. 260). They argue that the clothes that children wear are not the cause of paedophilia and rates of teenage sex are not rising dramatically.

It's probable that both sides of the debate have a point—the sexualisation of children is exploitative but the nature of this exploitation may be relatively limited. We would argue that contemporary children are subject to the same wider changes in society that young people and adults are. The increasing influence of the market in shaping everyday life and the privileging of a dominant form of sexualised femininity are issues for both adults and children.

Children's agency and contemporary Western childhood

IN DOMINANT SOCIAL AND POLITICAL discourse, a sharp boundary is drawn between children and adults in contemporary Western countries. Children are largely restricted to subordinate and protected social roles. They have been removed from paid work and are now obligated to work on their own education for an extended timeframe (Mayall 2002). Qvortrup (2001) argues that childhood has been 'scholarised', which means that the dominant view is that the proper and appropriate central activity for children is to be learners rather than workers. In advanced industrialised countries, children's main activity is to undertake 'self-capitalisation' as learners in educational settings (Qvortrup 2001; Mayall 2002).

Despite the emphasis on childhood being a time of dependency, Mayall (2002) offers an alternative view. She outlines the ways in which children do in fact contribute to the social order and the economy from young ages, although many of these tasks are downplayed in much of the popular and academic literature on childhood. Mayall's (2002) research found that primary school children undertake a variety of work within the family, including housework, childcare and self care. Children also undertake 'people work' in the domestic setting. Children are active participants in constructing knowledge within the home 'through identifying and refining issues of justice, fair distribution, kindness and recognition of others' point of view' (Mayall 2002, p. 172). They act as reasonable people, and undertake practical and caring tasks (Mayall 2002). Mayall argues that children do have agency in advanced industrialised countries and this should be recognised and children's rights should be promoted more vigorously (Mayall 2002).

One important aspect of contemporary society that has very negative outcomes for children is their exclusion from public spaces. Issues such as 'traffic danger' and 'stranger danger' mean that in countries such as Australia and the UK, children are seen to require around-the-clock adult supervision. Gender and class have an impact on children's freedom in public spaces. For example, Mayall (2002) found that in the UK boys had more access to public space than girls and girls from an Asian background in particular. Mayall illustrates this claim in comparing the differences between 9-year-old children living in London and

9-year-olds living in Jyvaskyla in central Finland. The children in London were under continuous adult supervision at home and at school and their use of public space was only permitted under strict parental permission. The London children socialised mainly in each other's homes. By contrast the Finnish children managed their own way to school and home and had access to neighbourhood facilities without parental supervision:

> Most woke themselves up (with an alarm clock), made their breakfast, assembled their belongings and walked or cycled to school. Most of the journeys were on paths and tracks separated from car traffic ... After school, they went home; most then rang their mother to say they were back, and agreed to do their homework (each weekday) before any other activity. (Mayall 2002 p. 142–3).

At the end of the day Finnish families would meet at home for an evening meal. The independence and responsibility of the Finnish children stands in strong contrast to the everyday lives of the English children and from our observations children in Australia too. Australian children are expected to be under 24/7 supervision and intensive parenting has come to be seen as the norm, as we will explore in the following sections.

Parenting

SOMETIMES DOMINANT DISCOURSES, OR SOCIALLY dominant ways of thinking about experiences, are more easily identified by people outside the dominant group. One example of this is the people in Helen Marshall's (1993) Australian research who had decided not to have children. These people gave a clear account of dominant expectations of parenthood that they felt they would not be able to live up to. First, being a parent was considered to be 'natural' or an inherent disposition rather than something that could be learned. In this understanding you are either naturally the type to become a parent or you are not. Second, being a parent is an almost overwhelming commitment. This included the idea that children's needs should take precedence over adults needs. They discussed images of ideal parents, especially mothers, as ever present and self-sacrificing carers. Third, parenthood demands sacrifices. This involved the idea that children need time, and money and these are private sacrifices and private rewards (Marshall 1993). These ideas about the sacrifices required by people having children still have a large amount of influence as children are no longer seen as financial assets to families (Zelizer 1994). Nevertheless, expectations about 'sacrifice' and parenting remain profoundly gendered and the roles of mothers and fathers are substantially different.

Mums, 'proper mothers' and intensified mothering

A CULTURE OF MATERNALISM IS common in many Western cultures and appears to be particularly strong in the Australian context. A **maternalist culture** is one where mothers are exalted as the natural and indispensable carers of children (Flood 2003). This assumption is often taken for granted and has its roots in the modern family form that came to be dominant in the 1950s and 1960s. Women were expected to be 'homemakers', a vocation that involved both caring tasks and domestic labour. Raising and socialising children was a key part of a woman's homemaker role. These ideas about mothering have remained dominant even though the social landscape has changed dramatically in the last three decades. According to Pocock 'proper mothers' are still understood to be 'perpetually available, good and even-tempered, and the centre of loving family relations' (Pocock 2005, p. 126). The image of the ideal mother, who is patient, completely dedicated to her children's needs and always available, continues to resonate in Western societies (Hays 1996).

Deborah Lupton undertook research on first-time mothers before and after the birth of their first child in the 1990s. Before the birth women tended to emphasise putting their child's needs before their own. Anna provides an example:

> A mother to me is somebody that is always there for your child. Somebody that your child can come to at any time, a mother that can give love and care and advice and just be there for them to cuddle and help them develop (Lupton 2000, p. 54).

After the birth the women struggled to live up to their ideals and found that caring for a newborn was an 'all consuming' and challenging task and instead of coming naturally, motherhood involved learning a range of often difficult tasks including settling and feeding (Lupton 2000). Other researchers have also found that motherhood is learned on the job and that mothering involves a steep learning curve (Maher 2005; Everingham & Bowers 2006).

The organisation of the paid labour market has changed dramatically since the 1950s and the place of mothering in women's lives has also changed. According to Everingham, Stevenson and Warner-Smith (2007), who conducted research on three generations of women in NSW, the place of motherhood has changed over the lives of three generations of women. These changes are a legacy of the women's movement, interacting with the new economic conditions. For the older generation of women (aged 65–70) their identity in young adulthood was merged with motherhood and 'motherhood was just expected' (Everingham et al. 2007, p. 424). For women in the mid generation (aged 53–58) motherhood and identity were merged but paid work could be added to women's role with the expectation that paid work was fitted in around motherhood and 'nothing changed at home' (Everingham et al. 2007, p. 426). By contrast they found young women (aged 26–31), the most recent generation of mothers, have a different orientation to work and motherhood and the 'mother/worker' is emerging. These women seek autonomous selfhood prior to marriage and family and paid labour is more central to their identities. They engage in paid labour in a wider range of occupations than the previous generation of women. Again, in contrast to the previous generation, young women strive to fit mothering in around their commitment to paid work. They expect that they will work and be a mother at some stage and do not expect a breadwinner to take care of them. Instead they focus on building financial independence both before and after children (Everingham et al. 2007).

The emerging 'mother/worker' identity has tended to involve women adding together the tasks of mothering, caring, domestic labour and working in the paid labour market. Women have performed this complex reformulation of their role with limited support from the wider society. Men did not jump in to undertake half of the domestic labour or childcare tasks, leading to what Hochschild (1989) called the 'stalled revolution'. Public policy enabled equal opportunity within the workplace but the provision of childcare facilities and family friendly policies to support working mothers were patchy or absent (OECD 2002). In fact there is some evidence that mothering has become even more intensive in recent decades. 'Being there' and caring for children is no longer sufficient and women are expected to 'adopt the latest high standards of child-rearing and care backed by manuals, advice and instruction' (Pocock 2005 p. 127). Mothers, particularly middle-class mothers, are expected to engage in 'concerted cultivation' to successfully launch their children into adult lives (Lareau 2003; Gillies 2007). Ultimately, women continue to take more responsibility for parenting than men and under quite difficult circumstances, it seems.

The focus of public debate and academic discourse on mothering has tended to emphasise the difficulties in combining work and care. We are presented with 'images of women almost going crazy from the guilt and the pressure of the workload' (Summers 2003, p. 67) and claims that 'mother guilt' is in 'plague proportions' as 'women have had to shoulder the burden of guilt that comes from trying to overcome their natural nurturing instincts and combine conflicting roles' (Buttrose & Adams 2005, p. 4). However, Lindsay and Maher (2005) have argued that this 'crisis rhetoric' may have some unintended consequences. First, it silences an articulation of the strategies women use to combine work and family labour and their pleasure in being involved in both types of labour. Second, crisis rhetoric may have the unintended consequence of discouraging young women from having children and reducing the fertility rate and dissuading men from moving into simultaneous engaged parenting and paid work (Lindsay & Maher 2005). Quite different expectations and anxieties operate around fatherhood.

Dads, 'proper fathers' and involved fathering

IN CONTRAST TO MOTHERS, 'BEING THERE' for children is a relatively new expectation for fathers. As outlined in Chapter 2, the modern family form after World War II emphasised the 'father as breadwinner' ideal. The ideal father was expected to be

'the breadwinner, adviser, protector and disciplinarian' (Singleton 2005). Participating in childcare or domestic labour was not expected at all (Singleton 2005).

As gender roles changed with second-wave feminism the emotionally
uninvolved or absent father began to be criticised in academic and self-help
literature. Caring via 'breadwinning' was no longer considered adequate and the
absence of fathers was blamed for a range of psychological problems in boys
growing up (Singleton 2005). In the 1960s and 1970s a new ideal of the involved
father, or '**new father**' emerged: 'The new father is expected to be caring,
approachable and emotionally available to his children, and ought to achieve an
equitable balance between work and family life' (Singleton 2005, p. 144).

In the new ideal, fathers are expected to be active and engaged with their
children but in reality only a minority of men spend a substantial amount of
time caring for their children or taking major responsibility for child raising. It
is estimated that fewer than 10 per cent of fathers are highly involved in day-
to-day care of their children. In fact, the birth of a child is strongly associated
with men increasing their time spent in paid work rather than decreasing it
(Flood 2003). According to Australian time-use research, fathers spend much
less time with their children than mothers do; eight hours a day in comparison
to women's 12 hours a day, and two hours a day caring for their children in
comparison to over six hours a day by women (Craig 2006). Fathers spend under
one fifth of their time with children alone while mothers spend nearly half of
their time with children alone. This indicates that fathers are more likely to play
a 'helping out' role rather than taking major responsibility for childcare (Craig
2006). This statistical evidence supports the findings of qualitative research that
has found that fathers are likely to have a relationship with their children that is
'mediated' by the mother (Smart 2002). The mother translates information about
children's needs and preferences for the father rather than the father having a
direct relationship with the child.

Although most contemporary fathers express a desire to spend time with
their children and see this as important, there are cultural obstacles to men's
involvement in parenting. Michael Flood (2003) identifies four cultural barriers
to involved fathering in the Australian context. First, there is a culture of work
and materialism. A number of scholars have written about the intensifying work
culture where long hours spent at work is linked to successful masculinity (Pocock
2003; Flood 2003). Second, there is an absence of a culture of fatherhood and
accessible role models of involved fathers. Fathers who actively care for their
children are still seen as unmanly in many contexts (Flood 2003). Doucet (2000)
undertook research on men in the UK who shared the care of their young
children with their partners in the early 1990s. The men in this study talked
about their 'embarrassment' and feelings of being stigmatised when playing a
caring role. For example, Joe explained:

> I was actually slightly embarrassed as a bloke saying that I was going home
> to look after the children. I always had to qualify if with—'But I'm also

going to write a book'. Which is probably a male thing to do isn't it? (Doucet 2000, p. 173).

Third, there is a culture of maternalism described earlier where women are seen as the natural carers for children and men have a much more ambiguous role. Apparently some women are reluctant to allow fathers to play a major role in caring for their children. However, Everingham and Bowers (2006) argue that women are blamed for excluding men from caring for their children because 'new fatherhood discourses' promote unrealistic images of 'the new father' and fail to take into account the reality of early infant care. Early infant care involves an emotional intensity and a 'need to submerge the self of the primary caregiver in round-the-clock care of the newborn ... caregiving is not an instinctive skill possessed by women, but a skill acquired through an intensive period of immersion in the activity itself'(Everingham & Bowers 2006, p. 101). Everingham and Bowers (2006) ask 'how many fathers want to immerse themselves in this way?' Instead they found that men want to 'be there' or 'do their bit' or 'help out' rather than taking primary responsibility for infant care (Everingham & Bowers 2006, p. 101).

The final cultural barrier to involved fathering is suspicion that is directed towards men in caring roles as the awareness of sexual and physical abuse has increased over the last few decades. But as Michael Flood (2003) argues these cultural barriers to involved fathering are not insurmountable and some men are taking on a substantial amount of care for their children.

Diverse parenting contexts

As outlined in Chapter 2, as families become more diverse, parenting is practised in a wider range of contexts. Women make up the majority of single parents caring for their children whereas men are much more likely than women to live with step-children.

Gay and lesbian parenting is a relatively new phenomenon in the field of family studies. Intentional childbearing outside heterosexual unions is perhaps the most original and controversial type of family formation to have emerged in Western families in the last century, and lesbian parented families are much more common than families parented by gay men. During the 1980s a lesbian baby boom began in industrialised countries such as Australia and the United States (Stacey 1996). Biological constraints mean that lesbians construct their family forms with an exceptional degree of reflection and intentionality (Parks 1998). There are now a significant number of lesbian-parented families in North America, Western Europe, including Britain, and Australia. Lesbian families include families who conceive children within their relationship and also step-families—where parents bring children from previous heterosexual relationships. Lesbian and gay parents face many of the same issues as straight parents, in addition to the substantial challenge of living in a heteronormative context (Lindsay et al. 2006).

Childcare while at work

IN AUSTRALIA THERE IS SOCIAL pressure for mothers to care for their children at home, especially when they are very young. However, an increasing proportion of mothers are engaging in the paid labour market and the average time spent at home before returning to work is declining.

The strong maternalist culture operating in Australia has a negative impact on rates of maternal employment and causes many women to feel 'guilty' about working. Australia, along with the USA, is one of the few countries in the OECD that does not have paid maternity leave provisions for women workers. Moreover, childcare places are difficult to find and are frequently expensive. Although the provision of formal childcare places in day care centres and through family day care programs has grown steadily since the 1970s, the current demand for childcare far outstrips supply (McDonald 2002). Finally a moral panic about the effects of formal childcare is frequently and easily ignited in the Australian context. Consequently, Australian mothers are much more likely than mothers in the UK or USA to work part-time as a way of managing the constraints of the Australian work/care regime (Pocock 2003). About half of children younger than 12 use some form of care. Most of this is 'informal care' (37 per cent), which includes care by grandparents, other relatives or friends. About 24 per cent use 'formal care', including 8 per cent in long day care, 7 per cent in preschool and the remainder in before and afterschool care or occasional care services (Pocock 2003). According to Evans and Kelley (2002) 'many Australians, both men and women, have substantial moral reservations about the employment of mothers with children under school age—in the "nesting stage" of the lifecourse' (p. 188). But perhaps this is another example of a disjunction between parenting ideals and realities. The relentless movement of mothers into the labour market shows no sign of slowing down, but clearly social attitudes, policies and services need to catch up with the realities of contemporary family life in Australia.

Conclusion

IN INDUSTRIALISED COUNTRIES IN LATE modernity having children is a choice rather than a taken-for-granted option. Children interfere with the 'do-it-yourself' biography of people as mobile workers available to the market 24/7 (Beck-Gernsheim 2002). Middle-class young women, in particular, now talk about wanting to have a life first before having children. Children are seen as demanding of adult time and labour and they are expensive. However, in a world of falling fertility rates and family instability, children's symbolic value has increased—as Zelizer (1994) argues, children are now economically useless but emotionally priceless. Parenthood remains a major aspiration for young people but increasingly the challenge is to fit children around work and careers.

As in other times in history there is considerable anxiety about the way children are being raised in our society. Childhood is certainly different and our society is probably less child-friendly as children are excluded from public spaces, and healthcare, childcare and education are increasingly privatised. However, the moral panics about TV, sexuality and children being hurried through childhood exaggerate the negative implications of social change and idealise the social arrangements of the modern nuclear family of the 1950s and 1960s. Contemporary scholarship on children and childhood is beginning to pay attention to the ways in which children interact and shape the world around them—hopefully this will lead to more of their voices being heard in both academic research and public debate.

Key concepts

Sexualisation

Maternalist culture

New fathers

Discussion questions

1   What do sociologists mean when they say childhood is 'socially constructed'?

2   What do children represent to contemporary parents as opposed to parents in pre-modern times?

3   What are the main challenges facing heterosexual partnered women making the transition to first-time motherhood?

4   Should we be concerned about the fact that fathers continue to be less responsible and active in children's daily care than mothers? If so, what should be done about it?

Recommended further reading

Craig, L. 2006, 'Does Father Care Mean Father's Share? A Comparison of How Mothers and Fathers in Intact Families Spend Time with Children', *Gender and Society*, vol. 20, no. 2, pp. 259–81.

Holloway, S.L. & Valentine, G. 2003, *Cyberkids: Children in the Information Age*, Routledge Farmer, London.

Lupton, D. 2000, 'A Love/Hate Relationship: The Ideals and Experiences of First Time Mothers', *Journal of Sociology*, 36, 1, pp. 50–63.

Pocock, B. 2003, *The Work/Life Collision*, The Federation Press, Sydney.

10 | Families and Labour

Figure 10.1: Carol Porter, Man's Final Frontier—The Home

Introduction

IN THE POSTER REPRODUCED ABOVE, Carol Porter—in a humorous way—poses the question: 'Why are men so threatened by domestic labour?' The ideal family of the 1950s and 1960s in Australia involved a clear division of labour between two heterosexual parents. There was a male breadwinner and a female homemaker, who was also responsible for most domestic labour in the family home. This family ideal continues to shape the experiences of Australian families and the division of labour within families even though economic and social conditions have changed radically since then. In the last 40 years women have moved into the paid labour force with gusto but men have been reluctant to assume a substantially larger share of the domestic labour. In terms of work/life balance, current debate emphasises crisis and difficulty in the lives of working mothers and pressure on working fathers.

In this chapter we examine how the domestic division of labour operates in contemporary relationships and families and how this is linked to the gendered division of labour in the paid workforce. We outline key features of the contemporary work/family landscape and examine some of the theories sociologists have developed to explain why shifts in the paid and unpaid labour markets have been so uneven and challenging. We consider domestic divisions of labour between shared householders and same-sex cohabiting couples as part of the discussion, emphasising how similarities and differences in arrangements illuminate issues of how gender and sexuality relate to work.

A brief history of gendered work

IN CHAPTER 2, WE EXPLORED HOW the notion of separate spheres for homemakers and breadwinners emerged from the changing structure of work in early industrialised societies. Davidoff and Hall (1987) undertook a historical study of the English middle classes, showing how work and home became spatially separated spheres around the turn of the nineteenth century. Creating a division between work and home involved inventing specialised buildings to fulfil the function of being either homes or workplaces. However, this was not just a spatial shift in terms of how buildings were designed and work organised. It was connected with a moral and ideological shift that designated 'separate spheres' for women and men.

This separation of spheres had consequences for feminine and masculine identities as well as their work responsibilities. Women became housewives, and the permanently employed, full-time breadwinner became a central ideal for men. These identities have proved very resilient and have often been shored up by public policy. For example, in Australia, in the era between the two World Wars, institutionalised wage inequality became a key plank of social policy, in the form of the '**family wage**'. The Harvester Judgement of 1907 enshrined gendered wage differentials in legislation. A fair wage was considered to be one that gives a man enough money to support himself, a wife and three children in 'frugal comfort' (see Zajdow 1995). Women's wages were kept lower because it was assumed that they were not supporting families. According to Zajdow (2005), even at this time, one third of Australian women were the sole economic providers for their families. However, this notion of the family wage served to marginalise women in the paid workforce until they were needed in times of crisis such as during the War. We are still feeling the influence of the family wage today, as Australian men and women do not receive equivalent pay for equivalent work.

As the second-wave feminist movement developed in the 1970s, increasing numbers of Western women began looking for fulfilment beyond the home and moving into the paid workforce. This was the beginning of the contemporary blurring of the so-called 'public' and 'private' spheres. For instance, in contemporary families, domestic work is increasingly outsourced as paid labour, particularly tasks such as cooking, cleaning, mending and childcare. The forces of global capitalism have also challenged the feasibility of the breadwinner role. As Connell (2005) notes, the breadwinner is not just an image or ideology, it is an orientation to work that depends on being able to maintain a certain level of income and stable employment relations. Neo-liberal economic policies based on free market ideology now prevail in most Western democracies. With this there is a growing insecurity in permanent employment, workplace entitlements and a move towards casualisation of the workforce. If the housewife's sphere is in flux, as Connell (2005) observes, the breadwinner's is also considerably challenged. Accompanying this are indications of widespread social stress, anxiety and conflict focused on the relationship between the family and the labour market, and how women and men should participate in each.

The gendered division of public and private spheres has been broken down substantially but contemporary masculinities and femininities continue to be constituted by the historical ideals of male breadwinners and female carers. In the gendered division of paid and unpaid labour there has been both remarkable change and remarkable continuity at play in the last few decades. Although men and women both experience stress and strain with meeting their paid and unpaid labour responsibilities, there is broad agreement that women often shoulder a disproportionate burden of coping with domestic labour, including childcare. Many sociologists have tried to make sense of why women continue to do far more domestic labour than men, despite the extent to which women have moved into the paid workforce in increasing numbers over the past few decades. This remains the case, even in dual-career families where women work as many hours in paid work as men, in equally demanding jobs.

Families and the paid labour market

THE PAID LABOUR MARKET HAS had a profound impact on families. Since the 1970s the large-scale entry of mothers into the paid labour market has been one of the most major changes. From a situation of exclusion and discrimination, women have made huge gains toward equality with men. However, the labour market remains profoundly gendered. Men continue to earn more than women—on average women earn 85 per cent of what men do in full-time positions (Kee 2006). The wages gap is narrowing slowly and has decreased by four percentage points over the last decade (Kee 2006).

As illustrated in Figure 10.2 (below), some industries are firmly male dominated—such as mining, construction and manufacturing—while others are firmly female dominated—particularly education and health and community services. The industries in the middle have similar proportions of men and women workers (Office of the Status of Women 2004). The history of gendered specialisation explains why we often find a concentration of women in the kinds of service industries that echo their purported propensity for caring labour. Sociologist Rosemary Pringle did a classic study of secretaries in the late 1980s that showed just how much women's paid work becomes an extension of the caring labour they are supposed to do for free in the home (Pringle 1988). As illustrated in the graph below, contemporary women still tend to concentrate in caring and service industries such as health and education, where people's emotional and physical needs are looked after.

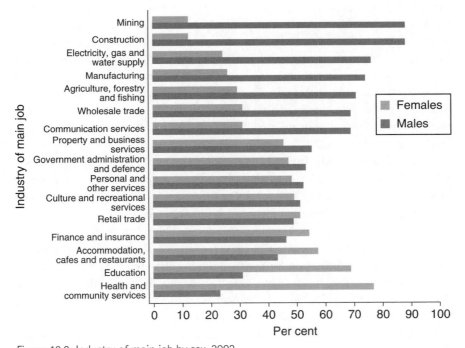

Figure 10.2: Industry of main job by sex, 2002

Source: Office of the Status of Women 2004

Most parents today are now in the paid labour market. Broomhill and Sharp (2005) argue that Australians have moved from male breadwinner model to **dual-earner families model**. In couple families with children, 62 per cent have both partners working and 32 per cent have the man in the labour market only (3 per cent have only the woman in the paid labour market, and 4 per cent have neither partner in the paid labour market). However men's participation in the labour market changes very little when having children, whereas women's participation changes markedly. Women with young children are less likely to be in the labour market than other workers.

The growth of part-time jobs since the 1960s has provided a platform for Australian women to enter the labour market. Three quarters of all part-time jobs in Australia are held by women. And 44 per cent of Australian women who have paid jobs work part time. The proportion of men working part time has also doubled since 1982, however, men in part-time work still constitute a much smaller proportion of the labour force, at about 14 per cent of all men in paid work. Part-time jobs in Australia have the following three characteristics: more than two thirds of them are casual rather than permanent part-time, they come with limited rights and entitlements and they provide negligible job security (Pocock 2003).

At the same time, there is a countervailing tendency with the development of a culture of long working hours in full-time jobs. Many Australians are working longer hours and experiencing a situation where the hours they are expected to work have begun to encroach on weekends. In 1982, average weekly working hours of Australians were 38.2 hours per week but in 2001 they were 41.3 hours per week. Across a range of industries, workers are coping with greater workloads and pressures from understaffing. For instance, teachers report their class sizes are larger, paramedics have more acute cases to deal with in each shift and public sector workers have more work and less time to do it in due to understaffing. Across the board, people are managed to expect and accept high levels of stress (Pocock 2003).

A **culture of long hours** was once the burden of manual and low-skilled jobs, but in recent decades it is professionals and managers who are working longer than a standard week (Pocock 2003). A culture of long working hours has a number of implications for gender relations and families. It reinforces the traditional male worker/female carer model. The result is that women are economically vulnerable, especially in the event of separation, and men are likely to lose intimate relationships with children and extended family if there is separation because they have not been able to play an active role in their daily lives. A culture of long working hours takes men away from families and it also makes it difficult for women with children to compete for recognition and promotion when they are compared to workers who do not have childcare responsibilities (Pocock 2003). As Barbara Pocock (2003) argues, long working hours are hostile to most forms of care that require time, predictability and energy.

Even though large numbers of mothers are in the paid labour market, Australian government policies over the last few decades have provided limited support for them. Maternity leave was not mandatory and the campaign for paid maternity leave by the Human Rights and Equal Opportunity Commission in 2007 failed to win the support of the former Howard government. Currently two thirds of women have no access to paid maternity leave and paid paternity leave for men or parental leave is even less available.

Workplaces are developing family-friendly policies but these often unintentionally reinforce traditional gendered expectations about work and care. It is mostly women who use family-friendly policies, despite the gender neutrality of the naming of these policies. Family-friendly policies include more flexible start and finish times for work, parental leave, part-time work and working from home arrangements. Connell (2005a) found in research in ten different public sector sites that it was largely women who make use of these policies, even though they are available to men. In their interviews with workers, it emerged that making use of these policies is generally perceived as a bad career move, even though it is a legitimate option in the policy framework established by these workplaces.

Smithson and Stokoe (2005) have argued that seemingly neutral 'work/ life balance' policies can entrench gender inequalities. On face value, work/life issues do not seem like gender equity issues given that employees make a choice as to whether they will make use of them and no 'sex discrimination' as such is involved (Connell 2005a). However, as Connell contends, they become gender equity issues when considered in the context of the relationship between work and home. Parents with children to collect from school, family dinners to cook and doctor's appointments to keep are not free to be available at short notice in a crisis or work the long hours that are often considered necessary to advancing up the career ladder. The ideal worker is thus still modelled on the breadwinner ideal from the middle of last century, as someone who has a person at home to take care of household and domestic needs. Connell argues that until men and women feel equally free to make use of these policies legitimately in their career interests, we do not really have gender equity.

Family-friendly policy in the European Union

The recognition that people need assistance to reconcile care and employment responsibilities has emerged in all Western countries and particularly in Europe. There is a widespread policy concern to raise employment rates in the context of the decline of the male breadwinner model and the ascendency of the dual-earner and single parent family (Fagan 2003). The major family-friendly policy initiatives that have been suggested are:

- Part-time work (including the right for workers to request an adjustment between full-time and part-time hours)
- Family leave and sabbaticals
- Flexi-time and other forms of 'time accounts'
- Compressed working weeks
- Term-time working

- Job sharing
- Tele-working
- Flexible retirement schemes
- Childcare support (Fagan 2003, p. 5).

Part-time work has been the major way that mothers have sought to combine work and family in Australia. The other policy initiatives are only available in a minority of workplaces and have been described as 'patchy' by the OECD (2002).

Domestic labour

As discussed in Chapter 2, with the development of industrialisation women were encouraged to become domestic specialists, undertake all inside domestic labour tasks and manage the emotional landscape of the family. These areas of specialisation came to be so strongly associated with the female role that caring for children, husbands and the home was seen as a 'natural' vocation for women.

With the development of the second wave of feminism, domesticity and the work of the housewife was radically critiqued and feminist sociologists such as Anne Oakley (1974) played a major role in making domestic labour visible as a form of labour that could be analysed just as paid labour was. Despite feminist analysis and critique of the allocation of unpaid domestic labour, change in unpaid work has been less rapid than in the sphere of paid work. More women than men engage in 'double burden' or 'second shift' of undertaking paid labour at work and then coming home to do a second shift of domestic labour (Hochschild 1989).

In Australia, scholarship on domestic labour is highly developed due to the existence of high quality sources of data. We have access to detailed housework longitudinal survey data such as Household Income and Labour Dynamics in Australia (HILDA) and time-use survey data is collected by ABS. It is well substantiated that women in Australia, and other Western countries, continue to do the majority of domestic labour, including childcare. As Pocock (2003) notes, in 1997 women performed nearly twice as much domestic and caring work as men. The average woman completed 33 hours a week of cleaning, shopping and childcare compared to men's 17 hours a week. According to Janeen Baxter (2002), women do three quarters of routine indoor housework tasks and two thirds of childcare tasks. Change in men's contribution to domestic labour has been slow and incremental and does not match the time that women have taken in the paid labour market (Maher et al. 2008). Hook (2006) compared men's unpaid work across 20 countries and found that Australian men's contribution to domestic labour and childcare had risen from 91 minutes in 1974, to 127 minutes per day in 1992.

Domestic labour in Singaporean families

Hing Ai Yun (2004) argues that both class position and ethnic identity shape the organisation of domestic labour in Singapore. The Singaporean state supports traditional family ideology, and new family forms and alternative lifestyles such as cohabitation and divorce are stigmatised. The key traditional family values include the male-headed household and the gendered division of labour, where men are breadwinners and women are homemakers. A man participating in housework upsets traditional norms and the culturally acceptable balance of power between husbands and wives.

For example, Ted was taught by his mother that his wife's duty was to care for all his needs. When his wife Isabel fractured her hand he began to 'help' with the domestic labour. However he still holds strong views about holding more power than his wife.

> As a man in the family, I am the head of the family. Even though Isabel is working, she is earning less than I am. Even if she is earning more than I do, I still cannot accept her having more power than I do. A man has to have pride, it is very demeaning for the husband to have less power than his wife (Ai Yun 2004, p. 387).

By contrast nearly all of the successful professional Singaporean women interviewed by Ann Brooks (2006) had part-time or live in maids to undertake domestic labour and childcare for them. This meant that many struggles between husbands and wives over contribution to domestic labour and childcare were avoided. Active participation by a husband was regarded as having novelty value (Brooks 2006). As a professor of medicine explains:

> She is a marvellous person and has worked for us for twenty years. She was my sister's domestic helper in the Philippines, and when my sister left for the United States she came to work for us. She was the nanny, she was the housekeeper, I trust her completely (Brooks 2006, p. 103).

'The stalled revolution'

AMERICAN SOCIOLOGIST ARLIE HOCHSCHILD COINED the phrase '**the stalled revolution**' in 1989, to summarise the considerable evidence at that time that as women moved into the paid workforce, men were failing to pick up the baton at home with domestic labour and childcare. There has been gradual change over the last couple of decades. Bittman and Pixley (1997) found that in the mid 1990s women were spending less time on some household tasks such as ironing, yet most of the observed changes in the amount of domestic labour women do have come about because women themselves have reduced the amount of time they spend on tasks rather than redistributing them. Either they outsource tasks like cleaning and ironing and pay others to do them, or they simply don't do them. Women use a range of strategies to lower the amount of domestic labour they undertake such as contracting out tasks, lowering their standards and taking shortcuts (Pocock 2003 p. 126). In other words, many women have turned to the market rather than their partners for help.

Groups of men known to do more than the usual amount of domestic work are divorced or separated men, single fathers and elderly men caring for their frail wives. The presence or absence of a spouse or partner can actually predict the amount of domestic work a man is likely to do and in general men who have wives or partners living with them do the least amount of domestic work (de Vaus 2004, Baxter et al. 2007).

The following table and graph show the extent to which inequities persist in the domestic and total labour burden carried by women.

Table 10.1: Hours per day on domestic work by family/life stage, gender and workforce participation (primary and secondary activities)

	Employed full time		Employed part time		Not employed	
Hours: domestic	Male	Female	Male	Female	Male	Female
Couple only < 35	1.2	1.9		2.2	1.0	
Lone person < 35	1.0	1.5	1.4		1.8	2.2
Couple, dependent children	1.5	2.7	1.3	3.3	1.6	3.8
Lone parent, dependent children		2.4		3.0	1.0	3.6
Couple only 35–64	1.8	2.6		4.0	2.8	4.6
Couple, non dependent children only	1.1	2.2		3.9	2.7	4.4
Lone parent, non dependent children only	1.0	1.8			3.1	4.0
Couple only > 64					3.0	4.2
Lone person > 64					3.4	3.6
Total	1.4	2.3	1.5	3.3	2.5	3.9

Source: 1997 Time Use Survey (Australian Bureau of Statistics, reproduced from de Vaus 2004)

Blanks = too few cases

The table illustrates that no matter whether they are employed full time, part-time or not in the labour force, women consistently do more hours of domestic labour per day than men. This pattern can be seen to carry through across various family configurations and stages in the life course. More recent evidence shows substantial variation in domestic labour across different types of couple households, though women do more than men in all household types. Baxter and colleagues (2007) found that in couple households, on average, women report spending 18 hours on housework in comparison to men, who report spending just below seven hours a week. The gender gap is the smallest where men are retired and women are employed full-time (women do two hours more than their partners). In households where both the women and men are employed full-time, women spend eight hours more on housework. In households where men are employed full-time and women do home duties, the gap is the highest at 23 hours (Baxter et al. 2007).

The gendered pattern is illustrated further by the graph below, which shows that women do substantially more unpaid labour and total labour than men over the course of a week.

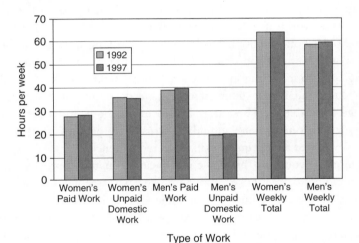

Figure 10.3: Women's and Men's Paid and Unpaid Hours of Work Per Week

Soure: Pocock 2003, p. 24

'Juggling' and 'emotion work' as invisible forms of women's labour

HOUSEWORK IS USUALLY THOUGHT OF as physical tasks such as cleaning, washing, cooking, and ensuring children are fed, clothed and changed. It is relatively straightforward to count how many hours are spent on these tasks using time-use diaries or asking people to estimate their hours spent on household labour. However, quantitative studies are not very good at capturing the complexity of the work associated with maintaining households.

There is a whole other layer of invisible labour involved that is difficult to quantify. Women are generally the ones who coordinate household schedules and are generally held responsible for managing the relationship between the household and the workplace. Many women use the word '**juggling**' to describe this complex management role. It involves not just doing the tasks but thinking ahead about what will need to be done tomorrow or next week. Coordinating children's schedules, making sure there is something to cook for dinner, remembering appointments and finding time for them, these are all examples of the coordination tasks that affect the interface between paid work and home life that tend to fall to women.

When men talk about their paid work, they don't tend to discuss fitting it in around children's routines or household schedules. They just don't see themselves as responsible in the same way as women tend to. Men tend to be 'helpers' who pitch in, leaving in many instances the identification and organisation of the domestic work load to women. In other words, women have to do the delegating.

'**Emotion work**' was a term coined by the American Sociologist Arlie Hochschild in her book *The Managed Heart* (1983). It is a term that has been applied to the world of paid work as well as domestic labour. In the context of household labour, emotion work describes looking after the feelings and emotional well-being of household members. For instance, making sure everyone is feeling OK, coordinating everyone's routines, keeping track of social events and schedules and feeling guilty if other's needs aren't put first. Sociologists encourage us to think of these tasks as a form of labour, and a form of labour that largely falls on women's shoulders. Organising people's routines, making sure they're looked after requires skill, time and patience.

Emotion work also has a second meaning in the context of domestic labour. Sociologists have talked about it as the work people do themselves to bring their emotions into line with an unpleasant reality. We can see evidence of this in the following quotations from Meg Carter's study, where women's desire to teach fairness to their children about domestic labour conflicted with the ideas of some men and some children that doing all the housework is 'the mum job' (Carter 2003). The women then found themselves trying to find a way to cope with the frustration of this by managing their emotional responses to the situation.

> We don't argue or disagree but we certainly differ. I can't be bothered with the hassle of trying to get the kids to do the housework. I'm happy with it the way it is. She can do it well and I'm happy for her to do it (Phillip Riley, 49, Carter 2003, p. 5).

> My voice becomes part of the wall. They don't hear it any more. It's easier not to pay attention to it [making husband and kids do housework], I get too stressed. Sometimes I do think about fairness and it gets me really angry,

so it's better for me not to think about it. I need to learn anger management. If the children expect me to do something and they say 'mum, it's your job', how do I manage that? (Angela Riley, 49, Carter 2003, p. 5).

Domestic labour and fairness

THESE DAYS MOST MEN AND women hold broadly egalitarian views but there is a large gap between beliefs and behaviour when it comes to actually doing domestic labour. For instance, in the 2001 HILDA survey, over 90 per cent of women and 80 per cent of men agreed housework and childcare should be shared equally when both partners worked full time (de Vaus 2004). However, the actual patterns of sharing were nothing like that. The sharing couples were actually in the minority, and many women were actually outsourcing the domestic labour in the so-called sharing couples.

This mismatch between 'equality talk' and the reality of unequal sharing of domestic work was noted by Bittman and Pixley in their book, *The Double Life of the Family* (1997). Bittman and Pixley coined the phrase '**pseudo-mutuality**' to describe the strategies men and women use to cover up the fact that there is a contradiction between ideologies of mutuality and actual practices. Pseudo-mutuality can be defined as the 'ideological embracing of mutuality without any adoption of mutual practices'. In other words, you don't reform the practice, you change the definition of the situation so the inequality becomes justified. Where pseudo-mutuality exists, men tend to minimise what their partners do around the house with statements such as 'women think cleaning toilets is 70 per cent of the housework' or inflate their own contributions. Women may express gratitude that their partners help at all rather than choosing to dwell on the unequal burden of labour. In other words, maintaining the semblance of equality between themselves and their partners may become a form of 'emotion work' that women do.

There is some evidence that the burden of doing most of the domestic labour but presenting your relationship as equal has intensified for Generation X couples. Generation X are typically defined as those born between 1968 and 1979. This generation is significant because they grew up during an era of rapid change in family life and became adults after the influence of second-wave feminism. Most are in their prime childbearing years now. The women in Maher and Singleton's study of young couples were acutely aware that their relationships should appear to be equal but struggled to achieve this in practice. Maher and Singleton (2003) suggest that ideals have changed much more substantially than practice in the area of domestic labour and observed that young women were very keen to present their partners as equal participants in housework despite the evident contradictions. For example, Rachel said, 'We share the cooking. We decide what to cook and then I cook it' (Maher & Singleton 2003, p. 73) and Lucy stated, 'I wouldn't want to give a bad opinion of Marcus' after describing their housework arrangements (Maher & Singleton 2003, p. 73).

To further complicate the picture, it's also true to say that many couples do not equate equal time spent on housework with the fairness of their arrangements. Both Australian and overseas studies indicate that about three quarters of women are satisfied with an unequal division of domestic labour between themselves and their male partners, in which they do more of the childcare and household labour and regard this as to some extent fair. The 2001 HILDA survey gathered information from both partners in households that contained a couple about whether or not they thought they did their fair share of the housework. On average, couples estimated that she did 15.1 hours of domestic work and childcare per week more than he did. At the same time there was clear evidence of a gender gap in terms of what is perceived as fair (de Vaus 2004).

Table 10.2: Feelings about fairness of domestic work distribution by gender, couples only, 2001

	Males %	Females %
I do *much more* than my fair share	6.7	32.0
I do a *bit more* than my fair share	9.8	24.2
I do my fair share	60.2	39.8
I do a *bit less* than my fair share	18.5	2.7
I do *much less* than my fair share	4.7	1.4
N	3850	4226

Source: HILDA, 2001 FaCS (2002) reprinted in de Vaus 2004, p. 287

Bittman and Pixley (1997) showed that the typical Australian couple is one in which it is regarded as fair for the female partner to do between 10.6 and 13.6 hours more domestic work per week than the male partner does. The fact that the male partner may spend more hours in paid work can only partly explain these perceptions of fairness (Craig 2006). This is because the pattern held for women employed full time, women employed part time and women who are not employed all. They all do much more housework than their male partners. Women in each category do more total labour hours than men per week.

- -

Explaining inequality

To SUMMARISE THE ABOVE, ALTHOUGH there has been some convergence in the paid and unpaid working lives of women and men in recent years, gender inequality persists. Sociologists have developed several theories to explain why this is the case.

Preference theory (Hakim)

ONE THEORY THAT HAS BEEN advanced to explain persistent gender inequality in public and private is **preference theory**. British sociologist Catherine Hakim (2000) has advanced this theory, which has been popular and influential with conservative family social policy-makers such as the previous Australian Prime Minister, John Howard. Hakim (2000) analyses labour market and care outcomes through personal types and preferences. She argues that women fall largely into three distinctive types of people. 'Home-centred' women mostly wanting to stay at home with their young children and do most of the domestic work. By contrast 'work-centred' women are very focused on careers, and the third type is 'adaptives' who choose to combine the two. Hakim (2000) argues that government policies should support all three types of women, but particularly home-centred women whom she sees as having been ignored in the push to get women into the paid workforce.

Hakim has been quite extensively criticised by feminist sociologists. First, her argument fails to look at how cultural values, gendered beliefs, government institutions and policies influence the choices people are able to make. Also, we would expect more women to think they did their fair share of housework rather than too much if her theory was correct and we know that only about 40 per cent of women believe this. Furthermore, Pocock (2003) criticises Hakim for emphasising types of women as if these types are stable for each woman over her entire adult life course. The theory does not capture the very dynamic nature of transitions into and out of the workforce by the same women over a period of time. For Pocock, it is far better to understand and cater to the fact that many women will experience within their lifetime a number of transitions into and out of the workforce. Pocock (2003) argues that we need to facilitate smooth family life and career-enhancing transitions into and out of the workforce, rather than focus on the preferences of static types of women.

'Doing gender'

ANOTHER EXPLANATION CONCERNS THE PERFORMANCE of gender identity through domestic labour (West & Zimmerman 1987). Berk (1985) has argued that the home is a 'gender factory' where we perform or enact gender through our everyday activities. The way we behave is influenced by our beliefs about gender-appropriate behaviour (Berk 1985). This may explain some of men's resistance to undertake housework if it is experienced as emasculating and it may explain women's apparent reluctance to give up domestic labour. The idea that gender is enacted through housework makes sense of the fact that Australian women who earn much more than their husbands also tend to do more housework.

This can be viewed as evidence of '**doing gender**'. High-earning women have to do housework to recuperate a sense of appropriate femininity (Bittman et al. 2003).

Unstable 'work/care regimes'

Pocock (2003) proposes that Australians' working life and caring life takes place within a complex social, cultural and institutional situation—or '**work/care order**'. We must understand how the various components intersect in order to come up with workable solutions. The work/care order is the larger economic and social context in which a set of institutions, values and behaviours play themselves out.

Work/care regimes operate within the larger work/care order and comprise the interplay between three main factors (Pocock 2003). The first is dominant cultural values or taken-for-granted beliefs about men, women and work: for instance what we believe is a 'proper' mother, 'proper' father or 'proper' worker. The second component of work/care regimes are institutions that shape what we do and where we do it in terms of family and work life, for instance, industrial laws, labour markets, childcare institutions, schools, workplace entitlements and government payments. Finally the third component Pocock believes is important is individual behaviour and preference, whether or not we want to do paid or unpaid work, how much we want to do and how we do it and how we care for our children. These three components overlap and interlock and cannot be viewed in isolation from each other.

Pocock (2003) attributes the continuing gender inequity and the increasing stress of contemporary family life to the fact that our work regimes are unstable in several ways. In the first place, there is a mismatch between behaviour and preferences, or in other words, what people do and what people want, and a mismatch between institutions and values. For instance, women's labour market behaviour has changed considerably and as a result, work itself has changed. However, our social institutions such as labour laws and workplace structures have channelled much of women's labour effort into insecure part-time or full-time jobs, without turning their attention to domestic labour or attempting to dismantle workplace roles that assume single workers who have no caring responsibilities.

Pocock's (2003) argument is that we need to change our values, institutions, and behaviour alongside preferences to achieve shared work/care goals. If institutions and values don't change then it is difficult for behaviours and preferences to change or be accommodated. In other words, institutions and culture need to genuinely reflect men's and women's identities as carer/workers. Both Pocock (2003) and Connell (2005) see a large role for institutions, notably government institutions, in this.

Domestic labour in shared households

Kristin Natalier's (2003) Australian research with young men living together in single-sex shared households also indicates that domestic activities are imbued with gendered significance beyond the heterosexual relational context. In other words, the 'slackness' that characterises the intersection between masculinity and housework among heterosexual couples persists in the absence of a cohabiting heterosexual couple relationship. The men in the shared households talked in similar ways to husbands in heterosexual relationships. They talked about opting in to housework when they felt like it rather than taking responsibility for it. As Jeremy, one of the study participants explains:

> We get around to it but yeah, it takes a while. We go 'nah' and leave it. We just get noodles up the road and if the plastic [container] lies around, it's not a hassle because it will get done when we're up for it (Natalier 2003, p. 260).

The men tended to give domestic labour a low priority in comparison to other work or leisure activities and 'consistently disengage from any systematic involvement in housework' (Natalier 2003 p. 265) Natalier concludes that 'these men behave as though they are husbands even in the absence of women who might act as wives' (Natalier 2003, p. 265).

Challenging dominant understandings about families and labour

THE DOMINANT MODE OF ANALYSING domestic labour in heterosexual relationships has been to focus on the persistence of gender inequality within the home and the relatively large gap in the amount of domestic labour men do in comparison with women. By contrast Oriel Sullivan (2006) compares time-use data from different countries (Canada, USA, UK, Netherlands, Norway and Finland) and argues that we should take the consistent change in gender patterns more seriously. Sullivan compares unpaid labour tasks from the 1960s to the 1990s and finds that the time that women devote to cooking, cleaning and clothes care has dropped by just under an hour a day during this period and there has been an increase of around 20 minutes that men devote to these core household tasks. '*Both* the upward trend for men and the downward trend for women in the core domestic tasks are consistent in direction across different countries and statistically significant when controlling for other relevant variables' (Sullivan 2006, p. 58). Sullivan's argument for change and plurality in domestic labour arrangements is reinforced by changing time-use patterns coinciding with change in the discursive context, including attitudes, language and symbolic representations over successive generations (Sullivan 2006, p. 39). Australian research on time-use over a shorter time-frame has found that men's childcare time is increasing, which suggests that men are moving into take up caring labour within the home (Craig 2006; Baxter 2002). Perhaps more qualitative research on the new ways that families are interacting with the labour market will provide a clear picture on how contemporary families are managing work and care (Maher et al. 2008).

The idea that housework and childcare should be regarded as primarily *labour* has become the dominant understanding in sociological and many feminist accounts of domestic tasks. However doing these tasks within the home may well be linked to pleasure, love, care and the production of meaning. These aspects of family life are underplayed in much of the sociological literature. For example, it is only relatively recently that the emotional experiences inherent in family life are being taken seriously by sociologists (Smart 2007).

Johnson and Lloyd (2004), in their historical analysis of Australian housewives in the 1940s and 1950s, challenge dominant understandings of what the housewife represents. They argue that rejecting the figure of the housewife was central to the development of second-wave feminism, which was important for rationalising women's entry into the paid labour market but has had the negative effect of limiting our analysis of the domestic sphere and contemporary selfhood. 'The individual unrestrained by private or domestic responsibilities, and possessing a rational mind freed from the distorting effects of the emotions and needs of the body, represents values and characteristics historically associated with masculinity' (Johnson & Lloyd 2004, p. 155). Instead, Johnson and Lloyd say we need to recognise a situated self: 'selfhood is formed precisely by a robust engagement with the social relationships of everyday existence, including those of domestic life' (Johnson & Lloyd 2004, p. 156). They argue that through making a home, developing rituals and daily practices, individuals are creating meaningful lives for themselves (Johnson & Lloyd 2004).

Domestic labour arrangements in lesbian and gay relationships

RESEARCH INTO DIVISIONS OF HOUSEHOLD labour in lesbian couple and single sex households indicate that gender and sexuality are implicated in complex ways in enactments and perceptions of domestic labour. Some researchers foreground sexuality in their analyses and others maintain gender is more important.

English researcher Gillian Dunne (1998) argues that an important dimension of understanding the gendered division of household labour is looking at the gender of the partner. In Dunne's research with coupled lesbian parents, she found each member of the cohabiting couple will often alternate between periods of full-time work and primary care, or each work part time in order to financially support the family (Dunne 1997, 1998, 1999). Dunne (1999) emphasises it is the lack of 'gendered scripts' in lesbian relationships that leads to greater egalitarianism in the sharing of economic resources, and domestic duties including child-rearing. Occupying the same position in the gender order gave the women in Dunne's study the space to make flexible and egalitarian arrangements. As Dolly, one of the participants, explained:

> I suppose because our relationship doesn't fit into a social norm, there are no pre-sex indications of how our relationship should work. We have to work it out for ourselves. We've no role models in terms of how we divide our duties, so we've got to work it out afresh as to what suits us ... We try very hard to be just to each other and ... not exploit the other person (Dunne 1999, p. 73).

In line with Dunne, other USA and UK research studies based on self-report data collected from lesbian parents also support relative equity in divisions of paid and unpaid labour between birth and non-birth mothers (see Reimann 1997; Dalton & Bielby 2000).

In gay men's relationships it has been found that personal resources had an impact on the division of domestic labour. Men who were older or wealthier tended to have more power and undertake fewer domestic tasks than their partners (Peplau & Fingerhut 2006).

> By contrast in lesbian relationships it is argued that partners feel uncomfortable with one partner dominating in their relationships and links between resources and domestic labour are less clear cut (Peplau & Fingerhut 2006).

However, to complicate these findings, others claim that the gender equity finding among same-sex couples may be more an artefact of the self-report interview or questionnaire as the main method of data collection. Christopher Carrington (1999) was able to live in with the North American lesbian and gay male couples in his study and thus base his findings on observational fieldwork and informal chats as well as more formal interviews with the couples. Carrington found that many lesbians employed in time-consuming, rewarding and challenging paid work did far less domestic work than their partners and expressed guilt about this as it deviated from their own expectations of egalitarianism. The partners, in turn, often tried to conceal the disparity and recuperate the semblance of egalitarianism by giving their work-focused mate credit for household tasks they did not perform. With regard to the gay male couples, Carrington found each partner was keen to emphasise his position of dominance in household decision-making, and reluctant to say he even cared very much about housework. In Carrington's view, 'doing gender' is more evident in the story told by these couples rather than their actual division of labour. His controversial contention is that lesbian couples perceive that two women living together should be more egalitarian than a heterosexual couple, and therefore have investments in presenting themselves as egalitarian to researchers. By contrast, gay male couples do gender in the sense that seeming to care too much about domestic labour is inappropriate, a conventionally masculine response.

Conclusion

WHEN WE EXAMINE THE WAYS in which families divide labour within their boundaries we see both remarkable change and remarkable continuity. Women have entered the paid labour market in huge numbers but men have been slow to take up domestic labour at home. Gender remains the most significant predictor of who will do domestic labour within all household types, including, it seems, shared households and gay and lesbian families. Women's and men's paid work trajectories are becoming more similar but it is unlikely that we will end up with a gender neutral worker. To achieve gender equality in both paid and unpaid labour, we need policy change by governments and workplaces and we may need to challenge the very constitution of our identities as women and men—so that mothers can earn money and fathers can care without guilt.

Key concepts
Family wage
Dual-earner family model
Culture of long hours
The stalled revolution
Juggling
Emotion work
Pseudo-mutuality
Preference theory
Doing gender
Work/care order
Work/care regimes

Discussion questions

1   Should parents be encouraged to work part-time as a way of managing the demands of paid and unpaid labour? Does it offer the best of both worlds or the worst?

2   What is a 'work/care regime'? According to Pocock, what are the main work/care regimes that characterise Australian society? Do you agree?

3   What is 'emotion work'? How useful is it in explaining gender disparities in domestic labour?

4   How men and women engage with unpaid or paid work is often framed with regard to 'choices' or 'preferences'. What are some of the broader social, economic or cultural factors that influence the choices we make?

5   What is 'doing gender'? How is doing gender relevant to the domestic labour debates?

Recommended further reading

Ai Yun, H. 2004, 'Ideology and Changing Family Arrangements in Singapore', *Journal of Comparative Family Studies*, 35 375–92.

Carter, M. 2003, '"It's Easier Just to do it All Myself": Emotion Work and Domestic Labour', paper presented at the *2003 TASA Conference*, University of New England, 4–6 December.

Dunne, G. 1999, 'What Difference Does Difference Make? Lesbian Experience of Work and Family Life', in J. Seymour & P. Bagguley (eds) *Relating Intimacies: Power and Resistance*, Macmillan, Basingstoke.

Hochschild, A.R. 1989, *The Second Shift: Working Parents and the Revolution at Home*, University of California Press, Berkley and Los Angeles, California.

Sullivan, O. 2006, *Changing Gender Relations, Changing Families: Tracing the Pace of Change over Time*, Rowman and Littlefield Publishers, Lanham USA.

11 | Separation, Divorce and Reconstituted Families

Figure 11.1: Divorce Reconfigures Family Life

In the event of divorce, and regardless of my private feelings about you, I promise I will always maintain a united front to our children. I promise never to use them, or arrangements involving them, as a weapon to get to you ... I solemnly promise to do this even if I think you are a philandering bastard/faithless bitch and I find myself rueing the day I first set eyes on you. I also promise to compromise about money, recognising that, in protracted rows about money, the only winners will be our respective lawyers.

Porter 2002, p.17

Introduction

IN THE NEWSPAPER EXCERPT QUOTED above, Liz Porter half-humorously argues that before couples marry they should be given preparation for divorce alongside preparation for marriage. This would enable them to avoid the bitter and attenuated battles over money and children that are viewed as an 'almost normal by-product of divorce' in Australia. When couples divorce, the organisation of love and care and the organisation of labour and resources within a family must be radically reconfigured. Moreover, most divorces are extremely painful personal experiences that have important social ramifications for the adults and children involved.

In this chapter we describe the rise of divorce in Western countries and the ways in which divorce reshapes families. We discuss what Beck-Gernsheim (2002) calls the '**normalisation of divorce**', where divorce is no longer a heavily stigmatised transition. We examine the broader social conditions that now support high divorce rates and then give an overview of the impact of divorce on fathers, mothers and children. We finish the chapter with a discussion of step- or **divorce-extended families**.

Divorce rates: Change and continuity

IN THE EARLY 1900S IN Australia, divorce was a rare experience. In the first decade of the twentieth century the number of divorces recorded each year fluctuated between 300 and 400. The crude divorce rate or number of divorces per 1000 residents rose slightly in the 1920s up to the mid 1940s, peaking in 1947 at 1.1. The number of divorces recorded in 1947 was 8705, or the highest it had been at any previous time during the first half of the twentieth century. This is believed to reflect the instability of wartime marriages (often entered into very quickly before the men went away to fight) and the disruptive effects of the war on marriage (Weston & Qu 2006). Gilding (1997) notes that the development of an Australian sociology of the family was strongly linked to post–World War II anxiety over levels of divorce.

The divorce rate fell in the early 1960s. By the early 1970s it began to rise again, spiking in 1975, which was the year 'no fault divorce' was introduced in Australia. The *Family Law Act 1975* allowed couples to divorce after 12 months of separation rather than having to prove why they needed a divorce. In 1976 the divorce rate peaked at 4.5 divorces per 1000 residents, the rate then dropped to 2.5 by 1985 and has remained relatively steady at between 2.5–2.9 per 1000 residents (Baxter, Hewitt & Western 2007). In 2006 the crude divorce rate was 2.5 per 1000 residents (ABS 2007a).

There are three divorce trends worth noting that have occurred over the last decade or so. First, just as people are marrying later, people are tending to divorce when they are older—in 2006 most of the males divorcing were in the 40–44 age group and most of the females divorcing were in the 35–39 age group. Second, the duration of marriage before divorce is increasing; the average length of marriage at divorce in 2006 was 8.9 years (ABS 2007a). Third, the number of divorces involving children is declining, down from 59 per cent in 1986, to 50 per cent in 2006, as illustrated in the graph (below).

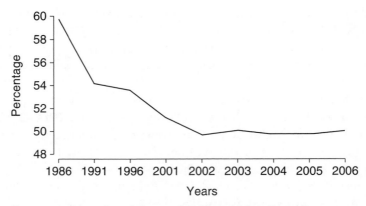

Figure 11.2: Proportion of divorces involving children, Australia

Source: ABS (2007a) *Divorces Australia 2006*, cat. no. 3307.0.55.001

Historically, women tend to initiate divorce more often than men but the pattern of lodging applications for divorce (or initiating divorce) is slowly changing. In 2006 more women (40.0 per cent) than men (29.5 per cent) lodged applications for divorce, but the number of joint applications for divorce has been increasing over time. In 2006, 30.3 per cent of divorces resulted from joint applications, up from 28.5 per cent in 2005, 21.5 per cent in 1996 and 7.4 per cent in 1986 (ABS 2007a).

Estimates of how many of today's marriages in Australia are likely to end in divorce vary according to the data and assumptions used. It has been estimated that between 32 per cent and 50 per cent of Australian marriages are likely to end in divorce. In 2000 the ABS demography newsletter stated that 46 per cent of marriages were likely to end in divorce (ABS 2000) while others estimate that 32 per cent of marriages will end in divorce (Hewitt et al. 2005). The latest estimate from the ABS is that 33 per cent of marriages entered into in 2001–2002 will end in divorce (ABS 2007d). As discussed in Chapter 6, fewer people are marrying and more are cohabiting, which has an impact on the divorce rate. It is reasonable to argue that divorce and separation from a long-term relationship will remain a common, but not a majority, experience in years to come.

Changes in the institutional basis of marriage

SINCE THE 1970S, FAMILY SOCIOLOGISTS have begun to document the massive change that has taken place in the institutional basis of marriage (Gilding 1997; Beck-Gernsheim 2002). Prior to the 1970s people had taken-for-granted expectations about the desirability of marriage and the behaviour and aspirations of husbands and wives. In this context, divorce was very much stigmatised. Over the last four decades these expectations and the associated social support for marriage has been undermined. The broader social conditions consistent with late modernity such as industrialisation, urbanisation and secularisation have radically changed society. Institutions such as the state, politics and the law have been forced to change as people sought divorce in growing numbers from the 1970s onwards.

According to Beck-Gernsheim there is now a tacit 'normalisation of divorce', in the sense that divorce is no longer socially unacceptable. Everyone who is married today knows there is a way out of their marriage and an alternative to it. This means that increasingly, marriage is under pressure to justify itself. A marriage needs to prove itself to be not just 'bearable' but 'better than a whole horizon of alternatives'. The pressure to justify a marriage or relationship means our standards of happiness are higher so the more our marriages appear inadequate and the more willing we are to contemplate divorce (Beck-Gernsheim 2002). For Beck-Gernsheim, low commitment to marriage or relationships or 'living with one foot out the door' is a particularly late-modern experience.

However, Carol Smart (2005) challenges Beck-Gernsheim's claim that the high divorce rate reflects a low commitment to marriage. Smart believes it is important to consider 'commitment' as a multi-dimensional concept involving different layers of commitment not only to the marital partner, but to relationships with extended kin and children of the marriage. Although divorce signals an end to the romantic and sexual commitment of the couple, this leaves open the question of how the commitments to children of the marriage or in-laws are reconceptualised in the post-divorce relational context. Smart's argument is that divorce reconfigures rather than severs the commitments of marriage.

Some research in the USA has found two distinct groups of people who divorce: those from traditional high-distress relationships (about half of couples divorcing) experiencing high levels of conflict or abuse and an emerging category of divorcees from low-distress relationships who report little conflict, moderate happiness but low commitment to their relationship (Amato & Hohmann-Marriot 2007). Family sociologists in the West have noted that people now have higher expectations about personal growth and self-actualisation from marriage. In addition, contemporary wives expect higher levels of gender equity and fairness in their marriages than previous generations. 'All things being equal, as people's expectations for marriage increase, an increasing number of people will be unsatisfied with their marriages' (Amato & Hohmann-Marriot 2007, p. 623). As the barriers to divorce have substantially weakened, couples in average—not just low—quality marriages may seek happiness alone or in new relationships. Change in social climate encourages a snowball effect. As more people divorce, social stigma is reduced and the chance of re-partnering increases because there are more men and women available on the marriage market. As the social costs of divorce diminish, more people consider it as a new life stage (Beck-Gernsheim 2002).

Causes of divorce

THE CAUSES OF DIVORCE ARE multilayered. On the one hand there are the broad demographic shifts and increasing individualisation outlined above. These provide an environment where divorce is seen as a relatively normal experience. On another level there are particular characteristics that are associated with marriage breakdown such as religiosity, ethnic background, cohabitation and birth cohort (Hewitt et al. 2006). Religious women and men are less likely to divorce than non-religious couples. In Australia immigrants from non-English-speaking countries are less likely to divorce than those born in Australia, while immigrants from English-speaking countries are more likely to divorce (Hewitt et al. 2005, 2006). In the USA, the pattern is slightly different and black people are much more likely to divorce than white people. People who cohabit prior to marriage are more likely to divorce than people who do not, perhaps because they have lower levels of commitment to marriage. Finally, your birth cohort or generation has an impact. Middle birth cohorts are more likely to divorce than older cohorts who value the permanence of marriage more. And middle birth cohorts are more likely to divorce than younger cohorts because they have had less time to experience marital disruption (Hewitt et al. 2006). In addition to these characteristics it has also been established that adult children of divorced parents are more likely to divorce themselves and those who marry at younger ages or experience unplanned pregnancies that motivate them to marry are also more likely to divorce (Hewitt et al. 2006; Amato & Hohmann-Marriott 2007). Having step-children in the household and holding liberal family values are also causes of divorce in the USA (Amato & Hohmann-Marriott 2007). There is some evidence that socio-economic factors influence divorce in Australia: it has been found that husbands with high levels of education and higher incomes experience more stable marriages than their peers with lower socio-economic status, whereas wives with higher levels of education are more likely to leave an unsatisfactory marriage than lower-educated women (Hewitt et al. 2005).

There are also factors that operate as constraining factors or barriers to divorce. Having young children and a higher number of children decreases the likelihood of divorce. There is also a body of research on the link between women's increasing financial independence in comparison to their husband's and a higher likelihood of divorce but the findings have been mixed (Hewitt et al. 2006).

Sociologists tend to concentrate on the social/structural characteristics outlined above, however when divorced people themselves are asked their reasons for divorcing, a slightly different picture emerges. The major reason for divorce people identify is infidelity, followed by incompatibility, alcohol or drug use, growing apart, personality problems, lack of communication and physical or mental abuse. Interestingly, men were more likely to report that they did not know why their marriages ended in divorce and women were more likely to report that abuse caused their relationships to end.

Table 11.1: Reported causes of divorce

Category	% Men	% Women
Infidelity	16	25
Incompatible	20	19
Drinking or drug use	5	14
Grew apart	9	10
Personality problems	10	8
Lack of communication	13	6
Physical or mental abuse	0	9
Don't know	9	0
N cases	**77**	**131**

Source: Data summarised from Amato & Previti 2003, p. 615

Divorce parties in Australia and Taiwan

As divorce becomes normalised, the divorce party is a new urban ritual beginning to be celebrated throughout the Western world. Many divorce party internet sites have sprung up in recent years, although little is known to date about how popular divorce parties actually are, and researchers have yet to investigate their content and meaning as celebrations.

In common, descriptions of divorce parties on Australian websites assume the celebrations are for only one member of the divorced couple and their supporters. As such they symbolise divorce as a 'clean break' between the couple, and the family members on each side of the partnership. According to the website divorceparty.com.au, there are many reasons for a man or woman 'untying the knot' to throw a party to mark this event, just as one would with marriage or on the birth of a child. Divorce celebrations are said to be a way to thank the friends and family members who helped the divorcing person through the emotional pain; they may provide a forum to vent anger at the former partner in the presence of a supportive audience; they can serve to tell the world that the divorced person is ready to leave behind the pain or anger of the separation and begin embracing a new stage in life, or, alternatively, friends can throw the party as a way of demonstrating their support for the divorced person at this very difficult time in their lives <http://www.divorceparty.com.au/why_divorce_party_nights_out.html>.

Sociologist Jui-shan Chang (2000) compares these Australian assumptions about divorce parties with those informing the divorce celebrations beginning to be conducted in Taiwan, noting that in Taiwan, as in other Asian industrialised societies, the divorce rate has also been high in recent years. In Taiwan, the divorce celebration takes the form of a multi-course banquet that each member of the divorcing couple attends. The extended family members of each party are invited; indeed, their approval to hold the banquet is sought. Unlike the Australian version, the Taiwanese banquet provides an opportunity for couples to announce their divorce to family members and friends, and to receive best wishes from both sides of the family for mutually beneficial futures post-divorce. In having both parties' families consent to, attend and share in the banquet, the possibility is opened up for a continuing relationship between the two families, although the marital relationship that brought them together has ended.

Each course in the banquet has a name that symbolises different aspects of the marriage, the process of divorce and hopes for the future. For instance, in the specific banquet Chang describes: the first dish was called 'waking up from the dream of a marriage'; the fourth 'all the good memories treasured'; the seventh, 'no regret to have had and ended this marriage'; and the ninth 'say goodbye and take care of each other'. The tenth dish expressed the wish that 'a decent friendship be maintained' (Chang 2000, p. 72).

Chang contends that this way of ritualising divorce is consistent with the traditional Confucian emphasis on marriage as a relationship between two families rather than two individuals. In Taiwan, most young couples seek marriage to a partner their parents approve of and the parents are still the hosts of the wedding. Although divorce can be particularly difficult in a cultural setting that emphasises the value of extended family connections and harmony, this ritual gestures towards the fact that the extended family relationships can potentially survive the individuals' divorce. Chang observes that the public ritual, affirming continuing ties and friendship between the divorcing parties, may have particular benefits for the children of the marriage, in that post-divorce contact with grandparents and other extended kin can proceed much more harmoniously when there is acknowledgment that some family ties continue on rather than 'break up' when a couple divorce. Her implication is that Western cultures could learn a lot about maintaining amicable and harmonious post-divorce relationships from this way of ritualising divorce, particularly when children are involved.

The impact of divorce

DIVORCE IS AN UPHEAVAL THAT involves considerable change for at least some of the family members. Because of this, it is often a painful process, whether or not it is also a relief. Often negative feelings of hurt, bitterness and rage escalate as couples divorce and many continue to experience these feelings intensely more than a decade after their divorce (Hughes 2007).

Divorce requires a re-negotiation of residence, possessions and arrangements for children's care, all of which can be a source of distress. When a couple divorce it is usually the man who moves to another dwelling. The most frequent pattern is that women and children remain behind in the first instance and later on they may move to somewhere cheaper and negotiate new surroundings as well

(Beck-Gernsheim 2002). When couples divorce they must organise a division of property and a division of household items and keepsakes. This can be a particular upheaval not only because it has economic implications for the divorcing couple and their children, but also emotional ones. Dividing possessions that have little monetary value can be a very fraught process because of the symbolic value attached to these possessions, particularly if they were acquired jointly in the context of the relationship (see Smart 2007, p. 168). There are also complex arrangements to be made about children's residence and contact, which generally means that one of the divorcing parties (usually the man) has to come to terms with the fact that he will see the children less often than before.

The impact of divorce may depend on the quality of the marital relationship before divorce. For example, partners who were in high-distress marriages characterised by high levels of conflict experience relief and an increase in happiness after divorce while those in low-conflict marriages experience a decrease in happiness following divorce (Amato & Hohmann-Marriott 2007). Historically in Australia and other Western countries, the tendency has been for mothers to provide the vast majority of care for children after separation and for fathers to discontinue contact and support for their children. However, over the past decade, Australia has moved from an assumption of primary care by one parent to presumptions of shared care and responsibility. To date, highly gendered patterns of care and responsibility within families continue to shape post-divorce family arrangements (Lacroix 2006).

In sum, as family life is re-configured the impact of divorce is experienced differently by fathers, mothers and children. Below we consider what is known about the impact of divorce on different family members.

Impact on fathers

DIVORCE SOMETIMES COMES AS A surprise to husbands. Women are much more likely to initiative divorce than men and men are much more likely to say they 'don't know' why their marriage ended in divorce than women. In general men tend to suffer financially from divorce and many will lose contact with their children.

Mothers' status as primary caregivers to children before divorce generally means the court awards them residential rights to children. The majority of children whose parents have separated or divorced live with their mothers rather than their fathers (87 per cent) (ABS 2006a). After divorce, there are two main patterns when it comes to contact between children and the non-custodial parent. While about 41 per cent of children have contact with the non-resident parent, about 30 per cent of children have no contact with the non-resident parent. The frequency of contact tends to decline further when children age beyond primary school into their teenage years. A secondary analysis of 2001 HILDA data found that 36 per cent of children had almost no contact with their fathers following divorce or separation, and dissatisfaction with the amount of contact tended to be much higher among fathers than mothers (de Vaus 2004, p. 241).

Smart and Neale (1999) argue that pre-divorce fatherhood is poor training for post-divorce parenthood in that fathers tend to have much less involvement in the day-to-day care of children than mothers. Furthermore, fathers' relationships with their children are often mediated by the mothers. This means that the mother may translate children's moods for the father or provide instruction on the emotional and physical needs of children. Following divorce, mothers may be less willing to do this work for fathers who have to create a direct and unmediated relationship with their children.

In Australia there is a child support scheme where the non-custodial parent (usually the father), is required to provide child support or will have money automatically deducted from their pay to the child support agency. Recent Australian research shows that the negative financial impact of divorce continues into old age but this impact is substantially reduced for people who remarry (de Vaus et al. 2007). Indeed divorced men are more likely to re-partner following divorce than women: 44 per cent compared with 29 per cent (Hughes, J. 2007).

The rise of the Fathers' Rights Movement

In the early 1980s, Australian researcher Peter Jordan conducted a study of 168 separated men and found that when women left, the men were often unprepared. The men least aware there was any problem before the break up were the most inclined to seek reconciliation and also more likely to stay distressed. Many men saw themselves as victims and were unwilling to take any responsibility for the break up. When Jordan repeated his study in 1996, including some of the original group of men, the results were very similar. Many of the original group clung to the feelings of bitterness and regret about the failure of their marriage, with a third saying they felt they would never get over the divorce. Divorced men with children felt particularly victimised, socially and financially, in their dealings with the legal system. They had a strong sense of loss in coming to terms with seeing children on a part-time basis.

Figure 11.3: Dads in Distress logo

Research such as Jordan's explains the emergence of the international **Fathers' Rights Movement** throughout the 1990s in a number of Western countries with high divorce rates. Men's advocacy groups have formed in response to the distress and anger that many non-custodial fathers experience through the divorce process. Following divorce, men frequently have less contact with their children and more limited emotional relationships with their children. For instance, 'Dads in Distress' is a support group for Australian men 'whose immediate concern is to stem the present trend of male suicide due to the trauma of divorce or separation'. They offer support services, local meetings and lobby governments on behalf of non-custodial fathers. The story of one of the dads on the website illustrates the high emotions experienced around divorce:

> I'm definitely a dad in distress, I'm, angry, I'm upset, I'm frustrated at a system that seems to forget fathers. We seem to be at the bottom level. I cannot afford to continue fighting through the courts when all my ex seems to do is breach orders time and again and gets a slap on the hand and then goes out and does it again. I have three kids who I adore but I am ready to walk away. There is no justice in this country for fathers going through a divorce (DIDS 2008).

Fathers' rights groups consistently lobbied Australian federal Members of Parliament in the early 2000s in the hope of effecting automatic 50–50 residence-of-children provisions for mothers and fathers in the event of divorce. This initiative received a great deal of endorsement from former Prime Minister, John Howard, who in June 2003 announced an enquiry into 'joint custody'. Changes to the Australian *Family Law Act* were introduced later in 2005. The changes promote shared parenting and shared responsibility for children between divorcing women and men although they stopped short of the initial proposition that children automatically spend equal time post-divorce with each parent (see Caruana 2005).

Many women's groups and researchers voiced concerns about the reforms, particularly for women and children leaving a husband and father due to domestic violence. However, some researchers see the reforms as an opportunity for reshaping the deeply entrenched gender roles in work/care patterns that may have existed prior to divorce.

Impact on mothers

THE IMPACT OF DIVORCE ON mothers is also devastating. Divorce usually means a sharp decline in income for mothers and an increase in childcare responsibilities. Mothers are more likely than fathers to become sole parents following divorce.

As discussed in Chapter 10, women are disadvantaged in the paid labour market because of gendered wage differentials and because women are more likely to take time out to care for children. Moreover, women are more likely than men to work part time or in casual positions. Following divorce, women are in an economically vulnerable position. In addition, as Smart and Neale (1999) argue, women must give up some of their mothering role to allow fathers to build a direct relationship with their children. Women can be anxious about father's capacity to parent when they are not there. Lacroix (2006) examined the experiences of parents in shared care arrangements but found that women continued to take a disproportionate amount of responsibility for caring for their children.

Impact on children

DIVORCE IS USUALLY A PAINFUL event for children but many are resilient and find ways to come to terms with their post-divorce family relationships. A moral panic about the negative impact of divorce on children is relatively easy to ignite and extreme claims about the impact of divorce receive substantial air time in the media in Australia and elsewhere (Lumby & Fine 2006). For example, the qualitative research by Wallerstein and colleagues from the USA presents children from divorced relationships as deeply psychologically troubled individuals who find it difficult to maintain stable relationships (Wallerstein, Lewis & Blakeslee 2000). However, the magnitude and lasting nature of the impact of divorce on children is much more complex than that—divorce is not always bad for all children.

There is a substantial amount of evidence for the negative impact of divorce on children. Children of divorced parents reach adulthood with lower levels of psychological well-being: they show more symptoms of depression and anxiety and have lower levels of self-esteem (Amato 2000). They are also more likely to experience discordant marriages and have a greater likelihood of experiencing divorce themselves. Finally, they tend to have weaker ties to parents, particularly their fathers, in comparison to children with continuously married parents (Amato 2000). Some research in the USA and Australia has found that divorce has a negative impact on educational attainment. One large Australian study found that on average divorce costs children 'seven tenths' of a year of education by reducing secondary school completion (Evans et al. 2001).

However, viewing divorce as a homogenous, overwhelmingly negative experience for children is also a mistake. Some recent research by Paul Amato and colleagues in the United States suggests that the outcomes of divorce for children depend on the nature of the marital relationship prior to divorce (Booth & Amato 2001; Amato & Hohmann-Marriott 2007). Divorce in low-conflict marriages has a strong negative impact on children whereas divorce in high-conflict marriages has a negligible or positive effect on children's well-being. For children whose parents are in high-conflict relationships, divorce may remove them from a stressful and sometimes abusive home environment but for children whose parents were in low-conflict relationships divorce may be experienced as an unexpected, unwelcome and uncontrollable event (Booth & Amato 2001). At the time of divorce most children hope their parents will get back together but this is often a vain hope. They must live with divided loyalties and many are drawn into the divorce battleground. As the dominant pattern is that children reside with their mothers following divorce they frequently lose contact with their father and paternal grandparents (Hughes 2007; Beck-Gernsheim 2002).

However, many children are resilient and learn to manage their feelings and relationships with their parents and new family members. Children must find ways of negotiating different family worlds as they move between the households of the main parent and the weekend parent—often navigating relationships with new partners and children (Beck-Gernsheim 2002). Children and families have mixed experiences of re-configuring family life. Carol Smart outlines both contented and discontented accounts of the outcome of divorce by children. Though the initial divorce was a stressful experience some children view their new family arrangements positively. For example, Jaime (age 13) said, 'I can remember sometimes that I wanted them to get back together, but now I don't want them to get back together in a way because, erm, we are settled and have got a new family and stuff' (Smart 2006, p. 161). Other children spoke about their complex new families and valued the new people in their families who had broadened horizons and provided positive resources. Smart (2006) also describes unhappy divorce narratives where children are caught between parents and have a 'blame' narrative for what has happened to their family life.

Beck-Gernsheim (2002) argues that children whose parents have divorced learn how to end relationships and cope with loss. For these children, divorce is a normal event that needs to be prepared for. They are more likely to take precautions against divorce but paradoxically their relationships are more likely to end in divorce (Beck-Gernsheim 2002). Kate Hughes has undertaken research with members of the first generation of Australian children who experienced their parents' divorce in the 1970s and her findings support the arguments put forward by Beck-Gernsheim (2002). These adults are now aged 27–41 (sometimes known as Generation X) and are establishing their own relationships and households. The majority of participants in this study held the view that 'relationships were about growth' and each relationship is a learning opportunity. As Susan explained, 'Every relationship is different because of the person that you are with and each person you are with brings out the different dimensions in you' (Hughes 2005, p. 75). The idea that 'all relationships end' was a sentiment expressed by most of the participants in Hughes' study. This is expressed succinctly by Steve: 'The thing is that I don't look at relationships as a lasting thing. To me, you're with someone while things are OK and if they get to a point where you don't like it anymore, then you leave' (Hughes 2005, p. 78). Many of the participants expressed a lack of faith in nuclear families providing the best form of domestic and emotional organisation. Instead they pointed to newer family arrangements characterised in the literature as 'families of choice' (Weeks, Heaphy and Donovan 2001), 'the divorce extended family' (Stacey 1990) or 'the post-familial family' (Beck-Gernsheim 2002).

In another paper from the same project, Kate Hughes (2007) examined the contemporary relationship between divorced mothers and their adult children and found that many of these relationships were ambivalent. Separated custodial mothers frequently develop closer relationships with their children than fathers do. The adults in Hughes' study were closer to their mothers than fathers but many expressed an irritation with their mother's inability to manage their feelings about their divorce and some expressed frustration about their mother's emotional immaturity and 'issues'. The experience of having to emotionally support their mothers and the role-reversal that this entails was described by many of the adults. As Alix explains: 'We don't feel we were very effectively parented at all, by any parents, at any time. We feel it how—we were often the grown ups' (Hughes 2007, p. 573). Susan expresses similar sentiments: 'It was probably a bit more difficult with my mother but I guess it's because of what's been going on in her life. I've had to mother her' (Hughes 2007, p. 573).

As sociologists we can make both a positive and a negative interpretation of the implications for family life at a time when divorce has become normal. The positive outcome is that children learn that a full and satisfying life is possible alone and they do not have to depend on the success of a long-term relationship for happiness. On the other hand the negative interpretation is that children of divorce lack security in relationships and ability to deal with conflict and are doomed to repeat their parents' mistakes (Beck-Gernsheim 2002). The normalisation of divorce has both positive and negative outcomes for children.

Step–families/blended families/ reconfigured families/post–divorce families

ESTABLISHING STEP-FAMILIES AFTER DIVORCE entails another radical reconfiguration of domestic life. According to Furstenberg and Cherlin, step-families are 'a curious example of an organisational merger, they join family cultures into a single household' (Furstenberg & Cherlin 1991, p. 83). Everyday rules and routines, and expectations on issues such as pocket money, TV watching and bedtime, have to be negotiated and agreed upon. It is likely there will be clashes in habits and expectations. There must also be negotiation about how various members should interact with each other within the family on trivial and profound issues, such as what to call step-parents, appropriate discipline and so on (Beck-Gernsheim 2002).

Step-families provide an example of new family arrangements where moral decisions must be negotiated on an ongoing basis and family relationships are carried out between households (Smart & Neale 1999). At the same time step-families are also profoundly shaped by broader gender and class relations within society (Ribbens McCarthy, Edwards & Gillies 2003). Mothers continue to be much more likely to retain the main responsibility for caring for children and the overwhelming majority of children living in step-families live with their mother and a step-father (Ribbens McCarthy, Edwards and Gillies 2003).

A step-parent/step-child relationship tends to be 'contingent' rather than 'positional' so that step-parents have to earn their place in the family by finding a way of taking an active and caring role in a child's life (Ribbens McCarthy, Edwards & Gillies 2003). Finch's notion of **displaying families** is useful for understanding this process—that family life is built and confirmed by the actions of participants within them rather than taken-for-granted roles (Finch 2007). Nevertheless gender continues to have an impact and step-mothers and step-fathers are positioned differently. Step-mothers are expected to be 'good mothers' and play a substantial role in caring and taking responsibility for their step-children. By contrast step-fathers occupy a more ambiguous role and their contribution may be limited to financial support (Ribbens McCarthy, Edwards & Gillies 2003).

Ribbens McCarthy, Edwards and Gillies (2003) conducted in-depth interviews with 'step-clusters' in the UK and found that most of the families did not like the term 'step-family' and preferred to see themselves as 'ordinary' families. They found interesting class differences in understandings of step- and biological relationships. Middle-class people were more likely to emphasise the importance of biological relationships in determining emotional relationships whereas working-class people were more likely to emphasise the sustained day-to-day care provided by a step-parent. Working-class step-fathers were more likely to treat step-children as their own and assert no difference between step and biological parenthood. As David, a working-class step-father explained:

> You don't just marry the other partner, you accept their children ... our family is myself and Joyce (wife) and five children, three of them are hers and two of mine, and their shouldn't be no difference between them (Ribbens McCarthy, Edwards & Gillies 2003, p. 86).

By contrast Frank, a middle-class step-father was wary of taking on an effective fathering role;

> I do provide for them on a practical day-to-day basis, but I don't provide for them in a parental loving arrangement. That is something that I couldn't or wouldn't attempt to take away from their father (Ribbens McCarthy, Edwards & Gillies 2003, p. 84).

Clearly step-families are diverse—many mirror nuclear families where fathers are primary breadwinners and mothers are primary carers while others involve complex and more fluid negotiated relationships. Judith Stacey's research on families in post-industrial America in the 1980s, found examples where women were able to turn divorce into a 'kinship resource', by establishing new relationships with ex-spouses' new partners (Stacey 1990, p. 254). Stacey reframes 'step-families' more positively as 'divorce-extended families', claiming it is possible that the divorce-extended family may offer a greater number of people to build relationships with than the isolated nuclear family was ever able to (Stacey 1990).

The normalisation of fragility?

BECK-GERNSHEIM ARGUES THAT THE '**normalisation of fragility**' is what lies ahead for families and relationships in the West. Generations X and Y are likely to experience various family trajectories that include cohabitation, marriage, divorce, more cohabitation and probably remarriage. Marriage is no longer a bond that lasts a lifetime but now a relationship that is maintained only under certain conditions.

There is evidence that young people, especially those whose parents have divorced, try to take precautions against divorce such as delaying and/or avoiding marriage and childbearing. The paradox is that these strategies may reduce the emotional or financial damage following on from divorce but serve to increase the likelihood divorce will occur. For example, when people try to minimise the risk of divorce they reduce the obstacles to separation, and actions that might limit their room to manoeuvre in the future. Two major commitments to be avoided are marriage and childbearing. But there is a snowball effect: if people invest less in a life together (for example by not having children or marrying), there is less to keep the couple together. The less there is to lose, the easier it is for them to separate (Beck-Gernsheim 2002).

Women's increased participation in the labour market is another example of a risk-reduction strategy. The fragility of the family has an effect on the way young women, in particular, now plan their lives. An orientation toward a career and independent income is a sensible precaution in an environment where you cannot rely on marriage as a central life occupation (Beck-Gernsheim 2002). Chris Everingham and colleagues' research on the life orientation of Australian women supports this argument. They found that young women, in contrast to older generations, no longer expected a breadwinner to take care of them and expected that they would need to fit childbearing and family life around their careers (Everingham, Stevenson & Warner-Smith 2007).

In summary, risk-reducing strategies have the paradoxical effect of making divorce more likely even if they reduce the emotional and social damage to individuals. For example, if you don't marry you do not have to go through legal procedures of divorce and if you don't have children you do not have to live as a single parent or make custody arrangements and so on. As Beck-Gernsheim (2002) argues, such precautions tend to work against the stability of the contemporary couple.

Conclusion

DIVORCE HAS BROUGHT GREATER CHANGE and uncertainty to family life than in the 1950s at the height of the nuclear family. However, the novelty of this should not be over-estimated. Looking back one century to a time in which life-expectancy was much lower, we would see the kinds of family changes brought about today by divorce, being created by death. In contemporary Western countries with our long life-expectancies, divorce is re-shaping the family lives of many. It is likely that family fragility will increase. In other words, there will be more instability, more change, more transitions and intermediate family forms (Beck–Gernsheim 2002).

In the post-divorce family it is not just parentage and marriage that determine relationships of care and connectedness. Family relationships must undergo some reordering and renegotiating following divorce. For example, different members of the family may have a different perspective of who is part of their family and who is not. A divorced wife might include her children and ex, children might include mother and father and new partners and step-siblings, a divorced husband may include children, new partner and step-children but not his previous wife. In this process, it is easy to see evidence of what Beck–Gernsheim calls 'the do-it-yourself biography': 'When divorce becomes normal and what used to be called normal starts to crumble at more and more levels, then life is a building site' (Beck–Gernsheim 2002, p. 41). In family life, people have more choices and experience more beginnings and more farewells.

Many post-divorce families are conflict ridden and difficult but there are other examples where people are able to make successful divorce-extended families that offer more support and certainly more family members than isolated nuclear families ever did. Divorce may also carry benefits for social change in gender relations. According to Kinnear (2002), new family arrangements post-divorce may serve to move us more, as a society, toward genuinely gender-neutral parenting. In this view, as fathers become more vocal about their desire to become more active and involved parents, they will be under greater pressure to demonstrate their capacity to follow these demands with action. They will need to demonstrate a willingness to trade paid work and financial considerations for the daily work of children's care, on a par with the caring labour mothers currently perform. Mothers may also be challenged to relinquish care as their prerogative and find strong sources of identity and fulfilment beyond their status as nurturers.

Key concepts

Normalisation of divorce

Fathers' Rights Movement

Step-families

Displaying families

Divorce extended families

Normalisation of fragility

Discussion questions

1   How does experiencing parents' divorce in childhood influence young people's expectations about marriage and relationships?

2   Do you agree couples should stay together 'for the sake of the children' and, if so, under what circumstances?

3   How does the high divorce rate explain the emergence of the international Fathers' Rights Movement? Evaluate some of the main arguments of Fathers' Rights activists.

4   Does divorce demonstrate a lack of commitment? Discuss the different kinds of commitment evident in family life post-divorce.

Recommended further reading

Hewitt, B., Baxter, J. & Western, M. 2005, 'Marriage Breakdown in Australia: The Social Correlates of Separation and Divorce', *Journal of Sociology*, vol. 41, no. 2, pp. 163–83.

Hughes, J. 2007, 'Repartnering After Divorce: Marginal Mates and Unwedded Women', *Family Matters*, vol. 55, pp. 16–21.

Smart, C. 2006, 'Children's Narratives of Post-divorce Family Life: From Individual Experience to an Ethical Disposition', *The Sociological Review*, vol. 54, no. 1, pp. 155–70.

12 Violence and Intimate Relationships

Introduction

In January 2008, ex-Australian Rules Football great Wayne Carey was arrested at his inner-Melbourne home after police intervened in a domestic dispute between himself and live-in girlfriend Kate Neilson (Ede & Turnbull 2008). For Carey, it was the second altercation with the law in the space of a year over violence inflicted on his partner. While on holiday in the USA in October 2007, he allegedly broke a wine glass in Neilson's face and was arrested soon after police arrived at their hotel. Later, Neilson changed her statement to police about Carey's violence, claiming instead that they were 'only having fun'.

To date, Carey's violent actions have cost him his media career. They have also eroded the hero status he attained at the height of his football fame. Overall, the police, employer and general public response to Carey's transgressions indicate the extent to which **domestic violence** against intimate partners is no longer publicly condoned in Australia. The controversy over Wayne Carey's behaviour is also valuable in making public a social phenomenon that is often hidden from view, and which constitutes the main theme of this chapter. There is a dark side to intimate relationships, as expressed in physical, sexual or emotional violence directed at family members, and partners. The pain of this is often privately borne by those who experience the abuse.

In this chapter we consider violence in intimate relationships, giving an overview of Australian patterns and trends in comparative context. We discuss the different kinds of relationships in which violence may occur, including those between parents and children, and intimate partners in same-sex relationships. Finally, we outline some contemporary sociological theories about violence, contrasting these with the explanations for violence characteristic of early feminist and psychological theories. Acknowledging the structural patterns in family/relationship violence and the relevance of the social and cultural context in which it occurs is important in a sociological analysis.

Defining and naming violence in intimate relationships

UNDERSTANDING VIOLENCE IN INTIMATE RELATIONSHIPS as a social problem has a relatively recent history. Historically, violence within relationships was considered normal, and until 1891 the law supported a man's right to beat his wife if she disobeyed him (Scutt 1983). One nineteenth century source explains that should a man be accused of assaulting his wife, he could defend the charge by explaining that the violence was punishment. The following list of 'bad behaviours' were at that time deemed worthy of wife-beating, and indicate the extent of the power imbalance that existed between husbands and wives:

> ... a bell not answered with the required promptitude, a dinner somewhat late or badly cooked, a pair of slippers not to be found when wanted, a book carried off, a set of papers disarranged (McGregor & Hopkins 1991, p. 122).

Social attitudes and laws may have changed, yet domestic violence remains one of the most significant social problems in the world today, and women, overwhelmingly, are the victims of this kind of violence. The United Nations estimates that between 20 per cent and 50 per cent of women worldwide have experienced violence from an intimate partner (Krug et al. 2002). Women's groups have worked very hard over the years to achieve public support for, and legal recognition of, the fact that relationship violence disproportionately affects women.

Historically, definitions have been politically important in the struggle to have **family violence** recognised as a serious social problem and a crime. The Women's Liberation Movement of the 1970s was intent to place 'private' issues, including domestic violence, on the public and political agenda. Redefining the terminology associated with men's violent behaviour in the home was an important part of this. During the 1970s, terms such as 'violence against women', 'male violence in the home' and 'spousal assault' were introduced. The radical feminist emphasis on the concept of patriarchy and the gendered nature of violence in the home informed this terminology. A major part of the feminist political struggle was to have violence in the home understood as a crime and to have police charge perpetrators with assault when they attended domestic violence incidents. The goal was to get the authorities to understand that violence was something that men do to women, and that violence in the home was 'assault', just as any other form of abuse that a stranger might inflict is thought of as assault (see McGregor & Hopkins 1991).

Many Australian social welfare agencies now use the gender neutral phrase 'domestic violence' to describe a situation in which one partner in a relationship uses physical or psychological means to dominate and control the other partner (Kirsner 2001, p. 7). 'Family violence' is also widely used due to its versatility in describing many forms of violence: for example, that occurs between partners, towards children, elder abuse and sibling abuse. However, Leone and Colleagues (2004) note that in the US literature, use of the term 'family violence perspective' has tended historically to distinguish between those who do not claim a feminist perspective in their explanations of why violence occurs, from those who do. In Australia, throughout the 1980s, family violence was a term associated with psychological rather than feminist responses to violence in the home. Many feminists believed it took the focus away from the fact that women and children rather than men were overwhelmingly the victims of violence in the home. This criticism has also been directed at the term 'domestic violence' (see McGregor & Hopkins 1991).

According to the Victorian Domestic Violence and Incest Resource Centre, the term 'family violence' is usually preferred by Indigenous communities in Australia. Within Indigenous communities, this emphasis on family violence is seen to differ from that of domestic violence in a number of ways including: a rejection of 'criminalisation' as the main strategy to deal with family violence on the grounds that Aboriginal men are already vastly over-represented in the Australian criminal justice system; a greater emphasis on the impact of colonialism, trauma, family dysfunction and alcoholism as primary causes; and attention to not only male partners but a range of potential perpetrators, also including sons, grandsons and other kin (Blagg 2000, p. 3).

A continuum of violent behaviours

JUST AS THERE HAS BEEN a range of opinions expressed about appropriate terminology to describe domestic violence, it has often been difficult to reach consensus on the behaviours that constitute domestic violence. For many years now, in Australia, for the purposes of policy, law and support services, domestic violence has been acknowledged to include a range of behaviours including verbal, emotional, financial, sexual and physical abuse. Again, feminists were in the vanguard of defining violence as the exercise of power and control over another person, which includes a much more extensive range of behaviours than physical beatings or sexual assault. A combination of abusive behaviours is often used in the exercise of power and control over the victims of violence.

Verbal and emotional abuse is known to include a range of behaviours that include: harsh criticisms or 'put downs' of appearance or personality, public insults and name-calling; social isolation such as refusal to allow access to family members or friends; and threats to hurt another family member or pet. Financial abuse includes controlling and withholding money, not allowing the partner to earn their own money, or rationing money for essential items in a demeaning or humiliating way. Violence in the home can also involve sexual abuse and stalking behaviour. It is common these days to talk about a **continuum of violence** that can involve some or all of the above abusive behaviours, and be directed at children or adults.

People tend to think of physical violence as the worst or 'real' form of violence, but physical violence is usually accompanied by other behaviours that may be more humiliating and long-lasting in their emotional effects. Many abused women report to women's crisis service workers that emotional or financial abuse can be as demeaning, degrading and painful as beatings. Recent Australian research has found that all forms of domestic violence have wide-ranging and long-term effects on women's lives. Negative consequences for finances, relationships, and physical, psychological and sexual health are reported long after the violent relationship has ended (Evans 2007).

Domestic violence and the Women's Refuge Movement

In the 1970s and early 1980s the Women's Refuge Movement in Australia emerged largely through the efforts of radical and liberal feminists, working together with religious organisations and 'femocrats' in government bureaucracies to bring about change in women's lives (McGregor & Hopkins 1991). Susan Evans claims that in Australia, women's refuges 'were synonymous with the fight against domestic violence and were constructed as *the* feminist intervention' (2003, p. 28). The first women's refuge in Australia was called 'Elsie', established in 1974 after a group of concerned feminists 'squatted' in an unoccupied inner-Sydney house. Many refuges came into being as group households organised along feminist collectivist lines, with a minimal hierarchy of positions among the workers, and shared decision-making with residents. The philosophy behind this comes from radical feminism and indeed many radical movements for social change. In this view, if violence stems from gender hierarchy, as the theory of patriarchy emphasises, non-hierarchical forms of organisation are to be encouraged as central to the struggle against domestic violence (see McGregor & Hopkins 1991, p. 23).

Figure 12.1: The Power and Control Wheel

The wheel pictured above was developed by a group of women's refuge and support workers in Duluth Minnesota, USA, in conjunction with their service users who had experienced domestic violence (see Pence & Paymar 1993). It represents the continuum of violence as a circle revolving around a central core of power and control. The spokes of the wheel depict the different behaviours that may constitute violence. The wheel is very widely used in domestic violence support services throughout the Western world. There are versions specifically developed to support Muslim and Jewish women, and versions available in a number of different community languages.

One behaviour that is represented on the wheel is abuse of animals as part of the continuum of violence and intimidation. Pet ownership is common among women seeking refuge accommodation and studies have established that cruelty or murder of domestic pets is part of the pattern of abuse (see Ascione, Weber & Wood 1997). At the same time, many refuges for women and children do not have the space or resources to accommodate residents' dogs and cats. Such is the extent of this problem that special services exist in a number of Australian states providing safe accommodation for pets when women and their children leave violent relationships to live in refuges.

Australian patterns and trends

IN AUSTRALIA, EXHAUSTIVE DATA SUPPORTS the fact that women and children are much more likely to be the victims of domestic violence than men. Due to the levels of shame and fear that tend to surround reporting violence in the home, it is generally believed official sources under-report the incidence of violence.

Domestic violence and adult women and men

THE AUSTRALIAN BUREAU OF STATISTICS *Personal Safety Survey* conducted in 2005 documents women's and men's experiences of violence from strangers, friends, partners and family members. Findings echoed a trend that has been apparent in Australian safety surveys for some time. When it comes to violence in general, men are overwhelmingly the victims, with one in ten men having experienced at least one incident of physical or sexual assault in the year prior to the survey, as opposed to one in 20 women (ABS 2006f). However, the type of violence men tend to experience is in public and at the hands of a stranger. In the ABS survey, 65 per cent of men who had experienced physical violence in the year prior were assaulted by another man whom they did not know, and only 4 per cent by a current or past female partner. By contrast, with regard to female victims of physical violence, 31 per cent were assaulted by a male partner or ex-partner as opposed to 15 per cent who were assaulted by a male stranger.

The most common setting in which women were victimised was domestic, with most women assaulted in either their own home, their partner's home or another familiar location (ABS 2006f).

One of the reasons violence in the home remains under-reported is that many women greatly fear further harm will come to their children or themselves if they tell anyone about the violence. This is not unfounded and domestic murder is an all too common occurrence, particularly in the period shortly after the woman takes the children and leaves home. The National Homicide Monitoring Program annual report for 2005–06 indicates that 66 Australian women (58 per cent of the 113 female victims) died that year due to a domestic dispute (Davies & Mouzos 2007).

Despite the sobering information that thousands of Australian women experience domestic violence, as Flood (2006) points out, there is also some good news. Comparing the ABS 2005 *Personal Safety Survey* with an earlier *Women's Safety Australia* study conducted in 1996, Flood contends that rates of violence against women have declined in the past few years. The ABS survey also found that women are more likely to report domestic violence to police than they were in the mid 1990s, which indicates the reduction in the incidence of violence is a genuine one, rather than the result of failure to report the violence. In 1996, only 35 per cent of women had reported the most recent incident of violence inflicted by a partner to the police; by 2005, this had risen to 61 per cent (Flood 2006, p. 3).

Unfortunately, we do not have comprehensive research on the links between domestic violence and socio-economic status. Incidence data collected from service providers has found that poorer families are over-represented. However, it can be argued that well-educated middle-class couples can more easily hide domestic violence from the surveillance of authorities. In Victoria, the well publicised Ramage case is an example where long-running abuse had been effectively hidden from friends, let alone state authorities by a relatively wealthy middle-class couple. James Ramage killed his wife Julie in 2004 and successfully avoided the charge of murder and was instead charged with manslaughter using the outdated principle of provocation. 'The jury found Julie Ramage had provoked her husband by criticising their sex life and saying she was leaving him' (Gough 2004). This finding caused outrage among Julie Ramage's family and friends, domestic violence service providers and legal and academic feminists and initiated a campaign for law reform in this area.

Children, young people and domestic violence

CHILDREN MAY DIRECTLY EXPERIENCE VIOLENCE and sexual abuse from adult parents or relatives, or indirectly, through witnessing violence between adults. Like domestic violence against women child abuse had to be 'discovered' and named.

Data is collected in Australia on the ways in which domestic violence can affect children. Indermaur (2001) conducted a survey of 5000 12–20-year-olds from all Australian states and territories. 23 per cent of the group were aware of at least one act of physical violence occurring against their mother or step-mother. Young people's awareness of male to female physical domestic violence occurring was higher in households where the male carer 'gets drunk a lot' and where the male carer 'hits children other than for bad behaviour', even though these represented a relatively small number of households: 14 per cent of households where male carer gets drunk a lot, 10 per cent where children are hit other than for bad behaviour. These figures also indicate that one in 10 young people also experiences violence directly in households where they observe violence occurring between the adults.

The Family Violence Intervention Program in the Australian Capital Territory maintains a database on incidents of family violence reported to the police. According to 2003–04 figures obtained from this database, 1625 children were recorded as present at 44 per cent of the domestic violence incidents police attended in that year. About half of these children were under the age of 11 years (Australian Institute of Criminology 2006).

Where young children are sexually or emotionally abused by parents, most of the available evidence about the incidence of such abuse comes from data collected by Child Protection Services in various states and territories of Australia. This means less is known about the prevalence of child abuse in the population at large, and more is known about those children who physically or emotionally display signs of abuse having occurred. A number of healthcare and education professionals such as doctors, social workers and teachers are mandated by law to notify the authorities when they come into contact with a child who is suspected of being abused. Mary Hood conducted a study of 334 referrals to the Child Protection Service (CPS) at the Women's and Children's Hospital in Adelaide, South Australia. She found a strong link between low socio-economic status and investigation by the CPS. 82 per cent of the 334 children under investigation came from the two lowest socio-economic areas of Adelaide.

Young people's experiences of partner violence

YOUNG PEOPLE ALSO EXPERIENCE VIOLENCE in the context of their dating relationships with boyfriends and girlfriends. Indermaur (2001) found that 70 per cent of young people who had had an intimate relationship had experienced at least one incident of physical violence in that relationship. There were no gender differences between young women and men with regard to this finding. However, 30 per cent of the young women had been frightened or hurt by this violence as opposed to only 12 per cent of the young men. Gender differences were also apparent between young men and women with regard to attitudes that could be classified as 'pro-violent'. Men were more likely than women to express pro-violent attitudes and to have witnessed parental domestic violence. Indermaur (2001) also found socio-economic status to be relevant with regard to young women's experiences of violence, in that young women from lower socio-economic areas were more likely to be the victims of relationship violence than those from higher socio-economic areas.

Domestic violence in same-sex relationships

It was my first relationship. First long-term relationship ... I was head over heels madly in love and I thought this was the relationship for life. It started out really good. This woman was nine years older than myself. [But it became] verbally abusive and then physically. I quite often had black eyes and ... she almost killed me once ... I was too young and insecure about the whole relationship, gay relationships, whatever ('Robyn', quoted in Ristock 2003, p. 335).

It is estimated that between 15 per cent and 20 per cent of lesbians and gay men in the USA have experienced domestic violence (Vickers 1996) although no such figures exist for Australia to date. The stigma attached to same-sex relationships has historically made it very difficult for lesbian and gay victims of domestic violence to speak out about their experiences.

Like heterosexual relationships, lesbian and gay domestic violence may include physical, emotional, financial and social abuse (Bagshaw et al. 2000). The abuse of power and tendency of the violent partner to control the victim in a manner that causes acute fear and distress are common to both gay and heterosexual patterns of violence. However, factors associated with the stigma attached to same-sex relationships may lead to specific patterns of abusive behaviour. Violent gay or lesbian partners may wield power through appeals to the homophobia or heteronormativity that exists in society at large. Examples of this include threats to 'out' partners to employers, family members or the Family Court. For HIV positive gay men, threats of outing may be about HIV status as well as or rather than sexuality. Renzetti (1992) found that emotional abuse was a factor in all the violent lesbian relationships she studied, in which abusive partners were often very jealous, and felt threatened by their partners' attempts to establish independent friendships.

The predominance of feminist explanations for violence in the research literature and the domestic violence support service system has not always made it easy to raise awareness about lesbian domestic violence. Janice Ristock, one of the most respected and active researchers of domestic violence in same-sex relationships in the USA, notes there can be fears among feminist service providers and researchers that publicly acknowledging the existence of lesbian domestic violence will undermine feminist analyses of men's violence against women. Ristock's own work has found that the dynamics of violence in lesbian relationships may follow the clear victim/abuser pattern characteristic of heterosexual relationships, or a more complicated pattern of fluctuating power dynamics where two women may be—at different times—victim and perpetrator. Ristock also found that where violence occurs in a lesbian relationship, the victim is often in her first relationship with a much older woman who has been openly lesbian for much longer, as in the quotation at the top of the page (Ristock 2003).

Most of what is known about domestic violence within the Australian lesbian, gay, bisexual and transgender communities comes from data collected by support services rather than research studies. For instance, an AIDS Council of New South Wales (ACON) counselling files audit revealed that 11 per cent of 54 sessions conducted between 2001 and 2003 with HIV positive gay men included discussion of violence from an intimate partner (ACON 2004). The NSW-based Domestic Violence Line estimated that in an average month, five calls out of 1000 were from lesbians experiencing abuse in the context of their relationship. Lesbian and gay victims of domestic violence are less likely to report the abuse to police, health care providers or other support workers, due to fear they will either not be believed or not taken seriously. Awareness campaigns within the lesbian and gay communities have received government funding in the past few years and are beginning to raise the public profile of intimate partner violence.

Explanations for domestic violence

THERE HAVE BEEN A NUMBER of explanations for why abuse and violence occurs so frequently between intimate partners. This is never merely an intellectual or academic exercise, given the way in which we understand violence impacts on the sense we make of available survey data, and the kinds of laws, policies and support services that are developed for victims. Because violence among family members causes death, pain and suffering, a huge amount of research has been conducted on this topic and there are a very large number of theoretical frameworks in existence that attempt to explain why violence occurs. In the following section, we consider just a few of the more influential feminist, psychological and sociological theories, and their critiques.

Psychological

PSYCHOLOGICAL EXPLANATIONS FOR DOMESTIC VIOLENCE tend to focus on the behavioural pattern of the person being violent, perhaps even their pathological tendencies, and the consequent powerlessness and passive behaviour of the victim. **Cycle of violence** theory, and the linked phenomenon '**battered women's syndrome**' (BWS) are principally associated with Lenore Walker's work (1979, 1984) and became very popular in the 1980s. Walker considered herself to be a feminist as well as psychologist, but the theory itself is primarily psychological. BWS is still extensively used as a legal defence when victims of domestic violence subsequently harm or kill their violent male partners. As both components of Walker's theories have been so influential, they are worth describing in some detail.

BWS describes a distinctively patterned set of psychological and behavioural symptoms resulting from prolonged exposure to domestic violence. Between 1978 and 1991, Walker conducted interviews with 435 women in Colorado, USA who had been victims of domestic violence, and developed and refined her theories based on these interviews. Among these women, Walker noted symptoms commonly associated with mental illness, such as depression, low-self esteem and a sense of powerlessness (Walker 1984). For Walker, the prevalence of this pattern of symptoms explained why so many women who had been abused by their partners stayed in the abusive relationship.

In Walker's theoretical perspective, BWS develops in tandem with the cycle of violence. Walker (1984) argued that domestic violence tends to occur in cycles characterised by a period of build-up and release, in which the victim and perpetrator both play a part. In the 'tension-building' stage, the victim will be exposed to verbal and/or emotional abuse and possibly minor physical violence, such as slapping. In response, she may attempt to pacify her abuser using a range of strategies based on past experience. Walker theorised that although the victim's aim is to avoid future conflict, her pacifying behaviour will instead tend to reinforce the abuser's violent tendencies until these culminate in a second phase of serious assault. She argued that it was at this time that victims became most fearful, and most at risk of death or serious injury. The discharge of tension in assault in this second phase, according to Walker, would lead to a third phase of 'loving contrition' in which the abuser would try to make up with his victim and possibly attempt to convince the victim he was sorry and intended to stop being violent (Walker 1984).

One of the main feminist criticisms levelled at Walker's theory is that it subtly implicates the victim's response as causative of the partner's violence. That is, the passivity, and pacifying behaviour displayed by the victim is part of the explanation for why the violence gets worse. Another criticism of Walker's theories is that they can only understand a decision to stay with an abusive partner as 'learned helplessness' or passivity, rather than a conscious and rational coping strategy some women may use after weighing up the alternatives to leaving a violent partner. For instance, it is possible to interpret some women's stories of living with violence as based on quite a rational analysis of the resources they have at their disposal, and importantly, the impact that leaving might have on their children, either emotionally or financially (see Rothenberg 2002 for a review of the main critiques).

In general, psychological theories tend to emphasise the individual traits of either victims or perpetrators of domestic violence. In doing so, they may overlook other social factors that could explain why women stay in violent relationships. For instance, the influence of poverty, unemployment or lack of affordable housing.

Feminist

FEMINIST THEORY HAS BEEN PARTICULARLY successful in legal, policy and crisis intervention approaches to domestic violence, to the point where feminism has become the dominant framework informing Australian public policy on violence (Evans 2003). Feminist theories of domestic violence depart from the standpoint that violence is a means by which men assert power and control over women in the home and in society at large. While claims that men are intrinsically violent characterised some strands of 1970s radical feminism, recent feminist writing about domestic violence make a more sophisticated distinction between biological or essential properties of men, and masculinity as a social construction. In a similar vein, while early feminist writing on domestic violence often drew on notions of a universal patriarchy, or social system in which all men wield power over all women, this argument has receded over time (Walby 1992). The strength of feminist theory in general is its identification of power and control as core issues in the use of violence against women. These insights have proved very useful in analyses of violence other than that occurring in men's and women's intimate relationships.

It is difficult to ignore some overtly patriarchal dimensions of how men express violence in the home. For instance, women often report that violence is sparked by men's anger at their housework incompetence or refusal to perform wifely duties appropriately, such as cooking meals or cleaning clothes. Perceived domestic transgressions such as burning the dinner or failing to have it ready when the husband gets home from work, are known triggers for many men's violent behaviour. This indicates that some men resort to violence in response to very rigid and patriarchal beliefs about their entitlements as men to discipline or punish their wives or partners, which as we have already seen, were actually legitimate entitlements in law just over a hundred years ago. As feminists also point out, many men who are violent to their partners are not violent in other areas of their lives, for example, towards work colleagues or friends or other family members.

Alternative explanations for domestic violence

CLASSIC FEMINIST THEORIES EMPHASISE MEN'S power over women in general as the most important factor in explaining violence. However, the usefulness of this perspective is to some extent challenged by the existence of violence in lesbian relationships and by the existence of female perpetrators of child murder and maltreatment. The data on female perpetrators of violence against men also challenges such oversimplified gender-based explanations for violence.

Furthermore, researchers and support workers involved with the issue of domestic violence in indigenous communities do not believe feminist theories adequately explain the influence of other structural issues in these communities apart from gender—which include generalised violence not only directed at family members, high poverty, homelessness, history of dispossession and considerable alcohol abuse. For instance, Indigenous Australian writer Melissa Lucashenko (1994) has criticised the emphasis on gender by white feminists in preference to race when levels of violence Indigenous men inflict on Indigenous women are so much greater than in other groups in the general Australian population.

The gender symmetry debate about domestic violence

In recent years, some researchers and men's rights groups have claimed that women are just as violent as men in domestic abuse contexts. This has given rise to what is known as the 'gender symmetry' debate in domestic violence studies (documented in Kimmel 2002; Flood 2006).

Several large scale social surveys conducted in different Western countries over a number of years have returned findings to ostensibly support the **gender symmetry thesis**. For instance, a survey conducted by Statistics Canada in 1999 found that 8 per cent of 14,269 women and 7 per cent of 11,607 men had experienced at least one instance of violence from an intimate partner in the 12 months prior to the study. Headey and colleagues (1999), in an Australian survey conducted in Melbourne, found that men and women reported experience of and performance of a similar number of violent acts in the previous 12 months. Several large-scale literature reviews conducted in the USA also claim to have found numerous published studies documenting survey findings in support of the gender symmetry thesis (see Kimmel 2002).

In a comprehensive analysis of the evidence, Kimmel (2002) notes that most, if not all, of the research supporting gender symmetry in domestic violence utilises a version of the Conflict Tactics Scale (CTS) developed over two decades by sociologist Murray Straus and colleagues in the USA. This scale contains questions about the frequency and nature of violent acts committed in the past year for example, 'I would like you to tell me how many times in the past 12 months you have punched, slapped, hit', and so on. Kimmel observes that while the CTS is useful in finding out about how many discrete incidents of violence occur between intimate partners, 'counting the blows' cannot in itself support the gender symmetry thesis, even if women and men appear to be equivalent on measures of how many blows they inflict.

The most important critique of the gender symmetry thesis is that counting acts of violence tells us nothing about the context in which the violence occurs, and context is very important for understanding the severity and impact of violence on the victim. For instance, Kimmel (2002) observes that counting acts of violence tells us nothing about who initiated the violence, the size or strength of the people involved, how fearful the people involved were, and whether the violent act was unprovoked or in self-defence. Bagshaw and Chung (2000) argue further that the CTS only counts violence over a 12-month period which may obscure a prolonged and systematic pattern of abuse experienced over a number of years. Dasgupta (2002) comments that there are substantial differences in the nature and severity of the injuries men and women receive from violence inflicted on a partner. The evidence here comes from hospital emergency room data that demonstrates women are much more likely than men to seek emergency medical help for injuries sustained from domestic violence.

Masculinities and men's relationship violence

MASCULINITIES THEORY HAS PROVED PARTICULARLY useful in recent interview-based research conducted with different groups of violent men. Connell (1987) coined the phrase '**hegemonic masculinity**', as a result of dissatisfaction with the feminist concept of 'patriarchy'. It refers to the fact that, in most social settings, there is a narrow range of dominant ways to express oneself as a man. Hegemonic masculinity is not a fixed characteristic or type of behaviour exhibited by men that has a foregone association with violence, power and control. Rather, the idea is that masculinities are relational and changeable. It is important to understand the detailed social context in which violent masculinities are enacted, not to condone or justify the behaviour, but in order to mount a challenge to the belief system that fuels the violence.

Mark Totten (2003) researched marginalised young Canadian men who belonged to gangs or violent male peer groups and used masculinities theory to explain the social dynamics of violence in their intimate relationships. Totten found that the abusive behaviour most of these young men directed at girlfriends (and also at racial minorities and gay men) was central to masculinity construction within the culture they inhabited. It served as a way of recuperating their masculinity in the absence of access to other sources of economic or social privilege. Most of these young men had been exposed to abusive behaviour in their immediate family environments and had developed very authoritarian beliefs about relationships between men and women. They had been unemployed and were likely to remain that way themselves, so they had few prospects of enacting masculine identity through more socially respectable behaviours such as breadwinning. As a consequence, the young men disagreed that there was anything masculine about jobs, material possessions and wealth. They could instead obtain status within their peer groups through sexual activity, physical toughness and keeping girlfriends 'in their place'.

Mullaney (2007) also drew on masculinities theory to study 14 men participating in programs for domestic abusers, speculating that the men's verbal accounts of the violence they inflicted on their wives and girlfriends could shed light on the workings of hegemonic masculinity in this setting. Mullaney expected that these men would attempt to *excuse* their behaviour when telling a researcher the story of how the violence came to occur. Instead, she found the men tended to *justify* it and this enabled them to locate the reason for the violence outside their 'true selves'. Much of what the men said to Mullaney about their violent behaviour focused on how their partner did not respect the duties they performed as men, for instance, in the work they did around the home or as financial providers. For Mullaney (2007), the men's accounts of their violence exposed a potential problem with the group programs for violent men that have become very popular in recent years. Rather than enabling men to take responsibility for the violence they inflict on partners, these programs may support men to blame their partners or circumstances beyond their own doing.

'Patriarchal terrorism' and 'common couple violence'

A RECENT BODY OF SOCIOLOGICAL work attempts to combine the most useful insights of feminist theory with the survey evidence of some 'gender symmetry' in violent domestic exchanges. This work was initiated by Michael Johnson in the USA, who believes it is no longer useful to discuss 'domestic violence' as a singular phenomenon, or only as 'male violence against women'. Johnson (1995) asserts that there are at least two distinct patterns in violent encounters between spouses and intimate partners, one that is more apparent in patriarchal families where men exert considerable power, and another among partners who generally share a far more equal relationship. In the patriarchal pattern, there is systematic violence that is clearly enacted in the interests of male control, as the feminist stance on domestic violence has always insisted. Johnson calls this '**patriarchal terrorism**' and 'intimate terrorism' in his later work (Johnson & Leone 2005). In the other main pattern, violence is characterised by occasional episodes or outbursts of conflict that sometimes get out of control. He calls this '**common couple violence**' or 'situational couple violence' in his later work (Johnson & Leone 2005). The main difference Johnson sees between the two patterns is that patriarchal terrorism tends to escalate over a number of years with regard to its frequency and severity. It is this type of violence that is most likely to lead to severe injury or death of the victim. Common couple violence, by contrast, is much more occasional and rarely intensifies in frequency or severity. Johnson also contends that the perpetrators of intimate terrorism are nearly always men, whereas rates of common couple violence tend to be more equivalent between women and men.

Johnson and Ferraro (2000), in an article about the progress made in domestic violence theory throughout the 1990s, argue that partner violence can no longer be understood without acknowledgement of the type of violence perpetrated, the motives of the person using violence, the social context in which the violence occurs and also its cultural context. They expand Johnson's earlier framework to include four different typologies of violence that may commonly fall within the category 'domestic violence'. In addition to common couple violence and patriarchal terrorism, they propose a third category of 'violent resistance', asserting that this type of violence is usually used by women towards their violent partners. Also, they argue for recognition of 'mutual violent control' or a situation in which two partners each demonstrate intimate terrorism tendencies and engage in a battle for control.

As Evans (2003) notes, a limitation of the work of Johnson and his colleagues, which could be levelled at any theory relying on the construction of 'types', is that the typologies can become too fixed, blinding us to other patterns of violent behaviour that may manifest, and become quite prescriptive in their effects. However, this work has certainly brought to light the very different contexts and circumstances that characterise the expression of domestic violence between men and women, and alerted us to the importance of being wary of broad explanations for why violence occurs and how it is used to exercise power and control.

Conclusion

INTIMATE RELATIONSHIPS AND FAMILIES ARE supposed to be safe, private and loving social relationships that provide a haven from the outside world. For victims of domestic violence these taken-for-granted expectations are not met. In the 1970s second wave feminism put domestic violence firmly on academic and public policy agenda. Nearly 30 years later, rates of domestic violence remain high and, as a society, our ability to analyse violence and intervene to stop it remains limited. Although expectations that intimate relationships should provide equality and self-actualisation for partners are now high, so too are experiences of domestic violence within relationships.

We emphasise that violence and abuse affect men and women, rich and poor members of society, children and adults, as well as family members of all ages. However, there is strong evidence that gender, culture and socio-economic status are important factors in how these phenomena are experienced and expressed. There is a need for more comprehensive sociological research on domestic violence to specify how violence is socially shaped in contemporary Australia.

Key concepts

Domestic violence

Family violence

Continuum of violence

Battered Women Syndrome

Cycle of violence

Gender symmetry thesis

Hegemonic masculinity

Patriarchal terrorism

Common couple violence

Discussion questions

1   'Cycle of violence theory' and the 'battered women's syndrome' have been criticised for individualising and pathologising women's experiences of violence. By contrast, what are some of the social factors that could explain why women stay in violent relationships?

2   What is the 'gender symmetry' thesis regarding violence in intimate relationships? Evaluate the arguments for and against this viewpoint.

3   What is hegemonic masculinity? How useful is this concept for understanding violence in intimate relationships?

Recommended further reading

Hird, M.J. & Jackson, S. 2001, 'Where "Angels" and "Wusses" Fear to Tread: Sexual Coercion in Adolescent Dating Relationships', *Journal of Sociology*, vol. 37, no. 1, pp. 27–43.

Kimmel, M. 2002, '"Gender Symmetry" in Domestic Violence: A Substantive and Methodological Research Review', *Violence Against Women*, vol. 8, no. 11, pp. 1332–63.

Johnson, M.P. & Ferraro, K.J. 2000, 'Research on Domestic Violence in the 1990s: Making Distinctions', *Journal of Marriage and the Family*, vol. 62, pp. 948–63.

13 Ageing, Care and Intergenerational Relationships

Figure 13.1: Post-retirement lifestyles now provide opportunities for older people to reclaim a 'life of their own' alongside their ongoing family responsibilities

----

Introduction

IN 2007, 'SEVENTY-SOMETHING' COUPLE Bill and Glenys Ferguson took part in a series of advertisements for Richard Branson's Virgin Money Home Loans. The ad campaign appeared in the Australian national press and featured Bill and Glenys enjoying themselves immensely in a number of sexual and scantily or unclad embraces. A subsequent newspaper article about the couple discussed the controversy these advertisements created, insisting 'old people don't lose their sex drive just because they're older' (Mangan 2007). It gives further details about Bill and Glenys' active and adventurous post-retirement relationship and lifestyle. We learn that they recently renewed their marriage vows in Sydney's Centennial Park alongside 277 other couples, breaking a world record for the number of couples doing so at the one time. They are planning a trip to New York to spend their Virgin money and will cruise home aboard the luxury ocean liner QE2. To cap this all off, Bill and Glenys would like to celebrate their upcoming 80th birthdays by treating themselves to a tandem skydive.

Bill and Glenys' story of a rewarding life beyond work or caring responsibilities exemplifies the extent to which retirement can now constitute a new beginning for older people, after the duties and identities associated with routinised paid work and rearing a family have served their purpose. A new breed of older people like Bill and Glenys see 'retirement' as anything but. It is a time for new forms of self-expression, personal productivity and hitherto unexplored sources of fulfilment. Older people today are better educated and healthier than the previous generation. They have greater access to global sources of information via the internet. They have generated considerable wealth. For these and other reasons, greater numbers of ageing Australians than ever before are well placed to maintain their independence until an advanced age.

Despite such change, a negative view of ageing and the idea that an ageing population is a burden persists. Older people are often regarded as a passive, needy and dependent group who are takers rather than givers, as recipients of pensions and welfare services, and funded by the declining proportion of younger people in the workforce (Tongue & Ballenden 1999). Furthermore, not all older people have benefited from the shift in perceptions and experiences of later life as a time of new lifestyle and self-reinvention opportunities.

In this chapter we explore the meaning and circumstances of ageing, beginning with an overview of demographic characteristics of ageing Australians. We follow this up with an introduction to some of the theories about what ageing represents, then turn to ageing as a gendered experience through discussion of the differences between men and women's social networks, and involvement in grandparenting. Along the way, we also consider ageing in comparative context, looking at issues of care and intergenerational support relevant to various Asian family relationships, and the gay and lesbian communities.

An ageing Australian population: Demographic characteristics and implications

MORE PEOPLE ARE LIVING LONGER in Australia, in keeping with trends in other industrialised societies such as the UK and USA. While older people constituted 4 per cent of the total population at the turn of the twentieth century, as of June 2004, the number of older people in Australia over the age of 65 years was estimated at 2.6 million, which is approximately 13 per cent of the population (ABS 2006a). An ageing population results from the historically unique combination of lower birth rates and longer life expectancy. Substantial growth is projected in both the relative and absolute size of the older population over the next 50 years. By 2051, 22 per cent of Australian men and 26 per cent of Australia women (6 million people in total) are expected to be aged 65 years and over (ABS 1999).

In Australia today, people over the age of 55 possess 25 per cent of the country's disposable income and almost 40 per cent of the total wealth (Commonwealth Department of Health and Aged Care 2001, pp. 49–63). Despite this, having adequate financial resources in years leading up to retirement is a major concern for many older people. Increased life-expectancy may mean continuing to work longer in order to meet living costs in retirement. Although a number of wealthier men and women are choosing to take earlier retirement provisions, other wage earners who have supported young families for many years are faced with the prospect of needing to remain in the workforce for as long as possible. Though the baby boom generation are thought of as wealthier than previous ageing generations, it is likely that there will be substantial economic inequalities within this group. Those who are less well off face the prospect of entering old age with higher levels of debt, little superannuation and the family home as their only major asset. In these situations, living longer may mean having to re-mortgage the family home. The proliferation in recent years of 'reverse mortgage' products available from banks and other lenders is testimony to the large numbers of retired people faced with dwindling finances due to their longevity (see Faulkner 2007).

Ageing can bring with it ill-health and vulnerability, particularly among groups of lower socio-economic status. With alarming regularity, stories erupt in the media about the ill-treatment and neglect of elderly people in aged-care facilities. Higgs and Gilleard (2006) contend that physically and mentally frail old people now constitute an underclass in Australian society, whose identity is bound up with their poor health status. These authors point out that 'if identity construction in later life is now part of the process of growing older, not all the choices are equal' (p. 234). Although long-term illnesses or physically debilitating conditions tend to increase with age, contrary to popular opinion, many older Australians over 65 are in very good health. Most older people (80 per cent of the population aged 70 and over) are not receiving any aged care services. In 2005, many rated their health as good (32 per cent), with more than a third rating it as good to excellent (36 per cent) (ABS 2006d).

Older people's marital status influences their living circumstances and the other supports they are utilising. The marital status statistics for older Australians reflect the fact that women tend to live longer than men. Across all older age groups, widows outnumber widowers and the proportion of both men and women who are widowed increases with age.

Sociological perspectives on ageing

SOCIOLOGY OFFERS SEVERAL BROAD THEORETICAL perspectives on ageing as a social process.

Disengagement theory and functionalism

As RUSSELL (2007) NOTES, FUNCTIONALIST assumptions about ageing dominated sociology until the 1970s, through an emphasis on **disengagement theory**. This theory held that as people get old, it makes sense that they should gradually be discharged from positions of responsibility in society. Talcott Parsons (1963) believed disengagement of the elderly was consistent with the demands of industrialisation. In pre-industrial societies, such as traditional Indigenous Australian societies, older people are considered as the repositories of knowledge and wisdom. There is respect and reverence for elders as they are the most knowledgeable members of the community. However, under conditions of industrialisation, the wisdom of older people soon becomes obsolete in the face of speedy technological change. For Parsons, this was functional because it promoted the smooth running of society, as it is the younger members of society who are best placed to keep up with the changing skill base. For instance, a compulsory retirement age serves to remove people from their work roles while they're still able to perform them, allowing young people to gradually take over and tasks to continue with little interruption to society. Consistent with disengagement theory, Parsons considered that the major social and emotional tasks facing older people revolved around how to adjust to retirement and the increasing separation from public life this entails.

Disengagement theory is largely rejected today for several reasons. In the first instance, the thought of social isolation or marginalisation may lead many older people to not want to disengage from paid work, particularly if they are in good health and enjoy their work. Disengagement theory also constitutes older people as passive victims of societal 'needs', ignoring the considerable diversity of this group and the varied skills and experiences they may have to offer the paid workforce. Furthermore, it is flawed in its implication that leaving the paid workforce means becoming a passive member of society in the sense of having no continuing role in public life. Available data on volunteering, for instance, indicates that over 20 per cent of Australians engaged in volunteer work are people aged over 55 (ABS 2006c). These people make a considerable contribution to public life although they are not in receipt of payment for their services. Finally, a range of feminist commentators noted how disengagement theory was largely a theory about older men given its emphasis on disengagement from the paid workforce.

Activity theory

MORE RECENTLY, SOCIOLOGISTS REJECTING DISENGAGEMENT theory have emphasised the positive dimensions of old age, and the ability of old people to successfully navigate the ageing process and resist age-related stereotypes. One example of this approach is **activity theory**, which holds that remaining active equates with successful ageing, and later life is regarded as the time for relative freedom from responsibilities and new opportunities. Broadly speaking, activity theory argues that old age requires the opposite of disengagement. It is a time when people reconstruct the meaning and purpose of their lives, and take on new challenges and identities. For instance, Peter Laslett (1987) coined the term '**third age**' to describe the positive opportunities afforded by post-retirement life. Laslett argues that there are four distinct ages or life stages that people navigate. The first is youth, during which dependency is viewed as the norm. The second is adulthood, characterised by independence, as well as considerable financial, family and work responsibilities. The third age is characterised as the time in which older people are relatively free to pursue their own interests after family and work responsibilities are largely over. In the fourth age, age-related ill-health marks a return to the dependence of youth.

A number of criticisms have been levelled at activity theory as exemplified by Laslett's focus on the 'third age' as a time of freedom and opportunity. Wray (2003) notes that successful ageing, activity and control in Laslett's conceptualisation of the third age appear to assume considerable wealth accumulation and participation in certain kinds of leisure activities constitute ageing well, when these may not be available to older people of lower socio-economic status. Recall Bill and Glenys Ferguson, whose story opened this chapter. Wray's critique draws attention to the fact that not all older people in Western societies have access to the financial resources, social confidence and degree of good health that facilitate participating in the activities enjoyed by Bill and Glenys. Yet should we deduce from this that they are not 'ageing well'? Calasanti and King (2005) go as far as to say an emphasis on activity as a recipe for ageing well is actually ageist and 'means that those who are chronically impaired, or who prefer to be contemplative, become problem "old" people, far too comfortable just being old' (p. 7). Furthermore, Laslett's theory neglects the fact that family responsibilities of a new kind may accrue after retirement, particularly for women who often take on considerable informal care-giving responsibilities for grandchildren, now so many of their daughters are in the paid workforce (see the Grandparenting section later in this chapter). Finally, Wray also makes the point that Laslett's use of concepts such as 'opportunity', 'control' and 'freedom' are very culturally specific terms, more in keeping with Western constructs of selfhood. This may limit our understanding of what successful ageing means to older people in different cultural settings.

Gender and ageing

DISENGAGEMENT THEORY AND ACTIVITY THEORY have been criticised for giving inadequate attention to the importance of gender as a lens through which older people's experiences must be viewed. Recently, a number of sociologists have turned their attention to the gendered dimensions of ageing, and the differing problems, challenges and opportunities facing older women compared to older men, particularly when it comes to participation in family and social relationships.

Cherry Russell's research over a number of years has explored the lived experience of older Australian women and men with regard to their concepts of home and social relationships in later life. During interviews with older people who were continuing to live in their homes, Russell found the meaning of 'home' was strongly gendered, with many women—more so than men—feeling a sense of identity attached to their home. This could be considered as a reflection of the greater work that women have traditionally done in the domestic sphere (Russell 2007). Russell observed that the stronger identity with, and attachment to, the home enabled older women to achieve greater power and agency over decision-making about living arrangements after their husbands had retired from the paid workforce. Similar to Russell's findings, Wray (2003) previously reported that older women had experienced agency and empowerment in diverse ways, both inside and outside the home. Rather than being concerned about loss of health or mobility, women interviewed by Wray were enjoying their later years as a time for self-fulfilment. This enjoyment was culturally varied and included grandparenting roles, religious activities, voluntary work and leisure (Wray 2003).

Gendered patterns of participation in social relationships have tended to characterise older women as social organisers (Russell 2007). Similarly to meanings of home, this is also a reflection of the greater social and emotional labour women have traditionally performed. Older men may defer to their wives, relying on them to make social plans and arrange family visits (Russell 2007). This can be problematic in the absence of women, leading to social isolation for older men who are divorced, widowed and unmarried (Davidson, Daly & Arber 2003). For example, in contrast to men who live alone, women living alone have been found to more frequently give and receive favours to neighbours (Perren, Arber & Davidson 2004). Gender differences in social participation outside the home also highlight the risk of social isolation for older men. Men have often been absent from community recreation centres designed to cater for the social needs of older people. Interviews with older men have indicated that they feel traditionally masculine activities are underprovided and they would prefer to form groups organised around tasks or clubs (Russell 2007; Davidson, Daly & Arber 2003).

Letting Go and the quality of adult child/ parent relationships

In the early 1990s, sociologist David de Vaus undertook a qualitative study of the relationships between adult children and their ageing or elderly parents and found that most adults' lives were emotionally interdependent with those of their parents, long after marriage or leaving home had severed household ties. De Vaus' study, *Letting Go* (1994), based on interviews with over 100 adult men and women, is a very rich and moving account of the lifelong and often difficult relationships men and women strive to maintain with their parents. De Vaus analysed his interviews around the central concept of 'letting go', which has some similarities with the psychological concept of attachment, and which he explained as follows:

> Letting go involves the differentiation of two people. It involves the capacity to see the other person as a person in his or her own right and the capacity to see oneself as a person in one's own right. It is not the denial of the relationship with the other person but the assertion of a particular type of relationship—one in which the person is valued for his or her own sake and in which one is able to act independently of the other person's approval or expectations (de Vaus 1994, p. 186).

For de Vaus, the emotional success or failure of the relationships his interviewees described hinged on whether or not the parent had been able to successfully distinguish his or her own needs from those of the child, and vice versa. In his study, de Vaus classified adult-child relationships into four main types: parent-centred, child-centred, remote and attached.

In the first two types of relationship, letting go had not been successful. In parent-centred relationships, a quarter of the 100 relationships considered, parents very much expected children to conform to their belief system and values. When this didn't happen, the adult children were criticised and put down by parents. The adult children in this group perceived their parents to have shown little interest in their ideas. They considered they had spent a great deal of time and energy trying to win parents' approval, as in the following quotation:

> I've got to guard myself against Mum. If I let my guard down I'll make a slip and then it will be on and I just don't have the energy to fight. I say 'Here I am, almost 50, and you're still trying to tell me what to do'. I'm still a child to her and she is still trying to keep me: still trying to own me (de Vaus 1994, p.1).

The opposite type to this was the child-centred relationships in which the children's lives provided the focus for the parents. Parents criticised, interfered, and emphasised children's inexperience. Adult children struggled to be left alone and to prove they could manage as independent adults.

> I resented them, both of them. They were very over-protective. I was an only child and they didn't have friends or anything to turn to for advice. I couldn't have anything that might cause me to get hurt ... Everything I did was watched. I felt like I was unjustly treated ... At the same time, they tried to buy my love. They were always showering me with gifts (de Vaus 1994, p. 36).

In the second two types, letting go had been accomplished, but to very different degrees. Remote relationships were those in which neither the children nor the parents wanted to be involved in each other's lives. In these relationships, the adult children perceived they had a great deal of autonomy, either because they had parental approval or had given up trying to get it:

> For a long time when I was young I didn't know he was my father. He slept on the verandah. I didn't know who he was. He's a nothing—a grey background figure who gives nothing and doesn't expect anything ... You can't reach out and touch him because he is not real. He is what everybody else wants him to be. I'm always pleased to see him and we have a very pleasant time, but he could be an uncle (de Vaus 1994, p. 61).

Finally, there were those with what de Vaus called attached relationships with parents. In these relationships, the parents did not interfere, treated their adult children as competent adults and acknowledged that they had a right to be different. These were the relationships described by participants as the least problematic and the most rewarding:

> My parents are reliable, loving, considerate, kind—always there. Things are nice and comfortable without being demanding in any way-in either direction. They are never imposing or demanding. I couldn't think of a better relationship ... There have been lots of times when they would like to have said 'Do that differently'. But never, ever from the day I got married have they once told me what I should or shouldn't do (de Vaus 1994, p. 87).

De Vaus' study captures adult-child/parent relationships from the perspective of the adult children only, and at one point in time, when (potentially) we could expect considerable change in the quality of relationships over time. However, it provides compelling reading as to the emotional resonance of older parent/adult-child relationships and remains one of the few Australian sociological studies to have considered intergenerational relationships between older adults.

Care and intergenerational relationships

FUNCTIONALIST SOCIOLOGIST TALCOTT PARSONS VIEWED the isolated nuclear family household form as relatively free from obligations to extended family, and saw this as a logical response to the industrial capitalist requirement for a mobile and flexible labour force. However, Litwak (1960) developed the concept of **modified extended family** to account for the interdependence discernible between family households of different generations. Despite the fact that extended family members tend not to cohabit in industrialised Western societies, it was evident to Litwak that substantial social exchanges of care and other resources continued to characterise intergenerational family relationships.

Contemporary Australian data indicates that many extended families who do not live in the same household interact with each other and offer support between the generations for prolonged periods of time. Increasing longevity is an important factor in this, as it provides greater opportunities for remarriage and grandparenting. For instance, 92 per cent of Australian 50–70-year-olds have weekly contact with an adult child, and provide a range of emotional, financial and practical supports to adult children. For those families who are income rich but time poor, the transfer of resources between generations may be financial with some families buying care for relatives. Among those who are time rich and income poor the transfers are more likely to come in the form of offers of informal care and other personal resources (Tongue & Ballenden 1999). In Australia, the flow of care and support still tends to work in favour of the adult children of retired parents. The older generation provides more unpaid care, financial support and resources to their middle-aged adult children than the other way around. This has been confirmed by numerous Australian studies of care and time use by men and women of different ages (see de Vaus 2004).

Despite the interconnections between adult children and their ageing parents, a degree of household and financial independence from adult children is considered ideal by most older Australian adults. Relatively few expect to or want to live with their adult children, in contrast to the expectations of older adults in other countries, for example, China (see Sheng & Settles 2006) and Italy (Baldassar 2007). In the Australian context, even carers of frail older relatives tend not to live with their parents. According to Wolcott (1998), for the current cohort of older Australians aged 50–70 'intimacy without dependence' best characterises their attitudes to family involvement and support.

- -

The 'sandwich generation'

GROWING NUMBERS OF MIDDLE-AGED women find themselves in the position of caring for or financially supporting their own dependent children or grandchildren and their elderly parents, while working full- or part-time jobs. They have come to be known as the '**sandwich generation**' because they are stuck in the middle of a considerable burden of care-giving for the younger and older generations. Because it has become increasingly popular to delay childrearing until you are in your late 20s or 30s, many Australians over 40 and even over 50, are in a situation where they have very young dependent children and elderly parents. Relatively young grandmothers in their 40s may have caring responsibilities for grandchildren and their ageing parents, once their own children are adults. Middle-aged women thus particularly face what some researchers have called a 'priority shuffle'. 'Who will I be?'; 'How do I fulfil all my roles?'; 'What are reasonable expectations on my time?'. There may be a particularly large gap between what women want to do and what they feel obliged to do when caregiving pressures come from older and younger generations.

Long–distance family relationships and aged care

Global technologies such as the internet, email, fax and Voice Over Internet Protocols (VOIP, or internet telephone), coupled with the decreasing costs of airline travel, have substantially increased the opportunities for relationships of care across geographic distance. Until recently, a strong assumption in the gerontology (aged care) literature was that care-giving requires close geographic proximity between aged people and their carers (Baldassar 2007). New literature on **transnational care-giving** has come into being in recent years, documenting and theorising the considerable social and emotional support migrant adult children provide to family members overseas. Gardner and Grillo (2002) have coined the phrase 'the transnational domestic sphere' (p. 179) as a way of considering the kinds of relationships and activities sustained between family members—notably, adult migrants and their elderly parents—from a distance.

Cora Vellekoop Baldock (2000), a Perth-based Dutch-born sociologist, began researching the characteristics of intergenerational care-giving in Australia in the mid 1990s, partly in response to her own experiences of caring for her elderly mother 'back home' in Holland:

> It was my father's death that brought a drastic change 25 years after I had left home. He died suddenly but I was able to attend the funeral, help comfort my mother, and assist my sister with some of the financial and other arrangements. This close contact and involvement in family continued after my return to Australia. I began a pattern of weekly phone calls with my mother, and my sister began to provide me with detailed information about my mother's well-being, financial matters, and any other issues requiring action. In this, my advice was sought, and it appeared that my involvement was appreciated. Return visits also began to accelerate, sometimes combined with research travel and conferences, but also specially arranged for family occasions (2000, p. 213).

Baldock, and colleagues Loretta Baldassar and Raelene Wilding, subsequently undertook a large study of transnational care-giving within a number of Australian resident migrant groups. The researchers included interviews with migrant adult children and family members in the country of origin as participants in the study (Baldassar, Baldock & Wilding 2007). The researchers found that male and female migrants were involved in care-giving for elderly parents in their country of birth. Their practices ranged from letters, phone calls to elderly parents and other family members or neighbours, emails, care-giving visits, and could also involve re-migration back to country of origin depending on circumstances. The impending death or serious illness of a relative often led to a prolonged return visit. Although transnational care was performed by men and women, there were discernible gender differences in the types of care and assistance provided. Men tended to be more involved in assistance to family members with business affairs, repairs and maintenance, whereas the women were more engaged with practical support connected to health issues and emotional support. The researchers concluded that transnational family relationships for all migrant groups are complex and substantial across space and time.

Baldassar (2007) also observes that migrants remain preoccupied with the influence their leaving has had on families and family relationships in their country of origin, and that maintaining the sense of connection relies on devoting considerable time and energy to sustaining social networks in the country of origin, in addition to sustaining an imagined or more symbolic and abstract sense of family ties. For this latter reason, Baldassar contends that there are connections between these domestic dimensions of transnational family relationships and the 'bigger picture' of transnational relations between migrants and their country of origin, with regard to the emotional and social benefits and costs of sustaining the connections:

> Unless there are functioning transnational networks, neither [the relationship to family or to the country of origin] can exist. Individuals and their emotional and affective attachments need to be able to transgress time and space. One [the country] may demand that you die for your motherland, the other [the family] that you perhaps surrender your chosen life to a kind of 'social death' in order to deliver your duty to your dependent parents or kin. The alternative is to effect a betrayal. They are both steeped in political and ideological baggage; one tied up in notions of obligation to an imagined nation, the other to an imagined family (Baldassar 2007, p. 283).

In other words, transnational care-giving may lead migrant adult children to experience a degree of ambivalence about identity and belonging. They may experience doubts about the migration decision, and also question whether their firmest allegiances are to the family ties in their country of residence or in the country of birth. A great deal of guilt was expressed about 'not being there' particularly if parents died and there had not been enough time to return before it happened.

Grandparenting

MORE OLDER PEOPLE LIVE TO see their children have children today than in previous times, due to increased life-expectancy, and will generally have some contact with grandchildren. A recent Australian study found that it was very rare for children to have no contact with at least one grandparent, and only 2.9 per cent of babies and toddlers, and 2.6 per cent of 4–5-year-olds were in this category (Gray, Misson & Hayes 2005). Grandparenthood is not a fixed life stage. Grandparents may be aged anywhere from their late 30s to their 90s, and thus barely middle-aged, ageing or elderly. They are a diverse group whose values and experiences as grandparents will be shaped by the social history they have lived through, the quality of the relationships with their own children, and their level of participation in the workforce.

Grandparenting as a social identity

GOODFELLOW (2003) SUGGESTS THAT GRANDPARENTS may base their beliefs about how grandparents should behave towards grandchildren on their memories of their own parents' behaviour as grandparents. She argues that many of today's grandparents who had their children in the 1950s or early 1960s may have formulated images of grandmothers (in particular) as nurturing, caring and available. Few of their mothers or mothers-in-law would have been in the paid workforce after marriage, in keeping with the prevailing expectations of women and the social policies of the times. Attias–Donfut and Segalen (2002), by contrast, suggest that the social climate in which grandparents became adults and undertook their parenting is more formative of the values informing their grandparenthood. In discussing the newer 'baby boom' generation of French grandparents born after 1940, who became adults during a considerable degree of social upheaval, these authors contend:

> The new generation of grandparents … have lived through a period of major social change that has seen new types of conjugal relations emerge, new styles of bringing up children, access to contraception and abortion for women, women participating massively in the labour market … and legal changes concerning conjugal relationships … Today's young grandparents were liberal parents … They opened the way to divorce and relationships without marriage. Their children were conceived voluntarily and in a planned way, and they became part of a new culture of intimacy (p. 283).

In this view, an affectionate and emotionally supportive grandparenting style is more likely to be influenced by adult experiences of changing social mores about relationship formation, contraception and abortion that enable more children to be planned and wanted. These authors also suggest the greater emphasis placed on intimacy and democracy in parent/child relationships from the 1970s onwards has bearing on grandparenting styles.

Grandparenting and childcare expectations

A MARKED CHANGE OVER THE past few years is in the number of grandparents, particularly grandmothers, providing regular care to grandchildren. As more families with children today are dual-earner families, increasing demands and expectations for childcare are placed on grandparents. In 2005, grandparents provided childcare to 20 per cent of all children, and constituted the main informal care providers (ABS 2005). Grandparents are also engaged in other kinds of support for their working children and grandchildren, which includes picking children up from school, kindergarten and childcare centres, and occasional care when children are sick (Gray, Misson & Hayes 2005).

Placing children in the regular care of their grandparents is known to be popular for a number of reasons. It is cheaper, more flexible and often more readily available than formal childcare (Gray, Misson & Hayes 2005). Perhaps more importantly, many parents assume that a relative, particularly a grandmother, will be more emotionally committed to the children and is able to provide more loving and attentive care than non-relatives (Goodfellow 2003). Grandparents themselves are known to consider their caring activities to constitute more than 'minding' or 'babysitting'. In Goodfellow's Australian study, grandparents spoke about the care they perform as valuable due to them having intimate knowledge not only about the children, but also the family. Many contrasted the care they could provide with the kind of care they believed would be provided by a paid carer:

> If you are caring for children in general, you are not emotionally involved.
> With strangers he's just another fee. With us, he is family (2003, p.11).

Goodfellow and Laverty (2003) found the there were four main perspectives on caregiving expressed by grandparents. 'Avid caregivers' were grandparents whose lives and identities tended to be centred around their grandchildren; 'flexible caregivers' were very involved with their grandchildren yet also gave some priority to having their own time; 'selective caregivers' enjoyed their grandchildren and considered them important yet did not want the grandparenting identity to define them; and 'hesitant caregivers' did not anticipate or want to care for grandchildren, in recognition of competing interests and concerns in their lives. The authors also found that grandparents who were not born in Australia—from both English and non-English-speaking backgrounds—were more likely to be in the 'avid caregiver' group. This may indicate the strength of cultural expectations that grandparents should provide childcare, or that grandparents want to hand down language, culture and traditions of the country of origin to grandchildren. It may also indicate that the migration experience shapes the sense of emotional investment in intergenerational ties.

Other researchers have found that the grandparenting/child relationship, and the grandparents' willingness to engage in childcare, has much to do with the quality of the relationships between the grandparents and the adult children, and their engagement with the paid workforce. Grandparents of lower socio-economic status tend to feel a greater degree of obligation to their children and grandchildren in terms of providing care. Higher socio-economic status grandparents, many of whom are still in the workforce or have very active education or travel lives in retirement, may see things quite differently, and feel more entitled to assert themselves in response to adult children's demands. Tensions may arise also when grandparents are perceived to interfere too much in the parenting and provide unwelcome and unsolicited advice about parenting styles (see Ochiltree 2006).

Just as mothers continue to take on greater responsibility for child rearing than fathers, so too it is with grandmothers. Grandmothers are more likely than grandfathers to be the 'hands-on' regular childcare providers, and to feel obliged to make personal sacrifices in order to provide care to children, for example, to reduce their working hours. Thelma's story (below), demonstrates very well the complex set of considerations about obligations to adult children that go into women's decisions to regularly care for grandchildren, and the frustrations and personal sacrifices this may entail:

My son starts work at five in the morning and he's home at 2.30. My daughter-in-law goes to work at 3 o'clock and works until half past eight. I said to them: 'Look, I intend to retire … [from my senior executive position] … as soon as I hit fifty-five, so if you can just hang in there and do this until I retire then I'll babysit full time for you until my husband retires.' I didn't want them to have to wait for years and years before having another child and all her salary needing to go to childcare. In the meantime, my other son and his wife had a child … So they said: 'We'll take up the offer.' And I thought, 'Hang on, it wasn't really an offer to you', because … my other son had a good job and so did his wife … However, you can't say, 'No, I'm not doing it for you, I'm only doing it for the others.' So that's how I ended up caring for the two children … They took me literally. I retired Thursday. I had Friday, Saturday and Sunday [off] and I came back on Monday and started babysitting. This year I have the children on four days of the week (from Goodfellow 2003, p. 7).

Finally, an issue beginning to attract research and legal attention concerns the considerable number of grandparents who are not only caring for but raising grandchildren in Australia today. There are a number of reasons why grandparents become primary carers of children, with maternal substance abuse accounting for over 50 per cent of Australian and 70 per cent of US grandparents acting as parents. According to unpublished ABS data, the Family Characteristic Survey in 1997 found that there were around 12,000 children aged 0–14 who were living with their grandparents but not their parents. However, a lack of previous Australian and international research and population data on grandparented families has contributed to insufficient policy, community services and government support for these grandparents (Horner, Downie, Hay & Wichmann 2007). Evidence from New Zealand, the USA, and European countries including the United Kingdom indicates that primary-carer grandparents all over the developed world are facing the same financial, legal and personal issues reported by Australian grandparents (Horner et al. 2007). They are usually not eligible for the payments and support services available to others who provide foster care or formal out-of-home care to children not their own, and their legal rights are often ambiguous and difficult to enforce. In their Grandparents Raising Grandchildren Study, Fitzpatrick and Reeve (2003) interviewed 499 grandparents raising grandchildren. Grandparents reported feeling that the legal system and government bureaucracy was unjust towards them and their grandchildren. For instance, parents continued to be eligible for Legal Aid and Centrelink payments while grandparents were not. Because parents can retain legal custody even though grandparents have been given responsibility for care, the grandparents reported that medical and educational care had been made difficult, for example, needing the child's birth certificate to enrol them in school. These difficulties are compounded by other stressors for grandparents, such as marital pressure, social isolation and their own declining health (Horner et al. 2007; Fitzpatrick & Reeve 2003).

Lesbian and gay experiences of ageing

According to Brian Heaphy (2007), previous sociological literature has assumed ageing to be similarly experienced by gay, lesbian and bisexual people, in over-emphasising sexual identity at the expense of gender and other material, social, and cultural realities. Heaphy was interested in finding out how gender norms influence social and personal relationships among older lesbian and gay adults. The participants in his study were British gay men and lesbians between the ages of 50 and 80, who were asked how they were faring with care and intimate relationships through a series of focus group interviews and questionnaires.

Heaphy found that older gay men demonstrated more acceptance of gendered inequities in relationships than lesbians, in the sense that the men believed it was natural for one partner to be more dominant and for older men to seek younger partners. Similarly to older heterosexual men, Heaphy found that some older gay men's social networks had narrowed with age, although some reported friendships were an important social resource.

Older lesbians were distinguished by a stronger sense of commitment to the principle of caring for others within their communities. Many women spoke of a shared history of feminist activism and volunteering that over time had evolved into a self-made supportive personal community of friends. This community was based on an ethic of mutual care and participation. Some older gay men who shared a history of political community building and HIV/AIDS activism also spoke about the importance of belonging to a community, such as forming support groups for older gay men. However, in contrast to women's stories of mutual care, men more frequently spoke of care as something they wanted to receive more of from their community, rather than give. Heaphy also found that when older gay men and lesbians tried to work together, conventional gender expectations such as the idea that women are carers and men are 'cared for' became problematic for the lesbian women. This was disappointing, as Jenny, aged 66 years explained:

> What I found was that ... nobody actually wanted to do the [caring] service. We certainly had more women offering to do this, but the men [were unwilling]. I don't say that men don't [care for people], because a lot of good men do, but they get lost within the power thing. That's what I found ... it was all about status and power (Heaphy 2007, p. 205).

Another theme Heaphy believed distinguished older gay men's experiences from lesbians' was the higher value attached to youthful behaviour and appearance in gay male communities. Older lesbians felt that lesbian communities were less bothered about youthfulness, which led to a more positive experience of ageing. In not monitoring the ageing process as closely as their gay male peers there was more freedom to feel affirmed as an older woman. By contrast, gay men spoke of feeling very conscious of their ageing bodies, and excluded from gay community activities due to the value attached to youth. Some men felt that only youthful bodies were valued and celebrated in the commercial gay 'scene'.

Conclusion

IN ANY DISCUSSION OF OLDER people in Australia, it is important to give due consideration to the diversity of their experiences and expectations with regard to family and intimate relationships. For some older people, like Bill and Glenys who opened this chapter, they may expect their old age to be a time of diminished family responsibilities, a time of 'doing their own thing'. Others, notably many older women, will be carers to a husband in poor health, or take on substantial informal caregiving to grandchildren. Also, the increasing incidence of divorce and remarriage means that older people cannot be considered part of a uniform 'life stage'. Some 70-year-old men, for instance, may still be parenting and financially supporting school-aged children as well as having responsibilities to older adult children from a previous marriage.

Researchers consistently find that many grandparents find their role a very emotionally significant and rewarding one in a number of ways. It can represent a new dimension to family experience, serve as a pleasing reminder of their longevity and provide an opportunity to provide guidance, support, and the benefits of one's wisdom to a new generation. However, it can also represent considerable social and emotional hardship, particularly when grandparents find themselves with responsibilities for care not entirely of their choosing, or wholly responsible for grandchildren's primary care.

In keeping with changing expectations of younger and older generations, the following key questions can be expected to increasingly come to the fore in adult child/older parent relationship and care considerations. How close should adults live to their ageing or elderly parents? How much should they visit one another? To what extent should older parents expect to be included in the activities of their adult children? Should adults expect their parents to help them out with childcare? Should parents help their adult children financially? What help should adults give their elderly parents, and which of the children will take the most responsibility in this? What is clear from the discussion in this chapter is that the degree of choice or negotiating power available to older people in finding answers to these questions remains unevenly distributed in Australian society.

Key concepts

Disengagement theory

Activity theory

Third age

Modified extended family

Sandwich generation

Transnational care-giving

Discussion questions

1   What are the main ways in which grandparenting has changed over the past 30 years? How do you account for these changes?

2   How are migrant and transnational families reformulating notions of caregiving? What kinds of social changes have made this possible?

3   What is the 'third age'? What are the arguments for and against this concept as it applies to post-retirement life?

Recommended further reading

Baldassar, L. 2007, 'Transnational Families and Aged Care: the Mobility of Care and the Migrancy of Ageing', *Journal of Ethnic and Migration Studies*, vol. 33, no. 2, pp. 275–97.

Higgs, P. & Gilleard, C. 2006, 'Departing the Margins: Social Class and Later Life in a Second Modernity', *Journal of Sociology*, vol. 42, no. 3, pp. 219–41.

Ochiltree, G. 2006, 'The Changing Role of Grandparents', *Australian Family Relationships Clearinghouse Briefing*, no. 2, pp. 1–9.

14 Conclusion: New Families, New Relationships?

THE SOCIOLOGY OF FAMILIES, RELATIONSHIPS and intimate life is a diverse and rich field, which includes labour, love, intimacy, care and connection but also power, exploitation, neglect and abuse. Intimate life carries our personal hopes and dreams but is not separated from wider social structures or social change.

Intimate life and the wider society

THE CENTRAL PREMISE OF THIS book is that families and intimate lives are shaped by the historical moment we are living in, and by our culture and social location—in terms of ethnic and religious background, our gender, our class and sexual identity.

Sociology offers a way of linking our personal lives with wider social forces such as the development of capitalism, individualisation and globalisation. It does this by thinking through broad theoretical frameworks such as functionalism, Marxism, feminism and individualisation. At the same time, sociology also offers a way of thinking about how people experience and make sense of their relationships by generating more nuanced accounts of everyday life. Social dynamics are captured with new concepts such as 'family practices' and 'display' rather than static 'social roles' that dominated our thinking in the middle of last century. We are all actively involved in creating, maintaining or letting go of relationships: 'even Sociologists fall in love' (Jackson 1993).

Gender remains central in the organisation of families and relationships. Women and men are positioned differently in families and tend to specialise in different tasks. The modern family form that reached its peak in the 1950s with its rigid gender specialisation of breadwinner and homemakers continues to influence family life. Mothers are expected to take major responsibility for childrearing, domestic labour and care within the broader family and community context. The link between masculinity and paid work remains strong and fathers are expected to play the major role of financially supporting their families. Nevertheless the profound changes in the organisation of care and labour within families should not be underestimated. Gender relations are being transformed; the 'mother/worker' identity has emerged and men are being called into caring as the 'involved father' is becoming the ideal.

Ethnic and religious backgrounds have a major impact on family size, family roles and intergenerational relationships. Family changes such as cohabitation and divorce are dominated by people from Anglo-Australian backgrounds in Australia and those without strong religious affiliations. Social class shapes family life in important ways too but these are often hidden from view. People from disadvantaged backgrounds sometimes struggle to form relationships and maintain them and there is new evidence that marriage is for the privileged— the more highly educated and financially stable.

Sexual identity is emerging as a new way of differentiating and shaping intimate life. Heteronormative values are being profoundly challenged as gay and lesbian couples are setting up households and forming families. Increasingly gays and lesbians are seeking social and legal recognition for their relationships and parenting roles. Indeed, family cultures have become more fluid, diverse and interesting.

Love and moral panic

FAMILIES AND INTIMATE RELATIONSHIPS ARE distinctive domains of social life because they are drenched with emotion. Love transforms the everyday practices of feeding, cleaning and washing into profoundly meaningful expressions of care and connection (Smart 2007). But families can also be the site for devastating abuse. Families provide the setting for our earliest social interactions and are often idealised or fantasised about. As Carol Smart argues, in dealing with families 'we are dealing with aspirations, yearnings, falsehoods and nostalgia, and this is emotive territory' (Smart 2007, p. 16).

The strong emotions surrounding everyday life within families carry over to public debates about contemporary families and whether they are providing enough care for the people within them, notably children. Moral panic about the so-called decline of the family has emerged at various times over history. In Australia in the early 1900s because of the decline in the fertility rate, in the 1970s because of the rising divorce rate and in this new century other concerns have emerged such as those about fatherless or motherless families, due to increasing numbers of single women and lesbian and gay people having children. It is likely that debate over the form and function of family and other kinds of intimate relationships will always be with us as a consequence of ongoing social change.

The future of families

IN CONTEMPORARY FAMILY LIFE THE cliché 'the more things change, the more they stay the same' also holds true. Most people aspire to form ongoing relationships with a partner (generally through marriage), have children and maintain connections with their family of origin. And most people will achieve these goals. Our commitment to families and relationships remains strong. However the social conditions shaping how we express and understand commitment have changed markedly.

Current research and theoretical work on families indicates that our commitments are more likely to be built through 'family practices' of mutual exchange and satisfaction for both partners rather than obligation or duty. Arguably we have more choice in how to construct our personal lives than in other times in history but our choices also remain constrained by our immediate social context. The stability of the 1950s family has gone but still families and relationships are important to us; in some ways they are better and in some ways they are worse for the people within them.

The individualisation perspective put forward by writers such as Giddens (1992) and Beck-Gernsheim (2002) holds that social structures have loosened and we can no longer look to older certainties about how to live provided by rigid gender roles, class structures and religion; instead we are forced to engage reflexively in family life and write our own biographies. This perspective allows for both a certain pragmatism and optimism among some sociologists that new ethical frameworks are emerging to inform decision-making and build relationships in reformulated family configurations. But we must also be careful to evaluate the claims of individualisation theorists, when considering the extent to which gender, class and other social categories have become 'de-traditionalised'.

English sociologist Carol Smart's work on post-separation family life is a good example of this kind of scholarship. Smart and Neale (1999), through in-depth qualitative study of men, women and children's views of post-separation family life, propose that adults and children are beginning to alter their moral frameworks for relating to each other and find new productive ways of resolving conflict and making decisions. Although they don't by any means romanticise post-separation family life or gloss over the considerable pain and conflict families experiencing divorce go through, their emphasis is on the capacity of post-divorce families for moral action. By this they mean 'critical self-reflection' and behaviour change that is not based on falling back on their old certainties or ways of doing things. So divorce and the forging of post-separation relationships can provide adults with a means to change and challenge previously more stereotyped gender roles, find ways to care about the other parent despite the absence of the intimate relationship, and view their children as active rather than passive people with their own needs and perspectives on the issues.

Jeffrey Weeks (1995), writing in the context of same-sex relationships, puts a similar emphasis on what he calls 'invented moralities'. In lesbian and gay communities, friendships may take on many of the roles traditionally fulfilled by families, and relationships of commitment support and care may ensue from friendships. In gay men's intimate relationships, emotional support and lifelong commitment may be separated from sexual intimacy without causing harm. In keeping with the possibilities afforded by Giddens' (1992) ideas, Weeks (1995) argues for the value of sexual choices and experimentation that enhance individual development and exploration if they do not infringe on the freedoms or well-being of others. The point here is that because relational forms don't fit our traditional notions of conventional family structure and morality, it does not mean that meaningful, workable and new kinds of intimate relationships are not being enacted and should not be recognised by law and policy-makers.

However these new ways of examining relationships and families also have their critics. Arguably, the choice-making individual pursuing personal satisfaction within democratic relationships and making new moral decisions about commitment and care is a model open to particular types of people but not everyone. Middle-class, educated, mobile, child-free and financially secure adults are more able to shape their intimate lives in these new ways. For the rest, the reality of family and community connections and responsibilities limit these choices and possibilities. For instance, Ribbens McCarthy and colleagues (2003) argue that parent/child relationships do not offer a fluid moral domain but one where attending to 'the best interests of the child' remains a key moral imperative. Individualism and negotiation are traits encouraged in children by middle-class parents while 'fitting in' and being 'in control' are valued by working-class parents because these are more workable in disadvantaged contexts (Gillies 2007). Indeed the family and personal life has become interesting again to sociologists (Smart & Neale 1999) as new scholarship examines the achievement of democracy and freedom within our intimate lives and the powerful constraints working against this.

When relationships are difficult, one of the consolations of sociology is that it enables us to see this is not all our own fault. There are wider social forces at play, and we are not in this alone. So too, different social, economic and historical contexts foster different ways of organising and participating in relationships and families. It is likely that our intimate lives will become more complex and multilayered as individuals live longer and experience greater geographic mobility and more types of living arrangements over their lifetimes. Blood ties may become less important for many people in the West but intimate relationships will remain highly significant.

This book has succeeded if it has challenged you to reflect on the tension between notions of the personal and the structural, commitment to others and individual satisfaction, choice and duty, democracy and inequity in contemporary relationships. We imagine these themes will be with us for many years to come, no matter what form the relationships themselves actually take.

Glossary

Activity theory: Theory that emphasises positive aspects of ageing, and proposes that older people achieve successful ageing by remaining active and taking on new challenges, identities and opportunities.

Arranged marriage: Practice whereby the selection of a suitable marriage partner is made by parents and/or the wider kinship group.

Assisted marriage: A newer adaptation of arranged marriage, in that parents or extended family members specify several suitable marriage partners, and the son or daughter to be married is able to choose from these.

Assisted reproductive technologies (ART): Technologies such as IVF, surrogacy and donor insemination, which enable people to conceive a child.

Baby boom: An era of high birth rates. Usually refers to the era following World War II in countries such as Australia, the USA and the UK.

Baby bust: An era of decline in the birth rate associated with people delaying having children and having fewer children.

Battered women's syndrome (BWS): Psychological concept that describes a distinct pattern of psychological and behavioural symptoms that women can experience as a result of prolonged exposure to domestic violence.

Blended family: A family containing two or more children where at least one is a step-child of one of the parents and one is the biological or adopted child of both parents.

Boomerang generation: Refers to the phenomenon whereby young people experience cycles of moving out of the parental home, then returning due to financial, emotional, educational or housing issues.

Breadwinner: A person, traditionally a man, who is solely responsible for financially supporting their family.

Circumstantial childlessness: Social phenomenon described by Leslie Cannold (2005) whereby women may be childless due to circumstance rather than choice (for example, they may be approaching the end of their reproductive years without a partner or having a partner unwilling to have children).

Closed domesticated nuclear family: Concept developed by Stone (1977) to describe a type of family characterised by strong emotional bonds between parents and children and privacy in the home.

Cohabitation: An arrangement whereby two people in a sexual relationship live together without being married.

Common couple violence: Michael Johnson's (1995) concept to describe the occasional episodes of domestic violence by men or women in relatively equal relationships.

Confucianism: An ethical and philosophical system of thought influential in a number of East and South-East Asian countries. It influences the form and expression of family relationships.

Continuum of violence: Contemporary term used to symbolise the wide spectrum of abusive behaviours that can be experienced by children or adults.

Contraceptive technologies: These technologies enable people to avoid conceiving a child.

Core culture: An immigrant's concept of the ideals and beliefs characteristic of their country of origin at the time of their departure.

Cultural diversity: Where people have different values, ideals and beliefs about family and intimate relationships, which are, in turn, expressed in their practices.

Cycle of violence: Concept associated with the work of Lenore Walker (1984), whereby domestic violence is argued to occur in cycles characterised by a period of build-up and release, in which the victim and perpetrator both play a part.

Demography: The study of population trends.

Demographic approach: An approach to social research in which broad social patterns are observed from historical records and census data.

Diaspora: Refers to the movement, migration and dispersal of people beyond their country of origin or homeland.

Disengagement theory: Based on a functionalist perspective, disengagement theory purports that it is in the best interests of society for older people to gradually move out of positions of responsibility, particularly paid employment.

Displaying families: Term used by Finch (2007) to describe how families are sustained by the visible actions of family members rather than taken-for-granted roles.

Divorce–extended families: Judith Stacey's (1990) term to describe the positive growth in the number of family relationships that can occur after divorce and remarriage (for example, multiple grandparents and parents).

Discourse: A term derived from Foucault's social theory. Discourses are ways of speaking or writing that constitute social reality.

Doing gender: Theory proposed by Candace West and Don Zimmerman (1987) that views gender as an ongoing accomplishment rather than a fixed role. In other words, it is sustained by behaviours and activities performed by men and women.

Domestic labour: Unpaid labour performed in the domestic sphere, such as housework.

Domestic violence: Term used to denote the physical and/or psychological domination and control within families and intimate relationships.

Dual-earner families: Families in which both partners engage in paid work.

Emotion work: Coined by Arlie Hochschild (1983), this refers to the management of feelings and emotional well-being in the context of family and intimate relationships that is typically the responsibility of women.

Ethnicity: Group of people with a shared cultural history and background (for example, a common language, food, customs) that provides them with a sense of belonging and identity.

Expressive role: From the functional perspective, the expressive role in families is characterised as feminine, oriented to the private world of unpaid work and responsible for the care of children.

Extended family: Refers to kin beyond the nuclear family (such as grandparents, aunts, uncles, cousins).

Family of origin: Family into which a person was born and raised.

Family practices: Concept from the work of David Morgan (1996) in which 'family' is defined by activities that are performed regularly rather than as a structure or form. Practices can have multiple meanings and may change over time.

Family wage: a concept from the Australian Harvester Judgement 1907. A fair wage was defined as sufficient for a man to support a wife and three children, effectively institutionalising gendered wage inequality.

Family-friendly policies: Working arrangements made available to employees by their employer that support the management of family responsibilities and paid work.

Fathers' Rights Movement: The growth of men's action groups during the 1990s, formed in response to the distress and anger that many non-custodial fathers experienced following divorce.

Feminist theory/feminism: A constellation of theoretical perspectives that share the view that women have historically been subordinated in society and that there is a conflict between the interests of women and men.

Filial piety: A concept about appropriate intergenerational relationships associated with Confucian philosophy in East and South-East Asian countries. It refers to the devout respect, obedience and gratitude expected of children towards parents and elders.

Friendship: A relationship between people that is not legally bound but may include qualities of care, commitment, interests and shared activities to varying degrees.

Functionalism: A theoretical perspective that emphasises the ways in which social structures shape behaviours and the roles that people play in society. A functionalist perspective views families as fundamental to the smooth functioning of society.

Gender regime: Concept from the work of R.W. Connell to describe the historical and structural ordering of gender relations. It takes into account the gendered division of labour, power relations, and the gendering of emotions within relationships.

Gender symmetry thesis: Theory that posits that men and women are equally violent in domestic contexts.

Gender: The social construction of masculinities and femininities.

Genealogical bewilderment: Concept used to describe the feelings of identity loss that people who do not know their biological heritage may experience.

Globalisation: Term used to describe the increasing interconnectedness of societies through media, telecommunications and other technological advances. Globalisation can include economic, political or cultural elements.

Group households: Household in which unrelated people live together.

Hegemonic masculinity: Concept developed by R.W Connell (1987, 2002, 2005). Hegemonic refers to the fact that in most social settings there is a narrow range of dominant ways to express oneself as a man.

Heteronormativity: The privileging of relational assumptions based on the majority experience of heterosexuals.

Heterorelationality: Refers to the privileging of the cohabiting, monogamous relationship as the most important relational form.

Homogamy: The tendency for people to marry people similar to themselves in class, age, race, ethnicity, religion and education.

Host culture: The dominant culture of the country where the immigrant now lives.

Household: A group of people who live together, usually sharing resources such as food. Householders may or may not be members of the same family.

Housewife/Homemaker: A person, traditionally a woman, who is solely responsible for domestic labour and care of children in the home.

Hypergamy: The social phenomenon of marrying someone of a higher social status or class.

Ideology: A shared belief system that advocates or justifies a particular way of living.

Individualisation: Refers to structurally necessitated decision-making, or the social process by which individuals form beliefs, values, morals, decisions and identity using their own resources, because traditional social categories, such as gender and class, no longer dictate clear life paths.

Industrialisation: Process of social and technological change during the late eighteenth and nineteenth centuries, in which manufacturing boomed and paid work became separated from the home.

Instrumental role: From the functionalist perspective, the instrumental role in families is characterised as masculine, orientated to the public world and responsible for paid work to economically support the family.

In vitro fertilisation (IVF): Medical process whereby fertilisation of an ovum by sperm occurs in the laboratory rather than in a woman's body.

Juggling: Describes the complexity of managing paid work, home, children, schedules and family relationships.

Kinship: An anthropological term to describe family connections/relations between people. Historically, it refers to the social organisation of biological ties. Contemporary approaches view kinship as relatedness based on many factors, including connectedness to place and the maintenance of care relationships.

Late-modern families: Term used to describe the pattern of families associated with the post-industrial era.

Liberal feminism: Feminist perspective that emphasises equal access for women to rights, education and paid work beyond the home.

Life experiments: Term used by Weeks, Heaphy and Donovan (2001) to describe the diverse ways in which lesbian women and gay men conduct intimate relationships and networks of care.

Living Apart Together (LAT): This phenomenon refers to couples who maintain a committed relationship while living in separate residences.

Marriage boom: Period of time during which greater numbers of people entered into marriage and married at a younger age.

Marriage bust: An era of decline in the rate of marriage and increase in the rate of divorce.

Marriage squeeze: Social problem whereby educated women and uneducated men have experienced increased difficulty in finding a partner they feel is suitable and this is due, in part, to enduring gender stereotypes.

Matriarchal society: Society in which women are more powerful than men.

Maternalist culture: Culture in which mothers are seen as the natural and indispensable carers of children.

Modern families: Term used to describe the pattern of families from the period of industrialisation until the mid twentieth century.

Modified extended family: Concept from the work of Litwak (1960) to represent the interdependent relationships between family members across different generations.

Monogamy: Sexual exclusivity, in the sense of being faithful to the one sexual partner. The principle of monogamy underpins marriage in many Western and some non-Western cultures.

Moral Panic: A term coined by Stanley Cohen (2002) to describe a public reaction based on the false or exaggerated perception of the behaviour of a minority that is seen as threatening to society.

Multi–family households: Household structure in which more than two generations of the same family live together.

New father: New ideal of fatherhood where men are involved carers for their children and they balance work and family life.

Normalisation of divorce: A shift in social attitudes whereby divorce is no longer considered socially unacceptable.

Normalisation of fragility: Concept coined by Elisabeth Beck-Gernsheim (2002) to denote the potential for current generations to experience marriage and relationships as impermanent.

Nuclear family: A social group comprised of a mother, father and their child/ children living together.

Open lineage family: Concept developed by Stone (1977) to describe a type of family characterised by a lack of privacy, extensive kinship and a lack of closeness between spouses and between parents and children.

Patriarchal family: Term used to describe a family form in which there is strong paternal authority over women and children and the interests of the family are emphasised over the individual.

Patriarchal terrorism: Michael Johnson's concept to describe the form of systematic domestic violence enacted in the interests of male control in patriarchal families.

Patriarchy: The power exercised by older men over women and children. In feminism this describes structural gender inequalities between women and men.

Patrilineal: Inheritance through male bloodline.

Patrilocal residence: Residence pattern in which a married couple and their children reside with the husband's family of origin.

Plastic sexuality: Giddens' (1992) concept that sexuality, having been separated from reproduction, is available as a creative expression of one's personality.

Political economy perspective: A structural theoretical perspective that emphasises how family and relationships are shaped by economic relations and social class.

Polygamy: The practice of a man having more than one wife.

Post-adolescence: A period of life in which the youth phase of freedom from responsibilities has been extended to prioritise careers, life experience and self-development prior to 'settling-down'.

Postmodernism: A theoretical approach that emphasises difference, diversity and contradiction. Postmodernism has been critical of grand theories and universal thought.

Preference theory: A theoretical approach used by Catherine Hakim (2000) to explain the enduring inequalities between men and women as being the result of people choosing to do what they prefer to do.

Pre-modern families: Term used to describe the pattern of European families prior to industrialisation.

Pseudo-mutuality: Bittman and Pixley (1997) coined this phrase to describe how men and women maintain a belief in equally shared domestic and paid labour, while their actual practices are unequal.

Pure relationship: A concept from the work of Anthony Giddens (1992) that refers to the qualities of contemporary relationships in which emotional satisfaction, personal fulfilment and equality are highly valued.

Queer Theory: A postmodern theoretical perspective predicated on the dismantling and reframing of conventional gender and sexuality categories (see *heteronormativity* and *heterorelationality*).

Radical feminism: Feminist perspective that views *patriarchy* as the central mechanism for understanding women's oppression.

Replacement level fertility: The estimate of the number of children a woman would need to have in her lifetime to replace herself and her partner.

Restricted patriarchal nuclear family: Concept developed by Stone (1977) to describe a type of family in which the father was the unquestioned head of the family and there were strong loyalties to the church and state.

Same-sex-attracted youth (SSAY): Young people who are attracted to or sexually active with the same sex. The term evokes the complex relationship between sexual behaviour, sexual attraction and sexual identities, rather than pinning down young people's sexuality to the rigid categories 'gay', 'lesbian', 'bisexual' or 'heterosexual'.

Sandwich generation: Term that describes the experience of the 'middle' generation who are in the position of caring for dependent children and elderly parents. In Western countries, it usually refers to women's caregiving responsibilities but it can also refer to the responsibilities of elder sons in Confucian influenced cultures characterised by *filial piety*.

Second wave feminism: Term used to denote the period of feminism from late 1960s to the 1980s, in which attention was drawn to the enduring inequalities experienced by women.

Sentiments approach: An historical approach to social research on families and households that seeks to understand how people related to and understood each other.

Sexual double standard: The existence of different standards for women and men regarding sexual behaviour. For example, until recently, young women were expected to remain virgins until they married while sexual experience was expected of young men.

Sexualisation of children: The idea that children are encouraged prematurely to become sexual beings, through the manner in which they are represented in advertising and popular culture.

Single: Describes people who are 'unpartnered' in the sense of not being in a cohabiting or committed intimate relationship. Historically, the term has meant 'unmarried', but this usage has considerably changed in recent years.

Social class: A form of social stratification in which groups of people are distinguished by differences in socio-economic position, social status or other social indicators.

Social structure: Sociological concept that refers to enduring or institutionalised patterns in social practice. It includes social divisions such as gender and class.

Socialisation: From a functional perspective, socialisation is a key function of families whereby children develop stable personalities and appropriate gender roles.

Socialist feminism: Feminist perspective that emphasises the gendered division of labour, particularly the exploitation of women's domestic labour under patriarchy and capitalist systems.

Sociobiology: A perspective that regards humans as a type of animal with biologically determined instincts, drives and roles.

Step-families: A family form whereby cohabiting or married adults live with a child or children who are the biological or adopted children of one of the adults.

Symbolic interactionism: This is a micro-sociological perspective originating from the work of George H. Mead and Erving Goffman. It focuses on how people experience and make sense of everyday life and their interactions in the social world.

The stalled revolution: Drawn from the work of Arlie Hochschild (1989), this describes the situation in which women have moved into the paid workforce but still do the majority of domestic labour and childcare.

The Stolen Generation: The generation of Indigenous Australians who were systematically removed from their families by the Australian government.

Total fertility rate (TFR): The number of children a woman would have during her lifetime if she experienced current age-specific fertility rates at each age of her reproductive life.

Transformation of intimacy: A concept from the work of Anthony Giddens (1992) used to describe the changing state of contemporary relationships.

Transnational care-giving: A social trend in the globalisation era whereby families provide support in a range of ways, including emotional, financial and social support, to family members in different countries.

Transnational families: Families whose members are dispersed across national borders due to immigration, education or work commitments in different countries.

Work/care order: Concept derived from Barbara Pocock's (2003) work. Refers to the Australian economic, social, cultural and institutional context in which working life and caring life occur.

Work/care regimes: Concept developed by Barbara Pocock (2003) to describe how dominant cultural beliefs about men, women and work, social institutions and individual behaviours and preferences interact within the work/care order.

References

ABS 2008, *Migration Australia*, cat. no. 3412.0, ABS, Canberra.

ABS 2007a, *Divorces Australia 2006*, cat. no. 3307.0.55.001, ABS, Canberra.

ABS 2007b, *Births Australia 2006*, cat. no. 3301.0, ABS, Canberra.

ABS 2007c, *Marriages, Australia 2006*, cat. no. 3306.0.55.001, ABS, Canberra.

ABS 2007d, Lincare, S. 'Lifetime marriage and divorce trends' Australian Social Trends, cat. no. 4102.0, ABS, Canberra.

ABS 2007e, *2006 Census QuickStats: Australia*, ABS, Canberra.

ABS 2006a, *Australian Social Trends 2006*, cat. no. 4102.0, ABS, Canberra.

ABS 2006b, Year Book Australia, cat. no. 1301.0, ABS, Canberra.

ABS 2006c, *Voluntary Work, Australia*, cat. no. 4441.0, ABS, Canberra.

ABS 2006d, *Health of Older People in Australia: A Snapshot*, cat. no. 4833.0.55.001, ABS, Canberra.

ABS 2006e, *Children's Participation in Cultural and Leisure Activities*, Australia, cat. no. 4901.0, ABS, Canberra.

ABS 2006f, Personal Safety, Australia 2005 [Reissue] cat. no. 4906.0, ABS, Canberra.

ABS 2005, *Childcare*, cat. no. 4402.0 [June reissue], ABS, Canberra.

ABS 2003a, *Year Book Australia*, cat. no. 1301.0, ABS, Canberra.

ABS 2001, *Census One Per cent Sample*, Confidentialised Unit Record File, ABS, Canberra.

ABS 2000, *Australian Demographic Statistics*, cat. no. 3101.0, ABS, Canberra. *Newsletters—Demography News—October.*

ABS 1999, *Year Book Australia*, cat. no. 1301.1, ABS, Canberra.

Ackerman, D. 1994, *A Natural History of Love*, Vintage Books, New York.

ACON 2004, 'Homelessness and Same Sex Domestic Violence in the Supported Accommodation Assistance Program', available at <http://ssdv.acon.org.au/providerinfo/documents/HomelessnessSSDVinSAAP.pdf>.

Agigian, A. 2004, *Baby Steps: How Lesbian Alternative Insemination is Changing the World*, Wesleyan, Connecticut.

Ai Yun, H. 2004, 'Ideology and Changing Family Arrangements in Singapore', *Journal of Comparative Family Studies*, vol. 35, pp. 375–92.

Albury, R. 1999, *The Politics of Reproduction: Beyond the Slogans*, Allen & Unwin, Sydney.

Allan, G. 2008, 'Flexibility, Friendship and Family', *Personal Relationships*, vol. 15, pp. 1–16.

Allen, L. 2003, 'Girls want Sex, Boys want Love: Resisting Dominant Discourses of (Hetero)Sexuality', *Sexualities*, vol. 6, no. 2, pp. 215–36.

Allen, L. 2004, '"Getting off" and "going out": Young People's Conceptions of Heterosexual Relationships', *Culture, Health and Sexuality*, vol. 6, no. 6, pp. 463–81.

Amato, P.R. 2000, 'The Consequences of Divorce for Adults and Children', *Journal of Marriage and Family*, vol. 62, no 4, pp. 1269–87.

Amato, P.R. & Hohmann-Marriot, B. 2007, 'A Comparison of High- and Low-distress Marriages that End in Divorce', *Journal of Marriage and Family*, vol. 69, no. 3, pp. 621–38.

Amato, P.R. & Previti, D. 2003, 'People's Reasons for Divorcing: Gender, Social Class, the Lifecourse and Adjustment', *Journal of Family Issues*, vol. 24, pp. 602

Anderson, M. 1980, *Approaches to the History of the Western Family 1500–1914*, Macmillan, London.

Anonymous 2002, 'How it Feels to be a Child of Donor Insemination', *British Medical Journal*, no. 324, pp. 7340 [data supplement].

Aries, P. 1962, *Centuries of Childhood: A Social History of Family Life*, Vintage, New York.

Arnett, J.J. 1997, 'Young People's Conceptions of the Transition to Adulthood', *Youth & Society*, vol. 29, no. 1, pp. 3–21.

Ascione, F., Weber, C. & Wood, D. 1997, 'The Abuse of Animals and Domestic Violence: A National Survey of Shelters for Women who are Battered', *Society and Animals*, vol. 5, no. 3, pp. 205–18.

Attias-Donfut, C. & Segalen, M. 2002, 'The construction of grandparenthood', *Current Sociology*, vol. 50, no. 2, pp. 281–94.

Australian Institute of Criminology 2006, Crime: Facts and Figures 2005, Australian Institute of Criminology, Canberra.

Avery, J. 2002, 'Jura Conjugalia Reconsidered: Kinship Classification and Ceremonial Roles in Adjacent Aboriginal Populations in the Northern Territory of Australia', *Anthropological Forum*, vol. 12, no. 2, pp. 221–33.

Bagshaw, D. & Chung, D. 2000, 'Women, Men and Domestic Violence, Partnerships against Domestic Violence Taskforce', Commonwealth of Australia, Canberra.

Bagshaw, D., Chung, D., Couch, M., Lilburn, S. & Wadham, B. 2000, 'Reshaping Responses to Domestic Violence: Final Report', Partnerships against Domestic Violence, Department of Human Services, South Australia, University of South Australia and Commonwealth of Australia.

Bailey, B. 1989, *From Front Porch to Back Seat: Courtship in Twentieth Century America*, The Johns Hopkins Press, Baltimore.

Baker, M. 2001, *Families, Labour and Love*, Allen & Unwin, Sydney.

Baldassar, L. 2007, 'Transnational Families and Aged Care: The Mobility of Care and the Migrancy of Ageing', *Journal of Ethnic and Migration Studies*, vol. 33, no. 2, pp. 275–97.

Baldassar, L., Baldock, C. & Wilding, R. 2007, *Families Caring Across Borders: Migration, Ageing and Transnational Caregiving*, Palgrave Macmillan, Houndmills.

Baldock, C. V. 2000, 'Migrants and their Parents: Caregiving from a Distance', *Journal of Family Issues*, vol. 21, no. 2, pp. 205–224.

Barnard, J. 1982, *The Future of Marriage*, Yale University Press, New Haven.

Barrett, M. 1992, 'Words and Things: Materialism and Method in Contemporary Feminist Analysis', in M. Barrett & A. Phillips (eds), *Destabalizing theory*, Polity Press, Cambridge.

Barrett, M. & McIntosh, M. 1982, *The Anti-Social Family*, Verso, London.

Batrouney, T. & Stone, W. 1998, 'Cultural Diversity and Family Exchanges', *Family Matters*, no. 51, pp. 13–20.

Bauman, Z. 2003, *Liquid Love: On the Frailty of Human Bonds*, Polity Press, Cambridge.

Bawin-Legros, B. & Gauthier, A. 2001, 'Regulation of Intimacy and Love Semantics in Couples Living Apart Together', *International Review of Sociology*, vol. 11, no. 1, pp. 39–46.

Baxter, J. 2002, 'Patterns of Change and Stability in the Gender Division of Household Labour in Australia 1996–1997', *Journal of Sociology*, vol. 38, no. 4, pp. 399–424.

Baxter, J., Hewitt, B. & Western, M. 2007, 'Post-familial Families and the Domestic Division of Labour: A View from Australia', HILDA conference.

BBC 2005, available at <http://news.bbc.co.uk/go.pr/fr/-/2/hi/americas/4081999.stm 2005/12/22>.

Beck, U. 1992, *Risk Society: Towards a New Modernity*, Sage, London.

Beck, U. & Beck-Gernsheim, E. 2002, *Individualization*, Sage, London.

Beck, U. & Beck-Gernsheim, E. 1995, *The Normal Chaos of Love*, Polity, Cambridge.

Beck-Gernsheim, E. 2002, *Reinventing the Family: In Search of New Lifestyles*, trans. P. Camiller, Polity, Cambridge.

Berk. S.F. 1985, *The Gender Factory: The Apportionment of Work in American Households*, Plenum, New York.

Berlant, L. & Warner, M. 2000, 'Sex in Public', in L. Berlant (ed.) *Intimacy*, University of Chicago Press, Chicago.

Berndt, R.M. & Berndt, C.H. 1977, *The World of the First Australians*, 2nd edn, Ure Smith, Sydney.

Birmingham, J. 2001, *He Died with a Felafel in his Hand*, Duffy and Snellgrove, Sydney.

Birrell, B., Rapson, V. & Hourigan, C. 2004, *Men and Women Apart: Partnering in Australia*, The Australian Family Association and Centre for Population Research, Melbourne.

Bittman, M. & Pixley, J. 1997, *The Double Life of the Family*, Allen & Unwin, St. Leonards.

Bittman, M., England, P., Sayer, L., Folbre, N. & Matheson, G. 2003, 'When does Gender Trump Money? Bargaining and Time in Household Work', *American Journal of Sociology*, vol. 109, pp. 186–214.

Blagg, H. 2000, 'Crisis Intervention in Aboriginal Family Violence', Summary Report Partnerships Against Domestic Violence Taskforce, Commonwealth of Australia, Canberra.

Boden, S. 2003, *Consumerism, Romance and the Wedding Experience*, Palgrave, Basingstoke.

Booth, A. & Amato, P.R. 2001, 'Parental Predivorce Relations and Offspring Postdivorce Well-being', *Journal of Marriage and Family*, vol. 63, no. 1, pp. 197–212.

Bottomley, G. 1997, 'Identification: Ethnicity, Gender and Culture', *Journal of Intercultural Studies*, vol. 18, no. 1, pp. 41–9.

Bottomley, G. 1979, *After the Odyssey*, University of Queensland Press, St Lucia.

Bradbury, B. 2004, *The Price, Cost, and Consumption and Value of Children*, Discussion Paper no. 132, Social Policy Research Centre, University of New South Wales.

Bradley, H. 1996, *Fractured Identities: Changing Patterns of Inequality*, Polity Press, Cambridge.

Brannen, J. 2002, 'Reconsidering Children and Childhood: Sociological and Policy Perspectives', in E. Silva & C. Smart 2002, *The New Family?*, Sage, London.

Brooks, A. 2006, *Gendered Work in Asian Cities: The New Economy and Changing Labour Markets*, Ashgate, Aldershot.

Broomhill, R. & Sharp, R. 2005, 'The Changing Male Breadwinner Model in Australia: A New Gender Order?', *Labour & Industry*, vol. 16, no. 1, pp. 105–30.

Budgeon, S. & Roseneil, S. 2004, 'Editor's Introduction: Beyond the Conventional Family', *Current Sociology*, vol. 52, no. 2, pp. 127–34.

Burke, T., Pinkey, S. & Ewing, S. 2002, 'Rent Assistance and Young People's Decision Making', Australian Housing and Urban Research Institute, Melbourne.

Butler, J. 1990, *Gender Trouble: Feminism and the Subversion of Identity*, Routledge, New York.

Buttrose, I. & Adams, P. 2005, *Motherguilt: Australian Women Reveal Their True Feelings about Motherhood*, Viking, Camberwell.

Byrne, A. 2003, 'Developing a Sociological Model for Researching Women's Self and Social Identities', *The European Journal of Women's Studies*, vol. 10, no. 4, pp. 443–64.

Calasanti, T & King, N. 2005, 'Firming the Floppy Penis: Age, Class, and Gender Relations in the Lives of Old Men', *Men and Masculinities*, vol. 8, no. 1, pp. 3–23.

Cannold, L. 2005, *What No Baby?*, Curtin University Books, Fremantle.

Cannold, L. 1998, *The Abortion Myth: Feminism, Morality and the Hard Choices Some Women Make*, Allen & Unwin, St. Leonards.

Carrington, C. 1999, *No Place like Home: Relationships and Family Life among Lesbians and Gay Men*, University of Chicago Press, Chicago.

Carter, M. 2003, '"It's Easier just to do it all Myself": Emotion Work and Domestic Labour', paper presented at the TASA conference 4–6 December 2003, University of New England.

Caruana, C. 2005, 'Changes to Federal Family Law and State Domestic Violence Legislation', *Family Matters*, no. 70, pp. 66–7.

Castles, F.G. 2002, 'Three Facts about Fertility: Cross National Lessons for the Current Debate', *Family Matters*, no. 63, pp. 22–7.

Chang, J. 2000, 'Making a Meal of Divorce: Chinese and Western Recipes', *Family Matters*, no. 57, p. 72.

Charsley, K. & Shaw, A. 2006, *Global Networks*, vol. 6, no. 4, pp. 331–44.

Cheal, D. 2002, *Sociology of Family Life*, Palgrave Macmillan, Hampshire and New York.

Cherlin, A.J. 2004, 'The deinstitutionalisation of American Marriage', *Journal of Marriage and Family*, vol. 66, pp. 848–61.

Coltrane, S. 1998, *Gender and Families*, Pine Forge Press, Thousand Oaks.

Commonwealth Department of Health and Aged Care 2001, 'Population Ageing and the Economy', AusInfo, Canberra.

Connell, R.W. 2005a, 'A Really Good Husband: Work/Life Balance, Gender Equity and Social Change', *Australian Journal of Social Issues*, vol. 40, no. 3, pp. 369–83.

Connell, R.W. 2005b, *Masculinities*, 2nd edn, Allen & Unwin, Crows Nest, New South Wales.

Connell, R.W. 2002, *Gender*, Polity Press, Cambridge.

Connell, R.W. 1987, *Gender and Power*, Allen & Unwin, Sydney.

Connell, R.W. & Messerschmidt, J. 2005, 'Hegemonic Masculinity: Rethinking the Concept', *Gender and Society*, vol. 19, no. 6, pp. 829–59.

Connor, J. 2004, 'Home among the Gum Trees: Securing the Future for Older People who Live in Residential Parks in New South Wales', Discussion Paper, New South Wales Ministerial Advisory Committee on Ageing, Sydney.

Connor, S. 2007, 'The Prospect of All-Female Conception', *The Independent on Sunday*, April 13, available at <http://www.independent.co.uk/news/science/the-prospect-of-allfemale-conception-444464.html> accessed 31 August, 2008.

Coontz, S. 2005, *Marriage, A History: From Obedience to Intimacy or How Love Conquered Marriage*, Viking, New York.

Craig L. 2006, 'Does Father Care mean Fathers Share?: A Comparison of how Mothers and Father in Intact Families Spend Time with Children', *Gender and Society*, vol. 20, no. 2, pp. 259–81.

Crawford, A. 2000, 'The Australian Nuclear Family could be Extinct by the End of the Century, True', *The Age*, 7 August 2000, Melbourne.

Crompton, R. 1998, *Class and Stratification: An Introduction to Current Debates*, Polity Press, Cambridge.

Cunningham, S. 2007, 'Sex and Sensibility', *The Age* [A2], 10 March, pp. 12–13.

Cussins, C. 1998, 'Quit Snivelling Cryo-baby, We'll Work out Which One's Your Mom', in R. Davis-Floyd & J. Dumit (eds), *Cyborg Babies: From Techno-Sex to Techno-Tots*, Routledge, New York & London.

Cwikel, J., Gramotnev, H. & Lee, C. 2006, 'Never-married Childless Women in Australia: Health and Social Circumstances in Older Age', *Social Science & Medicine*, vol. 62, pp. 1991–2001.

Dalton, S.E. & Bielby, D.D. 2000, '"That's Our Kind of Constellation": Lesbian Mothers Negotiate Institutionalized Understandings of Gender within the Family', *Gender & Society*, vol. 14, no. 1, pp. 36–61.

Daly, A. & Smith, D. 2003, 'Indigenous Families and Households in a Time of Welfare Reform', paper presented at the 8th Australian Institute of Family Studies Conference, 12 February, Melbourne.

Dasgupta, S.D. 2002, 'A Framework for Understanding Women's Use of Nonlethal Violence in Intimate Heterosexual Relationships', *Violence Against Women*, vol. 8, no. 11, pp. 1364–1389.

Davidoff, L. & Hall, C. 1987, *Family Fortunes: Men and Women of the English Middle Class 1780–1850*, University of Chicago Press, Chicago.

Davidson, K., Daly, T. & Arber, S. 2003, 'Older Men, Social Integration and Organizational Activities', *Social Policy and Society*, vol. 2, no. 2, pp. 81–9.

Davies, M. & Mouzos, J. 2007, 'Homicide in Australia: 2005–06', National Homicide Monitoring Program annual report, Research and Public Policy series, no. 77, Australian Institute of Criminology, Canberra.

de Vaus, D. 2004, *Diversity and Change in Australian Families: Statistical Profiles*, Australian Institute of Family Studies, Melbourne.

de Vaus, D. 1994, *Letting Go: Relationships between Adults and their Parents*, Oxford University Press, Melbourne.

de Vaus, D., Gray, M., Qu, L. & Stanton, D. 2007, *The Consequences of Divorce for Financial Living Standards in Later Life*, Research Paper no. 38, Australian Institute of Family Studies.

de Vaus, D., Qu, L. & Weston, R. 2003, 'Changing Patterns of Partnering', *Family Matters*, no. 64, pp. 10–15.

Delphy, C. 1977, *The Main Enemy: A Materialist Analysis of Women's Oppression*, Women's Research and Resources Centre Publications, London.

Delphy, C. & Leonard, D. 1992, *Familiar Exploitation: A New Analysis of Marriage in Contemporary Western Societies*, Polity, Cambridge.

Dempsey, D. 2006a, 'Active Fathers, Natural Families and Children's Origins: Dominant Themes in the Australian Political Debate over Eligibility for Assisted Reproductive Technology', *Australian Journal of Emerging Technologies and Society*, vol. 4, no. 1. available at <www.swin.edu.au/ajets>.

Dempsey, D. 2006b, 'Beyond Choice: Family and Kinship in the Australian Lesbian and Gay Baby Boom', unpublished PhD thesis, La Trobe University, Melbourne.

Dempsey, D. 2005, 'Lesbians' Right to Choose, Children's Right to Know', in G.H. Jones, & M. Kirkman, *Sperm Wars*, ABC Books, Sydney.

Dempsey, D. 2002, 'Reproducing intimacy and Kinship beyond Intercourse: Lesbians Practising Self-insemination', *Meridian*, [special issue: The Fertile Imagination], vol. 18, no. 2, pp. 103–21.

Dempsey, D., Hillier, L. & Harrison, L. 2001, 'Gendered (s)explorations among Same-Sex Attracted Young People in Australia, *Journal of Adolescence*, vol. 24, no. 1, pp. 67–81.

Dempsey, K. & de Vaus, D. 2004, 'Who Cohabits in 2001?: The Significance of Age, Gender, Religion and Ethnicity', *Journal of Sociology*, vol. 40, no. 2, pp. 157–78.

Dads in Distress (DIDs) 2008, available at <http://www.dadsindistress.asn.au/stories.html>.

Donovan, C. 2004, 'Why Reach for the Moon? Because the Stars aren't Enough', *Feminism & Psychology*, vol. 14, no.1, pp. 24–9.

Donovan, C. 2000, 'Who needs a Father? Negotiating Biological Fatherhood in British Lesbian Families using Self-insemination', *Sexualities*, vol. 3, no. 2, pp. 149–64.

Dow, S. 2005, 'All my Friends are Getting Married', *The Sunday Age*, 10 December, p. 7.

Doucet, A. 2000, '"There's a Huge Gulf between Me as a Male Carer and Women": Gender, Domestic Responsibility, and the Community as an Institutional Arena', *Community, Work and Family*, vol. 3, no. 2, pp. 163–84.

Du Bois Reymond, M. 1998, 'I don't want to Commit Myself Yet: Young People's Life Concepts', *Journal of Youth Studies*, vol. 1, no. 1, pp. 63–79.

Dunne, G.A. 1997, *Lesbian Lifestyles: Women's Work and the Politics of Sexuality*, University of Toronto Press, London.

Dunne, G.A. 1998, 'Introduction: Add Sexuality and Stir: Towards a Broader Understanding of the Gender Gynamics of Work and Family Life', in G.A. Dunne (ed.), *Lesbian Perspectives on Work and Family Life*, Harrington Park Press, New York and London.

Dunne, G.A. 1999, 'What Difference does Difference Make? Lesbian Experience of Work and Family Life', in J. Seymour & P. Bagguley (eds), *Relating Intimacies: Power and Resistance*, Macmillan, Basingstoke.

Dwyer, P., Smith, G., Tyler, D. & Wyn, J. 2003, *Life-patterns, Career Outcomes and Adult Choices*, Australian Youth Research Centre, University of Melbourne, Melbourne.

Ede, C. & Turnbull, J. 2008, 'Wayne Carey goes into Hiding', News.com.au, 30 January, <http://www.news.com.au/story/0,23599,23129246-2,00.html?from=mostpop> accessed 31 August, 2008.

Elkind, D. 2007, *The Hurried Child: Growing Up Too Fast Too Soon*, 3rd edn, Da Capo Press, Cambridge MA.

Encel, S. 2003, *Age can work: The Case for Older Australians Staying in the Workforce: A Report to the Australian Council of Trade Unions and the Business Council of Australia*, Business Council of Australia, Melbourne.

Engels, F. 1972 [1884], *The Origin of the Family, Private Property and the State*, Pathfinder Press, New York.

Entwisle, B. & Henderson, G.E. 2000, *Re-drawing Boundaries: Work, Households, and Gender in China*, University of California Press, Berkeley.

Evans, I.C. 2007, *Battle-Scars: Long-term Effects of Domestic Violence*, Research Report. School of Political and Social Inquiry, Monash University, Melbourne.

Evans, M.D.R. & Kelley, J. 2002, 'Attitudes toward Childcare in Australia' *The Australian Economic Review*, vol. 35, no. 2, pp. 188–96.

Evans, M.D.R., Kelley, J. & Wanner, R.A. 2001, 'Educational Attainment of the Children of Divorce: Australia 1940–1990', *Journal of Sociology*, vol. 37, no. 3, pp. 275–97.

Evans, S. 2003, 'Ways of Knowing about Domestic Violence: A Critical Review and Discussion of the Literature', Violence, Abuse and Neglect Prevention Service, Wentworth Area Health Service, New South Wales.

Everingham, C. & Bowers, T. 2006, 'Re-claiming or Re-shaping Fatherhood', *Health Sociology Review*, vol. 15, no. 1, pp. 96–103.

Everingham, C., Stevenson, D. & Warner-Smith, P. 2007 '"Things are Getting Better all the Time"?: Challenging the Narrative of Women's Progress from a Generational Perspective', *Sociology*, vol. 41, pp. 419–37.

Fagan, C. 2003, *Working-time Preferences and Work–life Balance in the EU: Some Policy Considerations for Enhancing the Quality of Life*, European Foundation for the Improvement of Living and Working Conditions, Dublin.

Farquhar, D., 2000, '(M)other discourses', in G. Kirkup, L. Janes, K. Woodward & F. Hovenden (eds), *The Gendered Cyborg: A Reader*, Routledge in association with The Open University, London and New York, pp. 209–20.

Faulkner, D. 2007, 'The Older Population and Changing Housing Careers: Implications for Housing Provision', *Australasian Journal on Ageing*, vol. 26, no. 4, pp. 152–56.

Fielding, H. 1999, *Bridget Jones's Diary*, Penguin, Harmondsworth.

Finch, J. 2007, 'Displaying Families', *Sociology*, vol. 41, no. 1, pp. 65–81.

Finch, J. & Mason, J. 1993, *Negotiating Family Responsibilities*, Tavistock/Routledge, London & New York.

Finkler, K. 2000, *Experiencing the New Genetics: Family and Kinship on the Medical Frontier*, University of Pennsylvania Press, Philadelphia.

Firminger, K.B. 2006, 'Is he Boyfriend Material? Representation of Males in Teenage Girls' Magazines', *Men & Masculinities*, vol. 8, no. 3, pp. 298–308.

Fitzpatrick, M. & Reeve, P. 2003, 'Grandparents Raising Grandchildren: a New Class of Disadvantaged Australians', *Family Matters*, no. 66, pp. 54–7.

Flandrin, J.L. 1979, *Families in Former Times: Kinship, Household and Sexuality*, trans. R. Southern, Cambridge University Press, Cambridge.

Flannery, T. 2003, 'Beautiful Lies: Population and Environment in Australia', *Quarterly Essay*, vol. 9, Black Inc, Melbourne.

Flood, M. 2008, 'Bent Straights: Diversity and Flux among Heterosexual Men', in E.H. Oleksy (ed.), *Intimate Citizenships: Gender, Subjectivity, Politics*, Routledge.

Flood, M. 2006, 'Violence Against Women and Men in Australia: What the *Personal Safety Survey* can and can't tell us', *DVIRC Quarterly*, no. 4, Summer, pp. 3–10.

Flood, M. 2003, *Fatherhood and Fatherlessness*, Discussion Paper no. 59, The Australia Institute, Canberra.

Flood, M. 2002, 'Pathways to Manhood: The Social and Sexual Ordering of Young Men's Lives, *Health Education Australia*, vol. 2, no. 2. pp. 24–30.

Foucault, M. 1977, *Discipline and Punish*, Tavistock, London.

Franklin, S., 2003, *Are we Post-genomic?*, available at <http://www.comp.lancs.ac.uk/sociology/soc085sf.html>, accessed 18 September 2003.

Friedan, B. 1965, *The Feminine Mystique*, Penguin, Harmondsworth.

Furstenburg, F. & Cherlin, A.J. 1991, *Divided Families: What Happens to Children when Parents Part*, Harvard University Press, Cambridge Massachusetts.

Gabb, J. 2009, *Behind Closed Doors: Researching Intimacy in Families*, Palgrave, London.

Gardner, K. & Grillo, R. 2002, 'Transnational Households and Ritual: An Overview', *Global Networks*, vol. 2, no. 3, pp. 179–90.

Gerstel, N. & Gross, H. 1984, *Commuter Marriage: A Study of Work and Family*, Guilford Press, New York.

Gibson-Davis, C.M., Edin, K. & McLanahan, S. 2005, 'High Hopes but Even Higher Expectations: The Retreat from Marriage among Low-income Couples', *Journal of Marriage and the Family*, vol. 67, no. 5, pp. 1301–12.

Giddens, A. 2001, *Sociology*, 4th edn, Polity Press, Cambridge.

Giddens, A. 1992, *The Transformation of Intimacy: Sex, Love and Eroticism in Modern Societies*, Polity Press, Cambridge.

Giddens, A. 1991, *Modernity and Self-Identity*, Stanford University Press, Stanford.

Gilding, M. 1997, *Australian Families: A Comparative Perspective*, Longman, South Melbourne.

Gilding, M. 1991, *The Making and Breaking of the Australian Family*, Allen & Unwin, Sydney.

Gillies, V. 2007, *Marginalised Mothers: Exploring Working Class Experiences of Parenting*, Routledge, Abingdon.

Gittins, D. 1985, *The Family in Question: Changing Households and Familiar Ideologies*, 2nd edn, Macmillan, Houndmills.

Glezer, H. 1971, 'Changes in Marriage Sex-role Attitudes among Young Married Women: 1971–1982', *Australian Family Research Conference Proceedings*, vol. 10, pp. 49–62.

Goffman, E. 1959, *The Presentation of Self in Everyday Life*, Anchor Books, New York.

Goodfellow, J. 2003, 'Grandparents as Regular Child Care Providers: Unrecognised, Under-valued and Under-resourced', *Australian Journal of Early Childhood*, vol. 28, no. 3, pp. 7–17.

Goodfellow, J. & Laverty, J. 2003, 'Grandparents Supporting Working Families: Satisfaction and Choice in the Provision of Childcare', *Family Matters*, no. 66, pp. 14–19.

Goodwin, R. & Cramer, D. 2000, 'Marriage and Social Support in a British-Asian Community', *Journal of Community and Applied Social Psychology*, vol. 10, no. 1, pp. 49–62.

Gopalkrishnan, N. & Babacan, H. 2007, 'Ties that Bind: Marriage and Partner Choice in the Indian Community in Australia in a Transnational Context', *Identities*, vol. 14, no. 4, July, pp. 507–26.

Gott, M. & Hinchliff, S. 2003, 'How Important is Sex in Later Life? The Views of Older People', *Social Science & Medicine*, vol. 56, pp. 1617–28.

Gough, D. 2004, 'Ramage Manslaughter Verdict Under Attack', *The Age*, 30 October, available at <http://www.theage.com.au/articles/2004/10/29/1099028209531.html?from=storylhs>.

Gray, M., Misson, S. & Hayes, A. 2005, 'Young Children and their Grandparents', *Family Matters*, issue 72, pp. 10–17.

Grimshaw, P. 1983, 'The Australian Family: An Historical Interpretation', in A. Burns & J. Goodnow (eds), *Children and Families in Australia: Modern Perspectives*, Allen & Unwin, Sydney.

Gubrium, J.F. & Holstein, J.A. 1990, *What is Family?*, Mayfield, Mountain View, California.

Haebich, A. 2000, *Broken Circles: Fragmenting Indigenous Families 1800–2000*, Fremantle Arts Centre Press, Fremantle.

Hakim, C. 2000, *Work-Lifestyle Choices in the 21st Century*, Oxford University Press, Oxford.

Harris, A. 1999, 'Everything a Teenage Girl Should Know: Adolescence and the Production of Femininity', *Women's Studies*, vol. 15, no. 2, pp. 111–24.

Hartley, R. 1995, 'Families, Values and Change: Setting the Scene', in R. Hartley (ed.), *Families and Cultural Diversity in Australia*, Allen & Unwin, Sydney.

Hays, S. 1996. *The Cultural Contradictions of Motherhood*, Yale University Press, New Haven.

Headey, B., Scott, D. & de Vaus, D. 1999, 'Domestic Violence in Australia: Are Men and Women Equally Violent?', *Australian Social Monitor*, vol. 2, no. 3, p. 57.

Healy, J., Hassan, R. & McKenna, R.B. 1985, 'Aboriginal Families', in D. Storer (ed.), *Ethnic Family Values in Australia*, Prentice-Hall, Sydney.

Heaphy, B. 2007, 'Sexualities, Gender and Ageing: Resources and Social Change', *Current Sociology*, vol. 55, no. 2, pp. 193–210.

Heard, G. 2008, 'Partnerships at the 2006 Census: Preliminary Findings', *People and Place*, vol. 16, no. 1.

Heath, S. 2004, 'Peer-shared Households, Quasi-Communes and Neo-Tribes', *Current Sociology*, vol. 52, no. 2, pp. 161–79.

Heath, S. & Cleaver, E. 2003, *Young, Free and Single: Twenty-somethings and Household Change*, Palgrave Macmillan, Basingstoke.

Hertz, R. & Ferguson, F. 1997, 'Kinship Strategies and Self-sufficiency Among Single Mothers by Choice: Post Modern Family Ties', *Qualitative Sociology*, vol. 20, no. 2, pp. 187–209.

Hewitt, B., Baxter, J. & Western, M. 2005, 'Marriage Breakdown in Australia: The Social Correlates of Separation and Divorce', *Journal of Sociology*, vol. 41, no. 2, pp. 163–183.

Hewitt, B., Western, M. & Baxter, J. 2006, 'Who Decides? The Social Characteristics of Who Initiates Marital Separation', *Journal of Marriage and Family*, vol. 68, no. 4, pp. 1165–77.

Higgs, P. & Gilleard, C. 2006, 'Departing the Margins: Social Class and Later Life in a Second Modernity', *Journal of Sociology*, vol. 42, no. 3, pp. 219–41.

Hillier, L., Dempsey, D., Harrison, L., Matthews, L., Beale, L. & Rosenthal, D. 1998, 'Writing Themselves in: A National Report on the Sexuality, Health and Well-being of Same-sex Attracted Young People', Monograph series no. 7, Australian Research Centre in Sex, Health and Society, National Centre in HIV Social Research, La Trobe University, Melbourne.

Hillier, L., Turner, A. & Mitchell, A. 2005, 'Writing Themselves In Again ... Six Years On': A Second National Report on the Sexuality, Health and Well-being of Same-sex Attracted Young People, Monograph series no. 50, Australian Research Centre in Sex, Health and Society, La Trobe University, Melbourne.

Hochschild, A.R. 1989, *The Second Shift: Working Parents and the Revolution at Home*, University of California Press, Berkeley and Los Angeles, California.

Hochschild, A.R. 1983, *The Managed Heart: Commercialization of Human Feeling*, Viking Books, New York.

Holloway, S.L. & Valentine, G. 2003, *Cyberkids: Children in the Information Age*, Routledge Farmer, London.

Holmes, M. 2004, 'An Equal Distance? Individualization, Gender and Intimacy in Distance Relationships', *The Sociological Review*, vol. 52, no. 2, pp. 181–200.

Hood, M. 1998, 'The Interplay Between Poverty, Unemployment, Family Disruption and All Types of Child Abuse', *Children Australia*, vol. 23, no. 2, pp. 28–32.

Hook, J.L. 2006, 'Care in Context: Men's Unpaid Work in 20 Countries, 1965–2003', *American Sociological Review*, vol. 71, no. 4, pp. 639–60.

Horner, B., Downie, J., Hay, D. & Wichmann, H. 2007, 'Grandparent-headed Families in Australia', *Family Matters*, vol. 76, pp. 76–84.

Huang, S. & Yeoh, B.S.A. 2005, 'Transnational Families and their Children's Education: China's "Study Mothers" in Singapore', *Global Networks*, vol. 5, no. 4, pp. 379–400.

Hughes, J. 2007, 'Repartnering after Divorce: Marginal Mates and Unwedded Women', *Family Matters*, vol. 55, pp. 16–21.

Hughes, K. 2005, 'The Adult Children of Divorce: Pure Relationships and Family Values?', *Journal of Sociology*, vol. 41, no. 1, pp. 69–86.

Hughes, K. 2007, 'Mothering Mothers: An Exploration of the Perceptions of Adult Children of Divorce', *Australian Journal of Social Issues*, vol. 42, no. 4, pp. 563–579.

Human Rights and Equal Opportunity Commission, 1997, 'Bringing Them Home: The Stolen Generation Report', available at <http://www.hreoc.gov.au/social_justice/bth_report/index.html>.

Ikels, C. (ed.) 2004, *Filial Piety: Practice and Discourse in Contemporary East Asia*, Stanford University Press, Stanford.

Immigrant Resource Centre in the North East 2002, *African Communities: Ethiopia, Eritrea, Somalia and Sudan*, Immigrant Resource Centre in the North East, Melbourne.

Indermaur, D. 2001, 'Young Australians and Domestic Violence', Australian Institute of Criminology Trends and Issues Series no. 195, Australian Institute of Criminology, Canberra.

Jackson, S. 1993, 'Even Sociologists Fall in Love: An Exploration of Love: An Exploration in the Sociology of Emotions', *Sociology*, vol. 27, no. 2, pp. 201–7.

Jain, S., Montgomery, M. & Agius, O. 2004, 'Household, family and Living Arrangements of the Population of Australia, 1986–2026', Paper Presented to Australian Population Association, 12th Biennial Conference, 15–17 September.

Jamieson, L. 1999, 'Intimacy Transformed?: A Critical Look at the Pure Relationship', *Sociology*, vol. 33, no. 3, pp. 477–94.

Jamieson, L. 1998, *Intimacy: Personal Relationships in Modern Societies*, Polity Press, Cambridge.

Jenks, C. 2005, *Childhood*, 2nd edn, Routledge, New York.

Johnson, L. & Lloyd, J. 2004, *Sentenced to Everyday Life: Feminism and the Housewife*, Berg, Oxford.

Johnson, M.P. 1995, 'Patriarchal Terrorism and Common Couple Violence: Two forms of Violence Against Women', *Journal of Marriage and the Family*, vol. 57, pp. 283–94.

Johnson, M.P. & Leone, J.M. 2005, 'The Differential Effects of Intimate Terrorism and Situational Couple Violence: Findings from the National Violence Against Women Survey, *Journal of Family Issues*, vol. 26, No. 3, pp. 322–49.

Johnson, M.P. & Ferraro, K.J. 2000, 'Research on Domestic Violence in the 1990s: Making Distinctions', *Journal of Marriage and the Family*, vol. 62, pp. 948–63.

Jones, G. 1995, *Leaving Home*, Open University Press, Buckingham.

Josephson, J. 2005, 'Citizenship, Same-sex Marriage, and Feminist Critiques of Marriage', *Perspectives on Politics*, vol. 3, no. 2, pp. 269–84.

Katz, C. 2004, *Growing Up Global: Economic Restructuring and Children's Everyday Lives*, University of Minnesota Press, Minneapolis.

Kee, H.J. 2006, 'Glass Ceiling or Sticky Floor? Exploring the Australian Gender Pay Gap', *The Economic Record*, vol. 82, no. 259, pp. 408–27.

Kenway, J. & Bullen, E. 2001, *Consuming Children: Education-Entertainment-Advertising*, Open University Press, Buckingham.

Kenyon, E. & Heath, S. 2001, 'Choosing This Life: Narratives of Choice among House Sharers, *Housing Studies*, vol. 16, no. 5, pp. 619–35.

Kilmartin, C. 2000, 'Young Adult Moves: Leaving Home, Returning Home, Relationships', *Family Matters*, no. 55, Autumn, pp. 34–40.

Kimmel, M. 2002, '"Gender Symmetry" in Domestic Violence: A Substantive and Methodological Research Review', *Violence Against Women*, vol. 8, no. 11, pp. 1332–63.

Kinnear, P. 2002, *New Families for Changing Times*, Discussion Paper no. 47, The Australia Institute, Canberra.

Kirsner, A. 2001, *Working Together Against Violence: The First Three Years of PADV*, Panther Publishers and Office of the Status of Women.

Klein, D.M. & White, J.M. 1996, *Family Theories: An Introduction*, Sage Publications, Thousand Oaks.

Kohler, H.P., Billari, F.C. & Ortega, J.A. 2004, 'The Emergence of Lowest-low Fertility in Europe During the 1990s', *Population and Development Review*, vol. 28, no. 4, pp. 641–80.

Komarovsky M. 1987, *Blue-Collar Marriage*, Yale University Press, New Haven.

Krug, E., Mercy, J., Dahlberg, L. & Zwi, A. 2002, 'The World Report on Violence and Health', *The Lancet*, vol. 360, issue 9339, pp. 1083–88.

Kwok, H. 2006, 'The Son also Acts as a Caregiver to Elderly Parents: A Study of the Sandwich Generation in Hong Kong', *Current Sociology*, vol. 54, no. 2, pp. 257–72.

Lacroix, C. 2006, 'Freedom, Desire and Power: Gender Processes and Presumptions of Shared Care and Responsibility after Parental Separation', *Women's Studies International Forum*, vol. 29, pp. 184–196.

Langer, B. 2005, 'Children: The Consumer Generation', in M. Poole (ed.), *Family: Changing Families, Changing Times*, Allen & Unwin, Crows Nest.

Lareau, A. 2003, *Unequal Childhoods, Class, Race and Family Life*, University of California Press, Berkeley.

Lasch, C. 1977, *Haven in a Heartless World: The Family Besieged*, Basic Books, New York.

Laslett, P. 1987, 'The Emergence of the Third Age', *Ageing and Society*, vol. 7, no. 2, pp. 133–60.

Laslett, P. 1972, *Household and Family in Past Time*, Cambridge University Press, Cambridge.

Lawler, S. 1999, 'Children Need but Mothers only Want: The Power of Needs Talk in the Constitution of Childhood', in J. Seymour. & P. Bagguley (eds), *Relating Intimacies: Power and Resistance*, Macmillan, Houndmills and London.

Lee, J. 2005, 'Down the Aisle in Budget Style', *The Sun-Herald*, 17 January.

Lees, S. 1999, 'Will Boys be Left on the Shelf?', in C. Wright & G. Jagger (eds), *Changing Family Values*, Routledge, London.

Leone, J.M, Johnson, M., Cohan, C. & Lloyd, S.E. 2004, 'Consequences of Male Partner Violence for Low-income, Minority Women', *Journal of Marriage and the Family*, vol. 66, pp. 472–90.

Levin, I. 2004, 'Living Apart Together: A New Family Form', *Current Sociology*, vol. 52, no. 2, pp. 223–40.

Levy, A. 2005, *Female Chauvinist Pigs: Women and the Rise of Raunch Culture*, Schwartz, Melbourne.

Lewis, M. 2005, 'Unilever Family Report 2005: Home Alone?', IPPR for Unilever, London.

Light Hearted Services 2007, LoveByte 2008, 'LoveByte's Formula for Romance', available at <http://www.lightheartedservices.com/cms/index.php?option=com_content&task=view&id=19&Itemid=36http://www.lovebyte.org.sg/web/host_p_1main.asp> accessed 27 July 2007.

Lindsay, J. 2002, 'Don't Panic! Young People and the Social Organisation of Sex', in G. Hawkes & J. Scott (eds), *Perspectives in Human Sexuality*, Oxford University Press, Melbourne.

Lindsay, J. 2000, 'An Ambiguous Commitment: Moving into a Cohabiting Relationship', *Journal of Family Studies*, vol. 6, no. 1, pp. 120–34.

Lindsay, J. & Maher, J.M. 2005, 'Beyond the "Crisis" Rhetoric: Designing Policy for Work and Family Integration for Employed Mothers', *Just Policy*, vol. 38, pp. 21–6.

Lindsay, J., Perlesz, A., Brown, R., McNair, R., de Vaus, D. & Pitts, M. 2006, 'Stigma or Respect: Lesbian-parented Families Negotiating the School Setting', *Sociology*, vol. 40, no. 6, pp. 1059–77.

Lindsay, J., Smith, A.M.A. & Rosenthal, D.A. 1997, 'Secondary Students, HIV/AIDS and Sexual Health', Centre for the Study of STDs/National Centre in HIV/AIDs Social Research, La Trobe University, Melbourne.

Litwak, E. 1960, 'Geographic Mobility and Extended Family Cohesion', *American Sociological Review*, vol. 25, pp. 385–94.

Lloyd, J. & Johnson, L. 2004, 'Dream Stuff: The Postwar Home and the Australian Housewife, 1940–60', *Environment and Planning D: Society and Space*, vol. 22, no. 2, pp. 251–72.

Logan, J.R., Bian, F. & Bian, Y. 1998, 'Tradition and Change in the Urban Chinese Family: The Case of Living Arrangements', *Social Forces*, vol. 76, no. 3, pp. 851–82.

Lucashenko, M. 1994, 'No Other Truth? Aboriginal Women Australian Feminists', *Social Alternatives*, vol. 12, no. 4, pp. 21–4.

Lumby, C. & Fine, D. 2006, *Why TV is Good for Kids: Raising 21st Century Children*, Macmillan, Sydney.

Lupton, D. 2000, 'A Love/Hate Relationship: The Ideals and Experiences of First Time Mothers', *Journal of Sociology*, vol. 36, no. 1, pp. 50–63.

Lupton, D. & Barclay, L. 1997, *Constructing Fatherhood: Discourses and Experiences*, Sage, London.

Maher, J. 2005. 'A Mother by Trade: Australian Women Reflecting on Mothering as Activity, Not Identity', *Australian Feminist Studies*, vol. 20, no. 46, pp. 17–30.

Maher, J., Lindsay, J. & Franzway, S. 2008, 'The Family Time Economy: Toward an Understanding of Time, Caring Labour and Social Policy', *Work, Employment and Society*, vol. 22, no. 3, pp. 544–52.

Maher, J.M. & Singleton, A. 2003, '"I Wonder What He's Saying?": Investigating Domestic Discourse in Young Cohabiting Couples', *Gender Issues*, pp. 59–77.

Mak, A. & Chan, H. 1995, 'Chinese Family Values in Australia', in R. Hartley (ed.), *Families and Cultural Diversity in Australia*, Allen & Unwin, Sydney.

Mangan, J. 2007, 'Sex and the Septuagenarian Coming to our Screens', *The Age*, 30 September, available at <http://www.theage.com.au/articles/2007/09/29/1190486635566.html> accessed 13 December 2007.

Mansfield, P. & Collard, J. 1988, *The Beginning of the Rest of Your Life? A Portrait of Newly-wed Marriage*, Macmillan, London.

Marr, D. 1981, *Vietnamese Tradition on Trial, 1920–1945*, University of California Press, Berkeley.

Marshall, A. & McDonald, M. 2001, *The Many-sided Triangle: Adoption in Australia*, Melbourne University Press, Melbourne.

Marshall, H. 2005, 'Fertility: Changing Pressures and Choices', in M. Poole (ed.), *Family: Changing Families, Changing Times*, Allen & Unwin, Sydney.

Marshall, H. 1993, *Not Having Children*, Oxford University Press, Melbourne.

Mayall, B. 2002, *Toward a Sociology for Childhood: Thinking from Children's Lives*, Open University Press, Buckingham.

McDonald, P. 2002, 'Issues in Childcare Policy in Australia' *The Australian Economic Review*, vol. 35, no. 2, pp. 197–293.

McDonald, P. 2000, 'Low Fertility in Australia: Evidence, Causes and Policy Responses', *People and Place*, vol. 8, no. 2, pp. 1–13.

McDonald, P. 1995, *Families in Australia: A Socio-demographic Perspective*, Australian Institute of Family Studies, Melbourne.

McDonald, P. 1991, 'Immigrant Family Structure', in K. Funder (ed.), *Images of Australian Families*, Longman Cheshire, Melbourne.

McGregor, H. & Hopkins, A. 1991, *Working for Change: The Movement Against Domestic Violence*, Allen & Unwin, Sydney.

McMichael, C. & Ahmed, M. 2003, 'Family Separation: Somali Women in Melbourne', *Refugee Rights Monograph*, Deakin University, Geelong.

McNair, R. 2004, 'Outcomes for Children Born of ART in a Diverse Range of Families', Victorian Law Reform Commission, Melbourne.

McNair, R., Dempsey, D., Wise, S., Perlesz, A. 2002, 'Lesbian Parenthood: Issues, Strengths and Challenges, *Family Matters*, no. 63, Spring/Summer, pp. 40–9.

McNamara, S. & Connell, J. 2007, 'Homeward Bound? Searching for Home in Inner Sydney's Share Houses', *Australian Geographer*, vol. 38, no. 1, pp. 71–91.

McVarish, J. 2006, 'What is the Problem of Singleness?', *Sociological Research Online*, vol. 11, no. 3, available at <http://www.socresonline.org.uk/11/3/macvarish.html>.

McWhinnie, A. 2001, 'Should Offspring from Donated Gametes Continue to be Denied Knowledge of their Origins and Antecedents?', *Human Reproduction*, vol. 16, no. 5, pp. 807–17.

Mead, G.H. 1934, *Mind, Self and Society*, University of Chicago Press, Chicago.

Millet, K. 1970, *Sexual Politics*, Ballantine, New York.

Mitchell, D. & Gray, E. 2007, 'Declining Fertility: Intentions, Attitudes and Aspirations', *Journal of Sociology*, vol. 43, pp. 23–44.

Moore, S.F. & Meyerhoff, B.G. 1977, *Secular Ritual*, Van Gorcum, Netherlands.

Morgan, D.H.J. 1996, *Family Connections: An Introduction to Family Studies*, Polity Press, Cambridge.

Morgan, D.H.J. 1985, *The Family, Politics and Social Theory*, Routledge and Kegan Paul, London.

Mullaney, J.L. 2007, 'Telling it like a Man: Masculinities and Battering Men's Accounts of Their Violence', *Men and Masculinities*, vol. 10, no. 2, pp. 222–47.

Mullati, L. 1995, 'Families in India: Beliefs and Realities', *Journal of Comparative Family Studies*, vol. 26, pp. 11–25.

Mulroney, J. & Chan, C. 2005, 'Men as Victims of Domestic Violence', Australian Domestic and Family Violence Clearinghouse Topic Paper, Australian Domestic and Family Violence Clearinghouse.

Murstein. B.I. 1977, 'The Stimulus-Value-Role (SVR) Theory of Dyadic Relationships', in S. Duck (ed.), *Theory and Practice in Interpersonal Attraction*, Academic Press, London.

Natalier, K. 2007, 'Independence, Individualism and Connection Among Share Householders, *Youth Studies Australia*, vol. 26, no. 1, pp. 17–24.

Natalier, K. 2003, '"I'm Not His Wife": Doing Gender and Doing Housework in the Absence of Women', *Journal of Sociology*, vol. 39, no. 3, pp. 253–69.

Newman, K.S. & Massengill, R.P. 2006, 'The Texture of Hardship: Qualitative Sociology of Poverty, 1995–2005', *Annual Review of Sociology*, vol. 32, pp. 423–46.

Nguyen, P.A. 2007, 'Relationships Based on Love and Relationships Based on Needs: Emerging Trends in Youth Sex Culture in Contemporary Urban Vietnam, *Modern Asian Studies*, vol. 41, no. 2, pp. 287–313.

Oakley, A. 1974, *The Sociology of Housework*, Martin Robertson, London.

Ochiltree, G. 2006, 'The Changing Role of Grandparents', *Australian Family Relationships Clearinghouse Briefing*, no. 2, pp. 1–9.

OECD 2002, *Babies and Bosses: Reconciling Work and Family Life*, vol. 1, Australia, Denmark and the Netherlands. OECD.

Office of the Status of Women 2004, *Women in Australia*, Commonwealth of Australia, Canberra.

Pahl, R. 2000, *On Friendship*, Polity Press, Cambridge.

Pahl, R. & Pevalin, D.J. 2005, 'Between Family and Friends: A Longitudinal Study of Friendship Choice', *British Journal of Sociology*, vol. 56, pp. 433–450.

Paice, J. 2003, 'Fertility: A Baby Bounce for Australia?' Current Issues Brief no. 1 2003–04, Parliament of Australia, available at <http://www.aph.gov.au/LIBRARY/Pubs/CIB/2003-04/04cib01.htm>.

Pakulski, J. & Waters, M. 1996, *The Death of Class*, Sage, London.

Pallotta-Chiarolli, M. & Skrbis, Z. 1993, 'Authority, Compliance and Rebellion in Second Generation Cultural Minorities', *Australian & New Zealand Journal of Sociology*, vol. 30, no. 3, pp. 259–72.

Pallotta-Chiarolli, M. 1990, 'From Coercion to Choice: The Personal Identity of the Second-generation Italo-Australian girl', *Multicultural Australia Papers*, 68, Ecumenical Migration Centre, Victoria.

Paradies, Y. 2006, 'Beyond Black and White: Essentialism, Hybridity and Indigeneity', *Journal of Sociology*, vol. 42, no. 4, pp. 355–67.

Parks, C.A. 1998, 'Lesbian Parenthood: A Review of the Literature', *American Journal of Orthopsychiatry*, vol. 68, pp. 376–89.

Parsons, T. 1951, *The Social System*, The Free Press, Glencoe Illinois.

Parsons, T. & Bales, R. 1955, *Family, Socialisation and Interaction Process*, The Free Press, New York.

Parsons, T. 1963, 'Old Age as a Consummatory Phase', *The Gerontologist*, vol. 3, pp. 35-43.

Pateman, C. 1988, *The Sexual Contract*, Polity Press, Cambridge.

Pence, E. & Paymar, M. 1993, *Education Groups for Men who Batter*, Springer, New York.

Peplau, L.A. & Fingerhut, A.W. 2006, 'The Close Relationships of Lesbians and Gay Men', *Annual Review of Psychology*, vol. 58, pp. 405–24.

Percival, R. & Harding, A. 2003, 'The Costs of Children in Australia Today', Paper Presented at the *Australian Institute of Family Studies Conference*, Melbourne.

Perren, K., Arber, S. and Davidson, K. 2004, 'Neighbouring in Later Life: The Influence of Socio-economic Resources, Gender and Household Composition on Neighbourly Relationships', *Sociology*, vol. 38, no. 5, pp. 965–84.

Pocock, B. 2005, 'Mothers: The More things Change, The More they Stay the Same', in M. Poole (ed.), *Family: Changing families, changing times*, Allen & Unwin, Crows Nest.

Pocock, B. 2003, *The Work/Life Collision—What Work is Doing to Australians and What to do about it*, Federation Press, Annandale, New South Wales.

Poole, M. 2005a, 'Understanding the Family: Ideals and Realities', in M. Poole (ed.), *Family: Changing families, Changing Times*, Allen & Unwin, Crows Nest.

Poole, M. 2005b, 'Violence', in M. Poole (ed.), *Family: Changing Families, Changing Times*, Allen & Unwin, Sydney.

Porter, C. 1993, *'Man's Final Frontier–The Home'*, National Library of Australia.

Porter, L. 2002, 'Decency when Divorce us do Part', *The Sunday Age*, 8 September, p. 17.

Pringle, R. 1988, *Secretaries Talk: Sexuality, Power and Work*, Verso, London.

Qu, L. & Soriano, G. 2004, 'Forming Couple Relationships: Adolescents' Aspirations and Young Adults' Actualities', *Family Matters*, no. 68, Winter, pp. 43–49.

Quah, S. 2003, *Home and Kin: Families in Asia*, Eastern Universities Press, Singapore.

Qvortrup, J. 2001, 'School-work, Paid Work and the Changing Obligations of Childhood', in P. Mizen, C. Pole & A. Bolton (eds), *Hidden Hands: International Perspectives on Children's Work and Labour*, Routledge, London.

Radway, J. 1984, *Reading the Romance: Women, Patriarchy, and Popular Literature*, University of North Carolina Press, Chapel Hill.

Raymond, J. 1986, *A Passion for Friends*, Beacon Press, Boston.

Read, P. 1983, *The Stolen Generations*, New South Wales Ministry of Aboriginal Affairs, Sydney.

Reiger, K. 2005, 'History: The Rise of a Modern Institution', in M. Poole (ed.), *Family: Changing Families, Changing Times*, Allen & Unwin, Crows Nest.

Reiger, K. 1991, *Family Economy*, McPhee Gribble, Ringwood.

Reiger, K. 1985, *The Disenchantment of the Home: Modernising the Australian family 1880–1940*, Oxford University Press, Melbourne.

Reimann, R. 1997, 'Does Biology Matter? Lesbian Couples' Transition to Parenthood and their Division of Labour', *Qualitative Sociology*, vol. 20, pp. 153–85.

Renzetti, C. M. 1992, *Violent Betrayal: Partner Abuse in Lesbian Relationships*, Sage, Thousand Oaks.

Reynolds, J. & Wetherell, M. 2003, 'The Discursive Climate of Singleness: The Consequences for Women's Negotiation of a Single Identity', *Feminism & Psychology*, vol. 13, no. 4, pp. 489–510.

Reynolds, J., Wetherell, M. & Taylor, S. 2007, 'Choice and Chance: Negotiating Agency in Narratives of Singleness', *The Sociological Review*, vol. 55, no.2, pp. 331–51.

Ribbens McCarthy, J., Edwards, J.R. & Gillies V. 2003, 'Moral Tales of the Child and the Adult: Narratives of Contemporary Family Lives under Changing Circumstances', *Sociology*, vol. 34, no. 4, pp. 785–803.

Rich, A. 1976, *Of Woman Born: Motherhood as Experience and Institution*, Virago, London.

Richards, L. 1990, *Nobody's Home: Dreams and Realities in a New Suburb*, Oxford University Press, Melbourne.

Richards. L. 1985, *Having Families: Marriage, Parenthood and Social Pressures in Australia*, Penguin Books, Ringwood, Melbourne.

Richters, J. & Rissel, C. 2005, *Doing It Down Under: The Sexual Lives of Australians*, Allen & Unwin, Sydney.

Rissel, C., Richters, J., Grulich, A.E.; De Visser, R. & Smith, A.M.A. 2003, 'Sex in Australia: First Experiences of Vaginal Intercourse and Oral Sex among a Representative Sample of Adults', *Australian and New Zealand Journal of Public Health*, vol. 27, no. 2, April, pp. 131–7.

Ristock, J.L. 2003, 'Exploring the Dynamics of Abusive Lesbian Relationships: Preliminary Analysis of a Multisite, Qualitative Study', *American Journal of Community Psychology*, vol. 31, no. 3 and 4, pp. 329–41.

Ritzer, G. & Goodman, D.J. 2004, *Sociological Theory*, 6th edn, McGraw-Hill, New York.

Roseneil, S. 2000a, 'Why We Should Care about Friends: Some Thoughts about the Ethics and Practice of Friendship', ESRC Research Group on Care, Values and the Future of Welfare, Workshop Paper no. 22, University of Leeds.

Roseneil, S. 2000b, 'Queer Frameworks and Queer Tendencies: Towards an Understanding of Postmodern Transformations of Sexuality', Sociological Research Online, vol. 5, no. 3, available at <http://www.socresonline.org.uk/5/3/roseneil.html>.

Roseneil, S. & Budgeon, S. 2004, 'Cultures of Intimacy and Care beyond "The Family": Personal Life and Social Change in the Early 21st Century', *Current Sociology*, vol. 52, no. 2, pp. 135–59.

Rothenberg, B. 2002, 'The Success of the Battered Women Syndrome: An Analysis of How Cultural Arguments Succeed', *Sociological Forum*, vol. 17, no. 1, pp. 81–103.

Rowland, R. 1984, 'Reproductive Technologies: The Final Solution to the Woman Problem', in R. Arditti, R. Klein & S. Minden (eds), *Test-tube Women: What Future for Motherhood?*, Pandora, London.

Rush, E. & La Nauze, A. 2006, *Corporate Paedophilia: Sexualisation of Children in Australia*, Discussion Paper no. 90 The Australia Institute, Canberra.

Russell, C. 2007, 'What do Older Men and Women Want?: Gender Differences in the "Lived Experience" of Ageing', *Current Sociology*, vol. 55, no. 2, pp. 173–92.

Sandfield, A. 2006, 'Talking Divorce: The Role of Divorce in Women's Constructions of Relationship Status', *Feminism & Psychology*, vol. 16, no. 2, pp. 155–73.

Sants, H.J. 1964, 'Genealogical Bewilderment in Children with Substitute Parents', *Journal of Medical Psychology*, vol. 37, pp. 133–41.

Sarantakos, S. 1984, *Living Together in Australia*, Longman Cheshire, Melbourne.

Schmidt, L. 2006, 'Happily Single', *The Age*, Sunday Life, February 12, pp. 12–17.

Schneider, D.M. 1980, *American Kinship: A Cultural Account*, 2nd edn, University of Chicago Press, Chicago.

Scutt, J. 1983, *Even in the Best of Homes*, Penguin, Ringwood, Melbourne.

Shen, H. 2005, '"The First Taiwanese Wives" and "The Chinese Mistresses": The International Division of Labour in Familial and Intimate Relations Across the Taiwan Strait', *Global Networks*, vol. 5, no. 4, pp. 419–37.

Sheng, X. & Settles, B.H. 2006, 'Intergenerational Relationships and Elderly Care in China: A Global Perspective', *Current Sociology*, vol. 54, no. 2, pp. 293–313.

Short, S.E., Fenyang, Z., Siyuan, X., Yang, M. 2001, 'China's One-child Policy and the Care of Children: An Analysis of Qualitative and Quantitative Data', *Social Forces*, vol. 79, no. 3, pp. 913–43.

Shorter, E. 1975, *The Making of the Modern Family*, Fontana/Collins, Glasgow.

Siedlecky, S. 1979, Sex and Contraception before Marriage: A Study of Attitudes and Experience of Never-married Youth in Melbourne, Australia', Department of Demography, Australian National University, Canberra.

Silva, E. & Smart, C. 1999, *The New Family?*, Sage, London.

Simpson, R. 2003, 'Contemporary Spinsters in the New Millennium: Changing Notions of Family and Kinship', London School of Economics Gender Institute Working Paper Series, issue 10, July.

Singh, S. 1997, *Marriage Money: The Social Shaping of Money in Marriage and Banking*, Allen & Unwin, St. Leonards.

Singh, S. & Lindsay, J. 1996, 'Money in Heterosexual Relationships', *Australian and New Zealand Journal of Sociology*, vol. 32, no. 3, pp. 57–69.

Singleton, A. 2005, 'Fathers: More than Breadwinners?', in M. Poole(ed), *Family: Changing Families, Changing Times*, Allen & Unwin, Crows Nest.

Skeggs, B. 1998, *Formations of Class and Gender*, Sage Publications, London.

Smart, C. 2007, *Personal Life: New Directions in Sociological Thinking*, Polity, Cambridge.

Smart, C. 2006, 'Children's Narratives of Post-divorce Family Life: From Individual Experience to an Ethical Disposition', *The Sociological Review*, pp. 155–70.

Smart, C. 2005, 'Textures of Family Life: Further Thoughts on Change and Commitment', *Journal of Social Policy*, vol. 34, no. 4, pp. 541–56.

Smart, C. 2004, 'Re-theorising Families', *Sociology*, vol. 38, no. 5, pp. 1043–8.

Smart, C. 2000, 'Divorce and Changing Family Practices in a Post-traditional Society', *Family Matters*, vol. 56, pp. 10–19.

Smart, C. & Neale, B. 1999, *Family Fragments?*, Polity Press, Cambridge.

Smart, C. & Shipman, B. 2004, 'Visions in Monochrome: Families, Marriage and the Individualization Thesis' *The British Journal of Sociology*, vol. 55, no. 4, pp. 491–508.

Smart, D. 2002, 'Relationships, Marriage and Parenthood: Views of Young People and their Parents', *Family Matters*, no. 63, Spring/Summer, pp. 28–35.

Smart, D. & Sanson, A. 2005, 'What is Life Like for Young Australians Today, and How Well are they Faring?', *Family Matters*, no. 7, Autumn, pp. 46–53.

Smithson, J. & Stokoe, E.H. 2005, 'Discourses of Work-Life Balance: Negotiating "Genderblind" Terms in Organizations', *Gender, Work and Organization*, vol. 12, no. 2, pp. 147–168.

Smyrnios, K. & Tonge, B. 1981, 'Immigrant Greek Mothers: The Anxiety of Change', *Australian Social Work*, vol. 34, no. 2, pp. 19–24.

Spender, D. 1994, *Weddings and Wives*, Penguin, Melbourne.

Stacey, J. 2004, 'Cruising to Familyland: Gay Hypergamy and Rainbow Kinship', *Current Sociology*, vol. 52, no. 2, pp. 181–97.

Stacey, J. 1990, *Brave New Families: Stories of domestic upheaval in late twentieth century America*, Basic Books, California.

Stacey, J. 1996, *In the Name of the Family: Rethinking Family Values*, Beacon Press, Boston.

Stack, C. 1974, *All Our Kin*, Harper & Row, New York.

Stone, L. 1977, *The Family, Sex and Marriage in England 1500–1800*, Weidenfeld & Nicholson, London.

Stone, W. 1998, Young People's Access to Home Ownership: Chasing the Great Australian Dream', *Family Matters*, no. 49, Autumn, pp. 38–43.

Storer, D. (ed.) 1985, *Ethnic Family Values in Australia*, Prentice-Hall, Sydney.

Strathern, M. 1992, *After Nature: English kinship in the late twentieth century*, Cambridge University Press, Cambridge.

Sullivan, O. 2006, *Changing Gender Relations, Changing Families: Tracing the Pace of Change Over Time*, Rowman and Littlefield Publishers, Lanham USA.

Summers, A. 2003, *The End of Equality: Work, Babies and Women's Choices in 21st Century Australia*, Random House Australia, Milsons Point, New South Wales.

Szego, J. 2007, 'Life at 15 Part One: Sex', *The Age*, Saturday 11 August, Insight p. 5.

Thompson, C. 2005, *Making Parents: The Ontological Choreography of Reproductive Technologies*, The MIT Press, Cambridge.

Tilly, L. & Scott, J. 1978, *Women, Work and Family*, Holt, Rheinhart and Winston, New York.

Tongue, A. & Ballenden, N. 1999, 'Families and Ageing in the 21st Century', *Family Matters*, no. 52, pp. 4–8.

Totten, M. 2003, 'Girlfriend Abuse as a Form of Masculinity Construction among Violent, Marginal Male Youth', *Men and Masculinities*, vol. 6, no. 1, pp. 70–92.

Trinca, H. & Fox, C. 2004, *Better Than Sex: How a Whole Generation got Hooked on Work*, Random House Australia, Milsons Point.

Vasta, E. 1993, 'Multiculturalism and Ethnic Identity: The Relationship between Racism and Resistance', *Australian and New Zealand Journal of Sociology*, vol. 29, no. 2, pp. 209–25.

Vickers, L. 1996, 'The Second Closet: Domestic Violence in Lesbian and Gay relationships: A Western Australian Perspective, *E Law: Murdoch University Electronic Journal of Law*, vol. 3. no. 4, pp. 1–24, available at <http://www.murdoch.edu.au/elaw/issues/v3n4/vickers.html>.

Walby, S. 1992, *Theorising Patriarchy*, Blackwell, Oxford.

Wallerstein, J.S., Lewis, J.M. & Blakeslee, S. 2000, *The Unexpected Legacy of Divorce: A 25 Year Landmark Study*, Hyperion.

Walker, L. 1984, *The Battered Woman Syndrome*, Springer, New York.

Walker, L. 1979, *The Battered Woman*, Harper & Row, New York.

Walkerdine, V., Lucey, H. & Melody, J. 2001, *Growing up Girl: Psychological Explorations of Gender and Class* Palgrave, Hampshire.

Warner, M. 1993, 'Introduction', in Warner M. (ed.) *Fear of a Queer Planet: Queer Politics and Social Theory*, University of Minnesota Press, Minneapolis & London.

Warr, D. 2006, 'Gender, Class and the Art and Craft of Social Capital', *The Sociological Quarterly*, vol. 47, pp. 497–520.

Warr, D.J. 2001, 'The Practical Logic of Intimacy: An Analysis of a Class Context for (Hetero)sex-related Health Issues', Unpublished doctoral dissertation, La Trobe University, Melbourne, Australia.

Weeks, J. 1995, *Invented Moralities: Sexual Values in an Age of Uncertainty*, Columbia University Press, New York.

Weeks, J., Heaphy, B. & Donovan, C. 2001, *Same-Sex Intimacies: Families of Choice and Other Life Experiments*, Routledge, London.

West, C. & Zimmerman, D. 1987, 'Doing Gender', in J. Lorber & S. Farrell (eds), *The Social Construction of Gender*, Sage, London.

Weston, K. 1991, *Families We Choose: Lesbians, Gays, Kinship*, Columbia University Press, New York.

Weston, R. 2004, 'Having Children or Not?', *Family Matters*, no. 69, Spring/Summer, pp. 4–9.

Weston, R. & Qu, L. 2004, 'Dashed Hopes? Fertility Aspirations and Expectations Compared', *Family Matters*, issue 69, pp. 10–17.

Weston, R. & Qu, L. 2007 'An Update on Partnership Formation Trends: What does the 2006 Census Suggest?', *Family Relationships Quarterly*, vol. 74, no. 6, pp. 6–19.

Weston, R. & Qu, L. 2006, 'Family Statistics and Trends: Trends in Couple Dissolution', *Family Relationships Quarterly*, no. 2, pp. 9–12. <http://www.aifs.gov.au/afrc/pubs/newsletter/newsletter2.html#family> accessed 28 May 2007>.

Weston, R. & Qu, L., 2001, 'Men's and Women's Reasons for not Having Children', *Family Matters*, vol. 58, pp. 10–15.

White, N.R. 2003, 'Changing Conceptions: Young People's Views of Partnering and Parenting', *Journal of Sociology*, vol. 39, no. 2, pp. 149–164.

White, R. & Wyn, J. 2004, *Youth and Society: Exploring the Social Dynamics of Youth Experience*, Oxford University Press, Melbourne.

Wolcott, I. 1998, Families in Later Life: Dimensions of Retirement, AIFS Working Paper no. 14, Australian Institute of Family Studies, Melbourne.

Wollstonecraft, M. 1992 [1792], *A Vindication of the Rights of Women*, Penguin, Harmondsworth.

Wood, E.J. & Guerin, B. 2006, 'Traditional or Western Marriage and Dating Customs: How Newer Migrants can Learn from Other Hindu Indian Female Immigrants', *New Zealand Population Review*, vol. 32, no. 1, pp. 1–20.

Wray, S. 2003, 'Women Growing Older: Agency, Ethnicity and Culture', *Sociology*, vol. 37, pp. 511–27.

Wyn, J. & White, R. 1997, *Rethinking Youth*, Allen & Unwin, St. Leonards.

Yeoh, B.S.A., Huang, S. & Lam, T. 2005, 'Introduction: Transnationalizing the "Asian" Family: Imaginaries, Intimacies and Strategic Intents', *Global Networks*, vol. 5, no. 4, pp. 307–15.

Young, M.D. & Willmott, P. 1957, *Family and Kinship in East London*, Routledge and Kegan Paul, London.

Zajdow, G. 2005, 'Families and Economies: What Counts and What Doesn't', in M. Poole, *Families: Changing Families, Changing Times*, Allen & Unwin, Crows Nest, New South Wales.

Zajdow, G. 1995, *Women and Work: Current Issues and Debates*, Deakin University Press, Geelong, Australia.

Zaretsky, E. 1982, 'The Place of the Family in the Origins of the Welfare State', in B. Thorne & M. Yalom (eds), *Rethinking the Family: Some Feminist Questions*, Longman, New York.

Zaretsky, E. 1976, *Capitalism, The Family and Personal Life*, Pluto Press, London.

Zelizer, VA. 1994, *Pricing the Priceless Child: The Changing Social Value of Children*, Princeton University Press, New Jersey.

Index